Additional Praise for *How Computer Games Help Children Learn*

"A must read for anyone who cares about learning. Game designers depend on having millions of people voluntarily learn more than anyone would dare put into a school curriculum. So studying games—how they are designed and how they are played—is one of the best sources of insight about learning, and Shaffer is an excellent guide to making the most of it."

—Seymour Papert, Professor Emeritus, Media and
Education Technology, MIT Media Lab

"Shaffer's book moves from vivid case studies and accessible accounts of key ideas from the learning sciences to practical advice on how parents can help their children learn more from the games they play. This book represents the logical next step in a conversation started by James Paul Gee's *What Video Games Have to Teach Us about Learning and Literacy* and Steven Johnson's *Everything Bad Is Good For You.*"

—Henry Jenkins, Director, Comparative Media Studies Program, MIT

"This well-written and important book will introduce parents and teachers to a radical idea: video games can be good for children. When children play games like *Sim City* or *The Oregon Trail,* they learn about urban planning or the American West in spite of themselves. But these games are just the tip of the iceberg; Shaffer describes a wide range of fascinating new learning games that are just now emerging. . . . Because these games give children the chance to creatively manipulate a virtual world, they can teach creativity and innovation, abilities that are more important than ever in today's competitive global economy. . . . Shaffer advises parents how to pick out a good learning game, how to play it with your children, and how to make sure they are learning from it."

—R. Keith Sawyer, author of *Group Genius: The Creative
Power of Collaboration*

"Shaffer's book points out forcefully a paradigm of future schooling: to better prepare our kids for a globally competitive world, we have to bring the thinking, practices, and cultures of various professions into school learning. With convincing examples of simulated professional games that can integrate learning, working, and playing, he proves that this is feasible."

—Tak-Wai Chan, National Central University, Taiwan

"This groundbreaking book raises fundamental issues concerning the goals of education and highlights the need for innovative thinkers in the twenty-first century. Written in a clear, lucid, and direct manner, Shaffer makes his ideas easily accessible to professional as well as lay readers. The book will benefit educators, school administrators, policy makers, and, most importantly, parents."

—Yam San Chee, Associate Professor, Learning Sciences & Technologies Academic Group & Learning Sciences Lab, National Institute of Education, Nanyang Technological University

"Deep learning, technical learning, learning that leads to the ability to innovate: these are the most important natural resources in our global high-tech world. Will our children be able to compete with kids in China and India? Shaffer shows us how to mine the potential of video game technologies to transform learning at home, in communities, and in schools."

—James Paul Gee, University of Wisconsin-Madison, author of *What Video Games Have to Teach Us about Learning and Literacy*

"Like Dewey, Piaget, and Papert before him, Shaffer challenges us to rethink learning in a new age. He uses vivid examples—backed by solid research—to show what education should look like in the twenty-first century."

—Kurt D. Squire, Assistant Professor of Education, University of Wisconsin-Madison, and Game Designer

How Computer Games Help Children Learn

David Williamson Shaffer

Foreword by
James Paul Gee

HOW COMPUTER GAMES HELP CHILDREN LEARN
© David Williamson Shaffer, 2006.

First published in 2006 by
PALGRAVE MACMILLAN™
175 Fifth Avenue, New York, N.Y. 10010 and
Houndmills, Basingstoke, Hampshire, England RG21 6XS
Companies and representatives throughout the world.

PALGRAVE MACMILLAN is the global academic imprint of the Palgrave Macmillan division of St. Martin's Press, LLC and of Palgrave Macmillan Ltd. Macmillan® is a registered trademark in the United States, United Kingdom and other countries. Palgrave is a registered trademark in the European Union and other countries.

ISBN-13: 978–1–4039–7505–8
ISBN-10: 1–4039–7505–1

Library of Congress Cataloging-in-Publication Data

Shaffer, David Williamson.

   How computer games help children learn / David Williamson Shaffer; foreword by James Paul Gee.
     p. cm.
   Includes bibliographical references and index.
   ISBN 1–4039–7505–1 (alk. paper)
    1. Career education—Computer-assisted instruction. 2. Career choice—Computer-assisted instruction. 3. Computer games. 4. Learning, Psychology of. 5. Virtual reality in education. I. Title.

LC1037.S32 2007
371.33'4—dc22   2006047629

A catalogue record of the book is available from the British Library.

Design by Newgen Imaging Systems (P) Ltd., Chennai, India.

First edition: December 2006

10 9 8 7 6 5 4 3 2 1

Printed in the United States of America.

For Amy, Nell, and Maya,
who let me play the best role of all:
Daddy

Indeed, what is a "career" or a "vocation" except a role-playing game extended over an adult lifetime?

—Merlin Donald,
Professor of Cognitive Science,
Case Western Reserve University

Contents

Foreword

Are today's schools preparing our children for tomorrow's world?

We do a better job today at teaching the basics. We have standardized our curricula and standardized the tests we use to make sure children can do basic mathematics and can read basic texts. But these days simple math and reading skills will, at best, get you a low-level service job, because standardized skills are not what they once were. Young people today need more. Much more. Even the capacity to learn new things quickly and well, important though it is, is not enough.

Young people today need to be able to use their learning muscles to innovate and create, and ultimately to adapt and transform themselves several times over in one lifetime. They need to be tech-savvy if they are going to have any hope of a secure future. This was not true for the Baby Boom generation. For Baby Boomers like me, being able to read books and engage with the liberal arts—while silently fearing math, science, and complex technologies—was, by and large, all right. But not anymore.

What does it mean to be tech-savvy? It means thinking that learning math and science and mastering new technology are completely natural, normal, and nonthreatening—even cool—because today science and technology are part of everything we do. Science isn't just in the lab, it's all over the Internet and the news. Art is digital, and many artists today are technical whizzes. Kids use mathematical and design thinking to reprogram the video games they play, modifying them to their own tastes and to challenge their friends.

These days anyone under thirty swims in a sea of technologies. They are networked around the world with people of different ages, races, nationalities, and genders: witness any raid group in the phenomenally popular massively multiplayer game *World of Warcraft*. Haven't heard of it? Then you fail to have what is, today, basic cultural literacy for young people across the globe—those same young people we want to educate and prepare for the future.

Our world today is full of complex—and dangerous—systems. Hurricane Katrina produced a "perfect storm" of controversy when global warming and poverty in the new global world combined with political failure at all levels. Natural disasters, global trade imbalances, and even international terrorism are problems where only the tech-savvy—only people who can link media, images, and design with science, math, and technology; only countries with people who can think about how to use new technologies in new ways—will survive. Our response to threats like these depends on innovation as well as advanced technology. Only those who can use technology to its fullest potential will be able to protect themselves, their families, and their country.

Are schools preparing our children to be tech-savvy?

The evidence, as far as I can see, is that many young children today are learning more about art, design, and technology from their video games and other digital technologies than they are from our technologically impoverished schools. Many of these kids don't just consume but also produce their own videos, animation, fan fiction, game modifications, Web sites, blogs, news commentary, and technical guides—sometimes ninety-page, single-spaced, highly technical strategy guides for video games.

But the fear—especially from older generations—is this: What about all that school content, all those important facts and dates that show up on school tests? Are kids going to know that stuff? Or are they going to be lost in a haze of networked technologies?

Here's the sad fact about that old-time school content, all those facts and equations on the tests: We have known for years now that most of the kids who can pass these tests—physics or social studies tests, say—cannot actually apply their knowledge to the real world. They can't use the rote learning and standardized skills they got in school to think in innovative ways. And that is nothing short of dangerous for a developed country like the United States in our high-tech, risky world.

David Shaffer has a radical answer. Radical, yes, but at the same time deeply conservative. He says: Let's get kids to learn not just to pass tests but to be able to solve problems in the real world, even to be able to transform that world. Let's do this in such a way that all kids can become tech-savvy innovators. In fact, while we're at it, let's use the best of what we know about video games and other powerful digital technologies that are already teaching our children. Let's use these technologies to enhance deep learning for content and skills we value in school and in society.

Technology of any sort, including video game and simulation technologies, is not adequate all by itself for deep learning. Shaffer shows us that we need to build these technologies into rich and well-designed learning systems. And he shows us how to do it.

What Shaffer asks us to consider is this: Take a profession—say architecture, or journalism, or engineering, or urban planning, or even video game design—and consider these facts. First, people in these professions know how to use skills—reading, writing, design, communication, research, and a bunch of other school-based skills—to solve real problems. Second, they know how to innovate. And, third, they know very well how to educate—to apprentice—their new members. Each profession owns and operates a tool kit of knowledge, skills, and values—what Shaffer calls its "epistemic frame"—that it uses to look at and act on the world in a distinctive way. If you want to look at and act on the world in that way, you have to master the tool kit.

So Shaffer proposes a recipe for a new pedagogy: If we can entice kids to role-play such professions, they'll get school-based skills and learning for innovation all in one go. But what would entice them? Here is Shaffer's brilliance: Let them play the game—the game of one or more of these professions. Let them take on the identity or role of a professional. Let them produce the products professionals produce—products they *can* produce thanks to new digital technologies. Let them take ownership of knowledge.

But Shaffer's games are special. They are not just virtual worlds, like the game *SimCity*. These games are, as Shaffer describes, "augmented by reality." Kids go back and forth between the virtual world and the real world as they play. When they redesign a city as urban planners, it is their city. They can walk the streets of their town in both real space and in the virtual world. When they write news reports as journalists, the stories are about the world around them. They walk the walk and talk the talk and, in the process, master the tool kit. They come to see the real world in a new way.

But the tool kit is, lo and behold, replete with school-based knowledge and skills, with tools for innovation and, in almost every case today, with technical skills and technological devices. You can't play these professional games without using, over and over again, lots of basic skills, facts, and information: the content of school tests. These things, which are in the foreground at school, come for free in Shaffer's epistemic games. In these games the focus is on solving problems by using the tool kit of a professional role that you think is "cool" and definitely worth inhabiting—games that you want to play because you want your shot at re-planning your downtown, facing an emergency like Katrina, or straightening people out on the science behind cloning.

But kids—middle school kids, or kids even younger—being professionals? Is Shaffer serious about this? Well, kids today already do something pretty similar when they play some of their video games. There they have to take on the skills and values of their avatar to transform a specific virtual world in distinctive ways to accomplish goals. Popular games like *S. W.A. T 4* and *America's Army* work this way—these are commercial games where you have to think like a professional in order to win the game.

What Shaffer shows so convincingly is that today's digital technologies—and research from the learning sciences—let us place kids in the shoes of professionals who don't shoot and kill, but instead transform the world for growth, development, justice, and survival. Why? Not for career management—though there's no harm in children getting to see early on what some of the alternatives to service work might be—but for learning beyond the basics and beyond standardized skills. For learning real problem solving and innovation.

Now, I said this is radical, but also a deeply conservative vision. It already sounds pretty radical, so how, for heaven's sake, is it conservative? Though Shaffer often works in out-of-school programs, his goal is to put pressure on schools to prepare children to be productive workers, thoughtful members of society, and savvy citizens. To be responsible members of the public sphere in a fast-changing, high-tech, science-driven, global world by learning the ways of innovation.

Today it doesn't get more back to basics than that. It comes down to our survival.

James Paul Gee
Madison, Wisconsin
April 2006

How Computer Games Help Children Learn

Introduction

The news is chilling. "Today," begins a recent report from the National Academies of Sciences and Engineering, "workers in virtually every sector must now face competitors who live just a mouse-click away in Ireland, Finland, China, India, or dozens of other nations whose economies are growing." The report examines the decline in American competitiveness in the global economy of the twenty-first century and concludes: "Without a renewed effort to bolster the foundations of our competitiveness . . . , we can expect to lose our privileged position. For the first time in generations, the nation's children could face poorer prospects than their parents and grandparents did."[1]

We are losing our competitive advantage and are in danger of falling behind in a world where work goes quickly and easily to countries with high skills and low wages. Young people today need to learn innovative thinking and high-tech skills in science and engineering to get high-paying jobs. Since 1980 the number of science and engineering jobs has grown four times faster than the labor force as a whole. But the number of U.S. citizens training to become scientists and engineers is actually declining.[2]

You don't have to read very deeply into the world of business to know that we are facing a national crisis. Books like *The Only Sustainable Edge* and *Evolve! Succeeding in the Digital Culture of Tomorrow*—plus more academic reports like *Offshoring and the Future of U.S. Engineering*—argue that technology now lets companies send overseas any job that can be done by a skilled worker according to some well-established process. As a result, we have to rethink what it means to compete in a global economy.[3]

As one professor of business management explains: "A standardized problem can be solved anywhere."[4] It doesn't matter if the job is low wage like an assembly line worker or call center operator, or high wage, like a radiologist. Other countries have call center operators, engineers, and computer scientists who are as well or even better trained as those in the United States and willing to work for less than their counterparts are here. In a connected world where even real-time face-to-face interactions can be done across time zones via video conferencing, it no longer matters where people are. Time differences can even be an advantage: Indian radiologists can read American X-rays while American doctors and patients sleep at night. Legal documents can be prepared, layout and graphic design projects executed, and a host of other high-skill jobs can be done in the same way.[5]

There is hope, though. The majority of the jobs that can be outsourced easily in this way are those that require only standard and standardized skills. As a result, America's competitive edge increasingly comes from how we can produce products, services, and technologies that are new, special, nonstandard—and thus not easily reproduced across the globe by competitors. The value of this kind of innovation is not in labor and materials, but in knowledge. The high end of the value chain in a global economy is the knowledge needed to design innovative products, services, and technologies that let people share information, work together, and do things in new ways. In the very near future, the only good jobs left will be for people who can do innovative and creative work.[6]

Yet despite this growing need for people who can think in innovative ways, the United States is rapidly losing talented foreign graduate students and is creating fewer native-born scientists and engineers.[7] In the early 1980s, when Deng Xiaoping came to power, he opened China's economy to capitalist competition and began a massive investment in science and technology as the foundation of economic—and thus national—power. A quarter century later, China is an economic dynamo. Major international corporations, including IBM and Microsoft, have set up laboratories in Beijing, and Microsoft's lab there is widely seen as the most innovative in an innovative corporation.[8] Indian pharmaceutical companies founded to reverse-engineer patented drugs are now becoming centers for outsourcing drug development—the very height of the value chain in the industry.[9]

This looming crisis has been the subject of a number of urgent policy reports, white papers, and books. Thomas Friedman's best-selling *The World Is Flat* talks about the challenge of innovation mostly in terms of foreign policy and global economics, examining how the new, high-skill, science- and technology-driven economies of many countries will soon outstrip that of the United States and what nation-states, governments, businesses, and workers must do to adapt to this changing world of the beginning of the twenty-first century.

At its core, though, this is a crisis in education. Young people in the United States today are being prepared—in school and at home—for standardized jobs in a world that will, very soon, punish those who can't innovate. Our government and our schools have made a noble effort to leave no child behind: to ensure, through standardized testing, that all children make adequate yearly progress in basic reading and math skills. But we can't "skill and drill" our way to *innovation*. Standardized testing produces standardized skills. Our standards-driven curriculum, especially in our urban schools, is not preparing children to be innovators at the highest technical levels that will pay off most in a high-tech, global economy.

The statistics are alarming. In China, 59 percent of undergraduate students get degrees in science and engineering. In Japan, 66 percent do. In the United States, only 32 percent do. We currently rank seventeenth worldwide in percentage of science and engineering degrees awarded each year. Thirty years ago, we were ranked third. Over 60,000 U.S. high school students compete each year in the Intel Corporation's International Science Fair. But lest you think that number is impressive, in China there are 6 *million* entrants—more than twice as many entrants per capita as in the United States. In the most recent Trends in International Mathematics and Science Study—an international test that compares academic preparation worldwide—44 percent of students in Singapore scored at the most advanced level in mathematics; only 7 percent of students in the United States did.[10]

A recent study showed that nearly half of all Native American, Hispanic, and African American students in the United States don't complete high school. One-third of all students drop out before getting their degree. In the study, those who dropped out said they were bored and classes were out of touch with their career goals. Over 80 percent said that more "real world" learning opportunities might have kept them in school.[11] Students who stay in school face a curriculum increasingly dominated by federally mandated, standardized tests that do little to prepare them for the kind of high-level thinking that is rewarded in the new global economy.

That's the bad news: We live in a time of economic change, but our schools are busy preparing students for the commodity jobs of the past—jobs that will be long gone by the time they finish school. We are in danger of leaving all of our children far behind in the new global competition for innovative work.

But while much of the writing about the coming crisis focuses on the problems in our schools, I want to look at solutions. Because here's the good news: *The very same technologies that are making it possible to outsource commodity jobs make it possible for students of all ages to prepare for innovative work.*

The computer is a truly transformative technology, one that changes nearly everything around it—a change on the order of the invention of the printing press, the development of writing, even the creation of language itself.[12] The same power for transformation that puts global competitors a mouse-click away also makes it possible for young people to prepare for life in the digital age.

When computers first appeared on the scene, educators argued that we should use them as tutors to help students learn the things they need to know. Thus was born the age of *computer-aided instruction*, where machines could help students just-in-time and on-demand, anytime, and anywhere that the computer was available. The computer could teach students to solve problems, answer questions on tests, and do better in school.[13]

In 1980 MIT professor Seymour Papert published his groundbreaking book, *Mindstorms*. Papert argued that we should use computers to help children learn by doing things that are meaningful and motivating—to solve real problems rather than just learning rote facts and basic skills.[14] Computers, he said, matter because they make it possible to think about learning in a new way.

Now, three decades later, learning to solve real problems is more important than ever, and this book is about how we can use computer and video games to do just that. It is about how a particular kind of computer and video game—*epistemic games*—can help young people learn the ways of innovation they need to thrive in a complex world.

What parents, teachers, and policy makers really need to know about education in the digital age, though, is not about computers and video games themselves. It is about learning, and about how new technologies make new kinds of learning possible. So this is not primarily a book about how computer and video games can help kids do better in school—although they can, and we'll talk about how. This is a book about how computer and video games can help adults rebuild education for the postindustrial, high-tech world by thinking about learning in a new way.

Beyond the Farm

We already know a lot about how to help young people learn to solve problems that matter. Early in my career, for example, I had the pleasure of teaching in a school that was also a working organic farm in rural Vermont. The students planted and harvested all of the school's produce. They fed and mucked the cows, sheep, and chickens, cleaned the school buildings, repaired walls and painted fences, took in hay or collected maple sap for syrup, and chopped and hauled wood to heat the buildings, depending on the weather and the season. This was an American high school, so students also took all the usual classes that high school students take. In science class, they studied ecology, and learned about the concept of sustainability they were practicing in their farm chores. In English class, they explored the relationship between humans and their environment through the work of Henry David Thoreau and John McPhee.[15]

It was truly amazing how hard these young people were working—and how much they were learning along the way. I spent a lot of time talking with students, and what I remember most vividly is that they were willing to work so hard because they saw the work as *authentic*. The chickens needed to be fed. Every morning. Even when it was 10 degrees below zero. If the tables weren't wiped down after breakfast, everyone got maple syrup on their elbows at lunch. Students saw the wood go from tree, to log, to neatly stacked cord, and, eventually, to the school's furnaces.

The chores were not arbitrary. The rhythms of nature and the realities of life on a farm determined the things that needed doing and the times they had to be done. Few of these students were going to be organic farmers when they graduated, so the chores were not something to be mastered now and used later on. They were things that needed doing. Right now, each morning. *Every* morning. As the great educator and philosopher John Dewey might have said, on this working farm, these tasks were not *about* life, they were life itself.[16]

These students were learning to *solve* real problems by *working* on real problems, learning how to think about things that matter in the world by actually doing things that matter in the world. But what would education "based on life itself"—learning to solve problems that matter by working on things that matter—look like in our high-tech, digital world?

Many parents already use modern technologies of all kinds—including games—to introduce their children early on to technical languages, skills, and knowledge. They help create and support their children's interests—whether in dinosaurs, mythology, computers, science, or art—by introducing their kids to books, video games, Web sites, videos, and other resources.

The books, video games, and movies of children's culture today demand strategic thinking, technical language, and sophisticated problem-solving skills.[17] Take a look, for example, at the language on a *Yu-Gi-Oh* card or Web site. The writing there is often more complex—more technical—than the language children see in their school books or hear in their classrooms. When my daughter, who is now in first grade, plays *Zoo Tycoon*—a game that lets players own and run a zoo, purchasing animals, building exhibits, and catering to visitors—she has an opportunity to learn about wildlife habitats, gain valuable design skills, and solve complex problems as she develops and expands a business.

Cultural critic Steven Johnson points out that there are more characters and more complex storylines in children's movies today than there were twenty and thirty years ago. Video games like *Civilization*, where players rule over a growing empire from hamlet, to city-state, to global dominion, are far more complex than *Pong* or *Pac Man* ever were.[18] Developmental psychologists have known for nearly a century that children learn from playing games. For example, Jean Piaget argued that the forms of children's play mirrors the stages of their intellectual development. Lev Vygotsky wrote about how play was critical to children's social and emotional development. In the field of cognitive psychology, Jerome Bruner and his colleagues showed that play is itself a form of learning: It helps us learn to solve problems by making us familiar with how things work.[19]

But good parenting and good teaching don't simply mean turning kids loose in a media jungle. Wise parents and good teachers read and play and talk with children. Psychologist Kevin Crowley and his colleagues at the University of Pittsburgh have studied how young children and their parents talk about science and technology. Their conversations, it turns out, are built up from short fragments of scientific talk: little exchanges in which the parent provides information to the child on a topic of interest. Crowley's work shows that as a child comes to understand more about the topic from each interaction, he or she becomes more interested in it—leading to further conversations and deeper understanding. These tiny and incomplete explanations, which are individually fairly unremarkable, come together to create what Crowley calls *islands of expertise*. An island of expertise is any topic—say rocket ships or dinosaurs—that a child cares a lot about and thus learns a lot about.

Crowley's point about these islands is that they are created over time as kids interact with parents and knowledgeable adults. Look, for example, at how one four-year-old boy in Crowley's study and his mother talked about some fossils in a museum exhibit:[20]

Max: Hey! Hey! A velociraptor! I had that one . . . !

Mother: I know, I know, and . . . remember, they have those—remember in your book, it said something about the claws . . . .

Max: No, I know, they . . . have so great claws so they can eat and kill . . . .

Mother: [T]hey use their claws to cut open their prey, right. . . . And that's from the Cretaceous period . . . .

Max: Cretaceous period.

Mother: Good. And that's 80 *million* years ago, which is a really very long time.

Notice how Max's mother is building and expanding his interests by engaging with him in ways of talking, thinking, and working that are technical, specialized, and academic. She turns her son's excitement about dinosaurs into an occasion for understanding the hypothesized biomechanics of a Cretaceous fossil. In conversations like these about kids' interests—about their games, about what they already know, and about what they want to know—adults help children see that learning matters and that they can be good at learning complex, technical, and specialized things.

In other words, play and exploration and experimentation matter. But adults have an important role in that process, and today too many young people lack role models and mentors.[21] Max's mother was able to encourage and support his interests into an island of expertise. Many parents are similarly skilled in mathematics, or design, or scientific and technical fields. But few parents and caregivers are experts in the wide range of professional and technical skills that kids need to master in today's world, and some have only limited expertise—perhaps almost none at all.

The key to solving the current crisis in education will be to use the power of computer and video games to give *all* children access to experiences and interactions that build interest and understanding—to give all children the kind of rich learning opportunities Max's mother gave him—but not just about Cretaceous fossils. Children need to learn about human biology, Internet technology, graphic design, information architecture, urban sprawl, global warming, political science, international relations, biomedical ethics, and a host of other forms of expertise that will prepare them for life in a world that is ever more complex, technical, and centered in the content of science, mathematics, computers, engineering, and art.

Epistemic Games

Computers have been in existence for over half a century and have been used in classrooms for decades. Yet there has been no wholesale transformation of education as we know it—as techno-skeptics like Larry Cuban, a professor of education who has studied the impact of new technologies in schools, are quick to point out.[22] Why? Because we have been looking at things the wrong way.

WHAT MATTERS ABOUT COMPUTERS

Media scholar Marshall McLuhan once said that "content" is like a juicy piece of meat that a burglar uses to lull a guard dog to sleep.[23] What he meant is that the things we do with a new technology, such as the printing press or television, are less important than the fact that we are using the technology at all. Reading and writing change us in ways more profound than the content of any single book. Television's power is its ability to bring the world to our living rooms—and it doesn't matter, in the end, which part of the world pays us a visit, because whoever comes to call makes the world seem like a smaller place. New technologies change the speed and kind of information we exchange and thus change the way we interact with each other and understand the world.

What matters about computers, then, isn't whether we use them to trade penny stocks for low commissions, shop on eBay, pay bills with online banking, check the weather, or play *Doom* with friends. These are just the content—the raw meat—good or bad, that distracts us from what computers are really doing.

What computers do, in all of these examples, and in every other way we use them, is let us work with *simulations* of the world around us.[24] Computers let us make models that work the way some part of the world does. These simulated models make it easier for us to get things done in the real world by letting the computer do some of the work we otherwise would have to do for ourselves. And these simulations let us play with reality by creating imaginary worlds where we can do things that we otherwise couldn't do at all. By letting us work and play with powerful simulations, computers change what it means to know something and what it means to be able to do something.[25] That's what McLuhan meant about the burglar, and that's why computers are a big deal. Using the real power of computers requires developing a new way of thinking about thinking—and thinking about learning.

Computer and video games can change education because computers now make it possible to learn on a massive scale by doing the things that people do in the world outside of school. They make it possible for students to learn to think in innovative and creative ways just as innovators in the real world learn to think creatively.

But they can do this only if we first understand how computers change what it means to be educated in the first place.

IN PRAISE OF EPISTEMOLOGY

Epistemology is the study of what it means to know something, and this is, fundamentally, a book about the epistemology—or rather, the epistemologies—of the digital age. The word *epistemology* comes from the Greek root words *episteme*, meaning "knowledge" or "understanding," and *logos*, meaning "word," "thought," "study," or even "meaning" itself. Epistemology is the study of knowledge, and here I argue that computers create both the means and the necessity to fundamentally rethink what it means to know something—and thus what is worth learning and how we teach it.

Computers are creating a world that places a premium on innovation and creative thinking, and computer and video games make it possible to prepare young people for life in that world—but only once we understand how people learn to think as innovators. We have to develop the tools to help young people learn the epistemologies of creative innovation. One way to do this is through *epistemic games:* games that are fundamentally about learning to think in innovative ways. This is surely not the only way to use new technologies to change education for the better, but it is the kind of solution we need: one that uses technology to think about learning in new ways appropriate for a postindustrial, global economy and society.

So this is a book about computers, and about games, and about the challenge of preparing students for life in an economy of global competition. But really it is a book about thinking. And more than that, about learning, and about how we can—how we *must*—use computers to make it possible for all of our children to learn in ways that are deeply authentic and fulfilling and powerful and motivating and, most of all, relevant. It is about using computer games to help students learn important ideas in ways that will be meaningful and useful in a changing world.

This book shows how we can use new technologies to give all children access to the kind of learning that Max had with the help of his mother and that students had at a very special and unique school in Vermont. It shows how computer and video games—though games of a very special sort—can transform education to meet the challenge of innovation in a global economy.

From Here to There

The view of learning this book presents—the idea that epistemology matters, and is central to the problem of education—has deep roots. Piaget, perhaps the leading developmental psychologist of the last century, didn't think of himself as a psychologist at all.[26] He called himself a genetic epistemologist, and his interest was in describing how children go through different stages in how they think as they grow up, coming to understand the world in increasingly abstract terms.[27] Similarly, Dewey wrote at length about the power of authentic activities—about the kind of learning taking place on the working farm in Vermont.[28] In the twentieth century, the progressive movement Dewey helped create has looked at how young people can—and should—learn through their own active work on meaningful problems.[29]

The view of learning presented here builds on work done over the last century to understand how people think and how we can best help them learn to think more deeply, more compassionately, and more effectively about the problems and situations they will encounter in the world. But the vision of education I offer here takes ideas about learning in two new and important directions.

First, it is about how learning can happen in games—primarily computer and video games, although I will also present examples of games that require very little technology. Second, it is about what children need to prepare for the economic and social conditions that new technologies are creating. It is a view of learning *in* virtual worlds and *for* a changing world.

The result is a way of thinking about education that is neither "progressive" nor "back to basics" in the traditional sense of those terms. Computers give children access to new worlds: to parts of the real world that are too expensive, complicated, or dangerous for them except through computer simulations, and to worlds of imagination where they can play with social and physical reality in new ways. The virtual worlds of the digital age require thinking about learning in new ways.

My argument is that we have to move away from thinking about education in terms of the traditional organization of schools. Schools as we know them developed in a particular place and time to meet a specific set of social and economic needs. But times have changed, and the way we need to think about education has changed too. The academic disciplines of history, English, math, and science are not the only way to divide up the world of things worth knowing, the forty-minute blocks of time in which they are currently taught using lecture and recitation are not the only way to learn, and standardized tests of facts and basic skills are not the only way to decide who has learned what they were supposed to learn.

To prepare for life in a world that values innovation rather than standardization, young people need to learn to think like innovators. Innovative professionals in the real world have ways of thinking and working that are just as coherent—and just as fundamental—as any of the academic disciplines. The work of creative professionals is organized around what I call *epistemic frames:* collections of skills, knowledge, identities, values, and epistemology that professionals use to think in innovative ways. Innovators learn these epistemic frames through professional training that is very different from traditional academic classrooms because innovative thinking means more than just knowing the right answers on a test. It also means having real-world skills, high standards and professional values, and a particular way of thinking about problems and justifying solutions.

The book is organized to look at each of the elements of innovative thinking—epistemology, knowledge, skills, values, and identity—in a separate chapter. While the point of an epistemic frame is that innovation requires combining these elements together, looking at parts of the frame separately makes it easier to see how computers, games, innovation, and learning fit together.

The first chapter looks at what it means to call something a game and at what it means to say that someone has learned to think. It brings these two ideas together to show how games can be more authentic than school: more realistic and more meaningful ways of thinking about problems that matter in the world.

The second chapter looks at how computers change what it means to know something and at the kind of knowledge that innovative thinkers need in the computer age. I bring these two ideas together to show how young people not only need to learn in new ways but need to learn different things in the digital age.

In the third chapter, I highlight how computers let us do more than we know how to do on our own and thus let us learn by doing the things that innovative professionals do. I look at how professionals learn to be innovative thinkers and show how the training of professionals provides a model for learning new things in new ways.

The fourth chapter is about how thinking and working like a professional means learning to value the things a professional thinks of as important, meaningful, and worth worrying about. It looks at what makes people want to work hard and want to learn: a view of computer games that goes beyond mere entertainment to show how they can motivate adolescents to develop the skills, knowledge, and attitudes they need to succeed in a changing world.

Chapter five explores what it means to be an innovative professional: how thinking and working like a professional means seeing oneself in that way. It is about how professional training helps people learn to identify themselves as professionals and why these kinds of experiences of innovation are so powerful for adolescents in preparing to be successful adults in the digital age.

The final chapter is about how epistemic games based on professional innovation can change the way we educate young people. It looks at what is special about these games, how they are different from ordinary commercial games and different from the usual school activities. The chapter shows how the next steps toward education for the digital age may not be in schools or even at home but with a new kind of game played by groups of children and the adults who care about their learning.

Each of these chapters also looks at a specific *monument game:* a game designed to test new ideas about learning that has been studied in detail. *Monument* is a surveying term for a permanently placed survey marker, such as a stone shaft sunk into the ground. Monuments serve as known reference points—places whose location has been very precisely determined—that can be used to establish the location of other points on a map.

These monument games serve two purposes. The first is to provide concrete examples of the concepts discussed in each chapter. As Papert has said, "You can't think about thinking without thinking about thinking about something."[30] The monument games give a specific context for the more general ideas in each chapter.

They also provide images of what a new way of thinking about learning might look like. These games are deliberately designed to be best-case scenarios. Building a new educational system for the digital age is a big undertaking—one that requires political, institutional, and intellectual changes. My hope is to begin that process of change by providing an image of what we need to do and how we might do it.

The inspiring news is that the games I describe in each chapter show how young people can play at being professionals to help them learn to think in innovative ways for a changing world. The disappointing news is that these games are not (yet) widely available. They were designed to be tested, not distributed. I hope and expect that, in the coming months, and certainly years, children will have easy access to these games and many others. At the moment they are quite deliberately images of possibilities, not blueprints or ready-to-use products.[31]

For this reason, each chapter also discusses a commercially available game that makes some of the same kinds of learning possible. My purpose is not to endorse these games in particular. In the first place, there are many other examples, and between the time I write these words and the time they are printed in book form there will surely be other, even better games. So any attempt to describe the "best games available" would be futile. More important, though, one of the points I will make is that a "game" is always more than what comes in a box. The games I describe here—epistemic and commercial—are only as good as the way they are played. So each chapter closes with a list of suggestions for parents, teachers, and other adults about how they can help children use games to prepare for life in a challenging world.

Of the fact that the world is changing there is little doubt. Many others have already argued that a crisis is coming, that young people need skills in innovation to find good jobs and lead fulfilling lives, and that the economic vitality of our country depends in the long run on their ability to do so. David Autor, an economist at MIT, and his colleagues have shown that computers have already changed the skills that individuals need for economic success. The job market increasingly values nonroutine work that requires complex thinking and pays high wages.[32] But it isn't only individuals who benefit from skills in innovation. A group of Canadian economists have shown that innovation is central to economic growth for high-wage countries.[33]

So while the data I draw on to frame the problem and the examples of solutions I present come mostly from the United States, I hope it is clear that these are not issues unique to this country. In a global economy, any nation interested in maintaining or even increasing its competitive advantage needs to think about innovation—and about how to prepare its young people for life in the digital age. We all need to learn from and about games.

My goal here is to look at how we can do that: to look at what we can do about those challenges, but not by focusing on what we can do in the short term today and tomorrow by changing the textbooks we use or closing failing schools. The real problem is bigger than that, and to solve it, we need to think about education in new ways.

With epistemic games like the ones I discuss, young people don't have to wait to begin their education for innovation until college, or graduate school, or their entry into the workforce. In these games, learning to think like professionals prepares them for creative thinking from an early age. But what role can (and should) such games play in how we educate children for life in a high-tech, global, digital, postindustrial world? Should they be part of the school curriculum? Should they be played at home—or on portable game players—like commercial video games? What should games for learning look like, and—more important—what kind of learning happens when children play them?

These are big questions, but the future of our kids and of our country depends on how we answer them.

CHAPTER ONE

Epistemology:
The Debating Game

On September 26, 1960, 70 million Americans watched the first televised presidential debate between Richard Nixon and John Kennedy. The moderator, journalist Howard K. Smith, began:

> Good evening. The television and radio stations of the United States and their affiliated stations are proud to provide facilities for a discussion of issues in the current political campaign by the two major candidates for the presidency. The candidates need no introduction. The Republican candidate, Vice President Richard M. Nixon, and the Democratic candidate, Senator John F. Kennedy. According to rules set by the candidates themselves, each man shall make an opening statement of approximately eight minutes' duration and a closing statement of approximately three minutes' duration. In between the candidates will answer, or comment upon answers to questions put by a panel of correspondents. In this, the first discussion in a series of four joint appearances, the subject-matter, it has been agreed, will be restricted to internal or domestic American matters. And now for the first opening statement by Senator John F. Kennedy.

This first of four debates between the two candidates was about domestic issues, but the substance was not what decided the victor. Nixon had been in the hospital for two weeks in August. He was twenty pounds underweight. His face looked pale, and he refused to use makeup to hide his perpetual five o'clock shadow. Kennedy, who had been campaigning in California, looked tan and well rested. Those who heard the debate on the radio thought that Nixon had outperformed Kennedy. Those who saw the debate on television thought Kennedy had won.[1]

Thirty-three years after Nixon and Kennedy's historic debate, a group of eighth graders filed into a school auditorium. On stage were two tables with two chairs each. On one table was a sign that said "Pro." The other table was labeled "Con." There was a podium and microphone in the center of the stage. The teacher was sitting at a table on the side of the stage with a second microphone.

Four students took their places behind the two tables at the center of the stage—Charles and Samantha at the Pro table, Adam and Louisa at Con.[2] The rest of the class sat in the front rows of the auditorium.

"Judges, debaters, and honored guests," began the teacher. "Welcome to the Annual Foreign Policy Debate. Our topic for today"—and here the teacher raised his voice—"*Resolved:* That the United States went to war with Spain for selfish reasons."

Solemn-faced, he continued: "Arguing in favor of the resolution will be Charles Lewis and Samantha Bell; arguing against the resolution will be Adam Markowitz and Louisa Medina.

"In our debate today, each speaker will have four minutes for opening statements. Speakers will alternate from each team, beginning with those supporting the resolution. There will be a five-minute intermission, then each speaker will have two minutes for rebuttal and concluding remarks. Judges will have five minutes to prepare their decision."

By this time the students onstage were sitting very still. Even though they had seen their peers go through this ritual earlier in the school year, they were clearly nervous. The large auditorium was quiet, except for the teacher's voice over the loudspeakers.

"As moderator, I will act as timekeeper," he continued. "I will use the following signals.

"This signal," he said, holding up one finger, "will indicate that a speaker has one minute remaining.

"This signal," he said, moving his hand in a circle, "will indicate that a speaker has thirty seconds remaining.

"This signal," he said, waving his hand across his neck, "will indicate that a speaker has five seconds remaining.

"At the end of a speaker's allotted time, the moderator will turn off the microphone at the podium.

"Debaters, good luck. We will hear first from the side supporting the resolution."

DEBATERS AND JUDGES

I remember the speech well, because by the time this particular debate took place, I had given it nearly thirty times in my teaching career. The speech was designed to give a sense of gravity to the occasion for these eighth-grade history students: to make the debaters and the judges take their job seriously. It was part of a game these students were playing, called *The Debating Game.*

A week before the debate, the Pro and Con teams had each received a detailed sheet titled "Advice to Debaters." The advice described the format of the debate and the criteria for victory: that the burden of proof in the debate is with the side arguing for the resolution:

> The Pro side will be arguing that the United States fought the Spanish-American War for selfish reasons. The Con team must try to convince the judges that the Pro side has not made its case. In order to win, the Pro side must prove its position to the judges (that America's reasons *were* selfish). The Con side need only show that a good case has not been made. The Con side does not have to show that the United States was *un*selfish.

The advice in this packet of material was *substantive*—"This debate centers on two key ideas: what makes actions in history 'selfish,' and information about the Spanish-American War"—but also *strategic*, suggesting how debaters might fashion their arguments to win the debate: "As for the meaning of 'selfish,' you are on your own coming up with a definition that works for you in the debate. Remember, though, in a debate you need not argue for what you believe in. Whatever argument will win is the argument you should use."

The judges similarly received a sheet of instructions, which included specific information about the criteria they should use for judging the debate: quality of the presentation, use of evidence, clarity of argument, and skill at rebutting the opposing team's positions. They were told explicitly that they were not supposed to judge based on their own beliefs but rather on the strength of the arguments presented by each side:

> The criteria for victory in a debate—the criteria on which you should make your decision—is not which team is *right*, but rather which team makes a better argument. . . . Debate is more like a court case than a class discussion. You should judge not on the *truth* of a debater's position, but on her presentation, use of evidence and sources of information, the clarity of her argument, and her skill at refuting points made by the opposing team.

The judges had to prepare a short paragraph justifying their decision immediately after the debate and then a full report explaining their decision in detail. As these reports were presented to the debaters, they had to be explicit, constructive, and sensitive.

This was not an easy game, in other words, and playing it meant following detailed instructions about how to be a debater and what it means to judge a debate fairly.

IS THIS *FUN*?

With this brief description of *The Debating Game*, let's ask a fundamental question: What makes this a *game*, not just a clever classroom assignment to help students learn about the Spanish-American War? Aren't games fun and about things that kids already care about? Isn't school about work and about doing things that you *have* to do rather than that you *want* to do? And by those criteria, isn't this schoolwork and not a game?

Well, actually, no. And understanding how and why *The Debating Game* is a game is an important part of understanding how computer and video games can change our educational system.

For starters, though, the game actually was fun. Students enjoyed playing, and not just because it was an excuse to avoid their regular history class for a day. This was a kind of fun that Seymour Papert characterized as *hard fun:* the kind of fun you have when you work on something difficult, something that you care about, and finally master it.[3]

But wait: Students really cared about the Spanish-American War? No—at least, not more than any other eighth graders. What these players cared about as debaters was winning and losing and the pride that goes with playing any game well in school and thus in the public eye. As judges, students cared because their opinions mattered. They were deciding who won and lost the debate, and their written assignment was not merely an exercise to be graded and forgotten; it was going to be read by their peers as an evaluation of their performance in the debate.

The point I want to emphasize here, though, is that while *The Debating Game* was fun, that isn't why it was a game—because fun is not actually the defining characteristic of a game. On some superficial level, we play games because we enjoy the experience overall. But quite often, much of the time we spend on a game isn't about having fun.[4]

Much of being on a football team is doing drills and calisthenics and weight training and running laps—things that, despite the coaches' protestations to the contrary, aren't much fun for most players. Video game players spend a lot of time repeating very basic maneuvers to be able to progress to the next level. When my daughter and I play the computer game *Spirit: Stallion of the Cimarron*, the only way to get the horse to gallop is to click the mouse button continuously. Since my daughter can't click fast enough to make the horse jump a fence or stream, the limiting factor on our enjoyment of the game is the stamina of my index finger. While I really like playing the game with her, that part isn't much fun for me at all.

Recently I was talking online with a colleague while he was playing *World of Warcraft*—one of the recent wave of massively multiplayer online games (MMOGs) in which literally thousands of people play online, moving their alter egos through life in a magical medieval world. When I realized he was playing,

I apologized for interrupting. He replied: "It's okay. I'm just running some boring errands in the game." Because it turns out that even in one of the most popular games of all time, judging by the total number of simultaneous players, you have to do a lot of things that don't, on their own, seem like much fun.[5]

If *fun* is not one of the defining characteristics of a game, then winning and losing aren't either. Many traditional games are a competition: most sports, for example; *Chess, Checkers*, and most board games; card games; and many children's games, like *Duck Duck Goose, Tag*, or *Hide-and-Seek*. You can even win or lose when there is no competition at all, as in some forms of *Solitaire*. But many games don't have winners and losers. In *The Debating Game*, the debaters win or lose, but the judges don't. If you listen closely to how children (particularly preschool and elementary school children) talk about their pretend play, they use the word *game* for all kinds of activities that are collaborative, ongoing, and have nothing to do with what we would consider winning in the traditional sense: "Let's play *The Firefighter Game*"; "Let's play *The Superhero Game*"; "Let's play *House*."

Similarly, winning isn't the goal in a game like *World of Warcraft*. You can become more powerful, but even the most powerful player in the game at any point in time isn't the winner. Game researcher Richard Bartle argues that there are at least four different types of players of multiplayer online fantasy games: players who like to succeed at tasks within the game world, those who like to find out as much as they can about the virtual world of the game, players who like socializing with others in the game, and those who like to gain power over other players.[6] Each of these different kinds of players enjoys different things about the game, and (particularly for the socializers and explorers) the game ends when you get tired of playing, not when you have "won."[7] Different players can have different *end states* for the same game—different ways to decide when they are done playing. For obvious reasons, games that let players find end states that are personally and socially meaningful are both more engaging and better for learning about things that matter in the world.

In a game like *Dungeons and Dragons*—the inspiration for many modern computer games—players take on a character: an elf wizard, a dwarf fighter, a hobbit thief, a human cleric. As is true of many video games today, players often spend a great deal of time at the beginning of the game customizing their character. In *Dungeons and Dragons*, this is done by rolling dice to determine the strength, agility, looks, and health of the character (which, of course, go by more techni-cal terms in the game). Clothes are chosen, equipment purchased, an entire past invented. In video games, players don't roll dice (although in some games there is actually a simulation of dice rolling on the screen!), but they still design a char-acter with various strengths and weaknesses, and often choose details down to specific facial features.

Once the characters in a game like *Dungeons and Dragons* are brought to life, players take on the role of their character within the rules of the game. Fighters can do things wizards can't, and vice versa. Players can be good or evil, accumu-late wealth, become more skillful, or die in their adventures. The outcome is determined by a combination of a player's choices, the decisions of other play-ers, and rolls of various combinations of dice within an elaborate system of rules. But in the end, no player can do everything. Becoming a master of one aspect of the game necessarily means not becoming good at another. As in life, there is no absolute state of victory. "Winning" is about playing the game well—not neces-sarily scoring more points than another player, accumulating the most treasure, or achieving some other predetermined end state.[8]

Roles and Rules

What makes a game a game is neither "fun" or "winning and losing" but rather the fact that it has some particular set of *rules* that a player has to follow. In a game, players are assigned particular *roles*—"white" and "black" in *Chess*, "dwarf fighter" in *Dungeons and Dragons*, "It" in *Tag*—and playing a role means follow-ing some set of rules for behavior. In making this claim, I am borrowing from developmental psychologist Lev Vygotsky, who argued that "there is no such thing as play without rules."[9] What Vygotsky meant is that in all play—even in what seems like open-ended play among very young children—a game creates some imaginary situation that has some implicit or explicit set of norms that determine what players can and cannot do.[10]

If you watch young children play, in fact, it often seems that more of the game is about deciding the roles and rules than about acting them out. One child will begin by saying: "Let's play we're orphans."[11] To which another will reply: "No, not orphans, but our parents have gone away and we have to take care of ourselves and our four cats all by ourselves." And then the first child again: "And one of our cats will be sick and I'll be an animal doctor and you can be a food cooker." And so on. They spend more time setting up an imaginary world they can inhabit than they do actually playing in the world they created.

The rules in these game worlds are, of course, the children's understanding of how orphans, pet owners, animal doctors, and food cookers behave in the world. To make this point, Vygotsky described two girls who are actually sisters and who also "play" at being sisters.[12] It is a situation I know well from playing various versions of *Family* with my daughters. My oldest child will say: "Let's play *Family*. I'll be the older sister, and she can be the younger sister, and you can be the daddy." We're supposed to "play," in other words, the actual situation in our real family by explicitly acting by the rules that govern the roles of sisters and father. They are supposed to be especially nice to each other (unless they are being stepsisters, in which case they are supposed to be especially mean), and I'm supposed to play either a transgressive father ("Let's have ice cream for dinner!") or an ideal one ("Let's clean up the house and then as a special treat go to the circus!").

Lest you think playing family in a game of this sort is just child's play, consider that this is essentially what the best-selling computer game of all time, *The Sims*, is all about. In the game, players live in a suburban town, where they have houses and jobs, buy and sell things, go to school, go to parties, date, marry, have children, and eventually die. The game's promotional materials tout the fact that players can "build relationships with other Sims and watch them blossom . . . or crumble. Hang with friends, throw parties, meet the love of your Sim's life, or just live the single life."[13] And, of course, you could also play an orphan who is a food cooker.

Games like these are fun, but their value is in letting children live in worlds that they are curious about, or afraid of, or want desperately to be able to try out. As Vygotsky explains, all games are "the realization in play form of tendencies that cannot be immediately gratified."[14] In playing games, children are doing explicitly, openly, and socially what as adults they will do tacitly, privately, and personally. They are running simulations of worlds they want to learn about in order to understand the rules, roles, and consequences of those worlds. They are learning to think by examining alternatives in play,[15] and from those experiences they are learning what it might mean to be social outcasts ("It"), war leaders ("white" or "black"), professionals ("firefighter" or "food cooker"), members of a family ("father" or "sister"), and a host of other real and imagined characters in the world.

It may seem odd to describe board games like *Chess* as worlds that players can explore by taking on particular roles, but when researchers study experienced game players, this is what they find. Consider, for example, how Herbert and Stuart Dreyfus, who have studied chess experts, write about the game. "Chess grandmasters, engrossed in a game," they explain, "can lose entirely the awareness that they are manipulating pieces on a board and see themselves rather as involved participants in a world of opportunities, threats, strengths, weaknesses, hopes, and fears. When playing rapidly, they sidestep dangers in the same automatic way that a teenager, himself an expert, might avoid missiles in a familiar video game."[16]

References and Rebuttals

What makes *The Debating Game* a game, then, is that the students step into the roles of debaters and judges and play by the rules that define those roles: They subordinate their own beliefs to the rules of evidence in a debate, focusing on who presented a better argument rather than who was right; they write an account of the debate not for the teacher but as feedback to their peers. They are, of course, not actually deciding on the merits of the Spanish-American War as historians, nor are they actually grading their peers. But they are acting as if they are doing so, just as *Dungeons and Dragons* players are not actually becoming elves and wizards but are acting according to the rules they (and the game's creators) think that elves and wizards live by.

Like *Dungeons and Dragons, The Debating Game* is a fantasy role-playing game—let's call it *References and Rebuttals*—in which players take on the roles of debaters and judges to inhabit an imagined world in which they are making judgments about the morality of historical actors and about the skill of their own peers. To see what this game tells us about games for learning, though, allow me to refresh your memory about the details of the Spanish-American War.

Here is a section of an eighth-grade history text that describes the conflict.[17] While you are reading, you might notice how often the passage uses the passive voice—there are few historical actors here, only vague historical forces. Motives are ascribed not to individuals but to large groups of people. The war is not actually started by anyone in particular; it just starts. Thus:

THE SPANISH AMERICAN WAR BROKE OUT. During the late 19th Century, Cuba and Puerto Rico were swept by revolutions. These two countries were all that remained of Spain's New World empire. Both islands now wanted their own independence. Americans supported this desire and grew angry that the Cuban and Puerto Rican rebels were treated so harshly by the Spanish. These American feelings were backed up by other facts: (1) Americans had invested some $50 million in Cuba, (2) Cuba was the largest supplier of American sugar, (3) Cuba was strategically important because it controlled the entrance to the Gulf of Mexico. . . . When the American battleship *Maine* was mysteriously sunk in Havana Harbor . . . the United States declared war and defeated Spain in less than five months. As a result of the Spanish-American War, the United States took over Puerto Rico as well as the Philippine Islands in the Pacific.

Now that you've learned again about the war, here are the review questions from the text to check your understanding:

What were three reasons that the United States entered the Spanish American War?

As a result of the Spanish American War, America annexed:

a. Mexico, b. the Philippines, c. Spain.

FOR EXAMPLE, ASK THEM WHY

Now let's compare that dry description of the war to how one player in *The Debating Game* looked at these events. I'm going to give a somewhat extended account here of one judge's report because the contrast in content and style is striking between what was written by a team of professional historians and educators for a textbook and this report produced by an eighth-grader as part of a game. Pay particular attention to the completeness of this description of the debate, and the way that the judge is not only writing about how the debaters used evidence to make their case, she is also using evidence to back up her analysis of the game.

Overall presentation

Pro side

The Pro side had a great overall presentation. Both speakers could have spoken slower and clearer because it was sort of hard to understand them and they were never short of time. . . . They sounded convincing by saying things like "The first casualty lists did nothing to diminish the patriotic fever of a nation aware it was on the high road to international eminence. In fact, coming just after the news of victory at Manila, they spurred enlistments and stirred the hearts of even the most conservative of citizens" (*The Spanish American War* by Allen Keller). This and other pieces of information made their argument sound convincing.

Con side

Both speakers did a wonderful job on their overall presentation. They both spoke well but it would have been better if they both spoke a little bit louder. The argument was very convincing; they used quotations and statistics. For example they said that 216 people died when the *Maine* sunk.

Quality of the argument

Pro side

Their argument was very well stated. They made it clear by saying the three main reasons for the United States to fight in the war: to gain wealth, land expansion, and power. Most of their argument made sense but it was not convincing how exactly the *Maine* sank and how the people who were on it died. They made their point clear that the United States went to war with Spain for selfish reasons.

Con side

Their argument also was very good. Their main argument was that the United States didn't want to become an imperialistic power and they made their point clear by saying that the United States wanted to help Cuba and not take over Cuba. They stated that historian Frank Freidal said, "That Cubans were not strong enough to win but not weak enough to surrender." This was a good statement because it is saying that the Cubans needed help and that is what the United States planned to do.

Use of sources

Pro side

They used very nice evidence. They both used many quotes, for example, one of them said, "It is the duty of the United States to demand, and the Government of the United States does hereby demand, that the Government of Spain at once relinquish its authority and government in the island of Cuba and withdraw its land and navel forces from Cuba and Cuban waters." (President McKinley sent a letter to Spain). . . .

Con side

They also used great evidence. It was helpful that they showed the judges their sources by laying the books in front of them. They used dates as well as quotes. . . . They might have not wanted to use as many quotes as they did because they could have just translated the quote into their own words because half of their debate was quotes. They said that the United States knew how it felt to be owned and that was a good piece of information.

Let's make a few observations about what this judge wrote. First, she was describing a debate in which players covered the essential elements of the war as reported by the text, including "the three main reasons for the United States to fight in the war: to gain wealth, land expansion, and power." But the debaters also clearly went far beyond the text, using primary source documents and secondary interpretations by historians to make their arguments. (As it turns out, this is even more impressive because the debaters had to prepare for the game *before* the class had read anything about the war in question.) Second, this judge was describing a debate in which the players were using evidence to argue for a particular interpretation of historical events, ascribing motives to historical actors to explain historical circumstances. They were arguing over whether we can call a nation's actions selfish and about whether that definition applies to the United States in its decision to declare war on Spain in 1898. Third, this judge's report itself was clearly organized to discuss the criteria by which she was asked to judge the debate. She was not talking about her opinion, or about which side was "right" or "wrong." She was evaluating competing interpretations of historical events based on the strength of the arguments presented. Fourth, this judge used specific evidence from the debate itself to make her points, giving concrete examples and using those examples to explain her analysis of the debaters' arguments.

Finally, keep in mind that these were eighth graders who, from the textbook, might otherwise have been expected only to be able to identify three reasons for the start of the war and to know that, as a result of the war, the United States annexed the Philippines.

For those interested in the outcome of the game, this judge (and the other judges) felt that although the side arguing for the resolution made a strong case that U.S. national interests played a role in the government's decision to declare war on Spain in 1898, there was not convincing evidence that its reasons were necessarily selfish. Victory was awarded to the con side.

The Debating Game matters here because it starts to capture, in game form, the kind of authentic and powerful learning that we saw on the farm in Vermont. It provides a bridge from learning in the world that matters to learning in games that matter.

Here's why: The rules of the imaginary world of the game do a better job of representing what it means to think like a historian than the traditional text-lecture-and-recitation of many history classes. When we read the report of this judge in the game—and read through the report to see how the debaters were making their arguments—we can see that these players of *The Debating Game* were thinking more like real historians than like students trained to answer multiple-choice questions about historical facts from a textbook.

Stanford professor Sam Wineburg has looked with some care at the differences between history as traditionally taught in school and as practiced by historians. In one particularly clever study, he gathered a set of documents about the "shot heard 'round the world" on the Lexington Green that started the American Revolutionary War: primary and secondary source texts as well as paintings of the scene of the battle made at different times. He gave this set of historical source material to eight historians and eight high school students and looked at how they used the documents to "try to understand what happened at Lexington Green on the morning of April 19, 1775."[18]

The differences were striking. The students read the texts "from top to bottom, from the first word in the upper-lefthand corner to the last word in the bottom-righthand corner." They saw the documents as "vehicles for conveying information." They thought of bias as a binary attribute: either a text is biased or it isn't—either it is, as one student explained, "just reporting the facts" (what another student described as giving "straight information") or it is a biased account and thus not to be trusted.

For the historians, the documents were not vehicles for reporting facts in this sense. They were accounts written by distinct people at specific points in time, each with a particular perspective. The historians saw a key part of their task as interpreting these documents in relation to one another. They saw the texts "not as bits of information to be gathered but as social exchanges to be understood." For the historians, the question was never "Is this source biased?" but rather "*How* does a source's bias influence the quality of its report?"[19]

Wineburg compared how a student and a historian dealt with an excerpt taken from Howard Fast's 1961 period novel *April Morning*, which tells a fictionalized story of the battle on Lexington Green. On reading the excerpt, both recognized it was a novel and said that they could not rely on the details from that source. Several minutes later, however, the student seemed to have incorporated information from Fast into his understanding of the battle scene. The historian, in contrast, came upon a claim in a later document that the colonists formed ranks in "regular order." He remembered seeing the claim earlier and went searching through the documents. When he found it was from the novel, he laughed: "Oh, that's from Fast! Forget it!" As Wineburg explained: "A detail is first remembered, but the historian cannot remember its source. This recognition sends the historian searching for the sources of this detail, and, when reunited with its author, the detail is rejected. The reason is that the historian knows that there are no free-floating details, only details tied to witnesses."[20] Contrast this with the student, who knew that information from a novel was suspect but used it anyway a few moments later, having forgotten the original source.

Wineburg concluded that what distinguished the high school students from the historians was not the number of facts that they knew about the American Revolution. Instead, the difference was in their understanding of what it means to think historically. For the students, history is what is written in the textbook, where "facts" are presented free of bias. For the historians, historical inquiry is a system for determining the validity of historical claims based on corroboration of sources in conversation with one another rather than an appeal to a unitary source of truth—it is a way of knowing based on using specific evidence to support claims rather than trying to establish a set of facts that exist without bias. As Wineburg said: "It is doubtful that teaching these students more facts about the American Revolution would help them do better on this task when they remain ignorant of the basic heuristics [guidelines] used to create historical interpretations, when they cannot distinguish among different types of historical evidence, and when they look to a textbook for the 'answer' to historical questions—even when that textbook contradicts primary sources from both sides."[21]

EPISTEMOLOGY

Wineburg argued that in learning history, these students did not, in fact, learn to think like historians. No amount of "learning to appeal to an all-knowing textbook" will teach students to understand historical texts in context with one another and with the period in which they are written. No amount of correctly remembered facts will prepare students to sift through the historical record of newspaper articles, partisan reports, contemporary documents, and later historical accounts and from this tangled web of information construct and defend a historical interpretation. In other words, the epistemology of most high school history classes does not match the epistemology of historical inquiry.[22]

Epistemology, in this sense, is what Harvard professor David Perkins has described as "knowledge and know-how concerning justification and explanation."[23] It is a particular way of thinking about or justifying actions, of structuring valid claims. Epistemology tells you the rules you are supposed to use in deciding whether something is true, and epistemology in this sense is domain specific: Mathematicians make different kinds of arguments than historians do.[24]

This may seem like an obvious point, but discussions of thinking often leave out the differences between ways of thinking within subjects. In his work on how children understand the world, Piaget, for example, focused on cognitive stages across domains. His theory was meant to describe a progression from thinking as a primarily physical experience, to symbolic thinking, to concrete concepts, and finally to abstract thinking. For infants, a ball is something that we throw and catch, and the infant's understanding of it is physical or *sensori-motor*. For toddlers, the ball becomes something we call a "ball." The toddler's understanding is symbolic but still *preoperational*. It is just a label. For preschoolers and elementary school students, a ball is something that is round and red and that could be blue instead but has to be round or it isn't a ball anymore. It is a concept the child can change or *operate* on, but those changes are limited to concrete features of the object. Finally, for teenagers and adults, the ball becomes an object that obeys Newton's Laws of Motion. It is an abstract or *formal operational* idea. But Piaget's point was that these modes of thinking are developmental stages: They are the foundation of thinking in any subject, in any context.[25]

To be fair, Piaget's stages are compatible with the idea that different subjects have different ways of thinking: Discipline-specific ways of thinking could have features in common for children of different ages. Emphasizing the distinctiveness of different epistemologies is important, though, if only because that is how academic subjects are organized—indeed, it is the very reason we have different disciplines in the first place. As Wineburg suggests, "The disciplines that lend us school subjects possess distinctive logics and modes of inquiry."[26]

Epistemology is also important here because it shows why Wineburg's results are such a fundamental criticism of history instruction in schools. In his study, high school history students and historians had different epistemologies. They used different criteria for deciding that a statement is true or a claim is valid. For Wineburg's students, true facts were presented in a nonbiased text. For his historians, truth depended on one's ability to support a historical interpretation with evidence from multiple sources. These high school history students and professional historians had different ways of justifying their actions—and thus were actually studying different disciplines.

Which brings us back to *The Debating Game*. To make a valid point in the game, a debater has to advance a specific historical interpretation. The debaters have to make interpretations about what happened in the Spanish-American War and why events unfolded as they did. Judges evaluate the validity of those claims based on the clarity of the argument presented and on the debaters' use of historical evidence from primary and secondary sources. Although the debaters are explicitly trying to win the debate, the terms by which they do so are a closer match to the epistemology of Wineburg's historians than to the multiple-choice questions of their textbook. Similarly, the judges themselves must advance an interpretation that they have to defend using specific evidence. Although the judges are making interpretations about (and using evidence from) the debate itself rather than the war, the epistemology is similar: What matters is presenting an interpretation and defending it with specific evidence rather than appealing to authority to establish the legitimacy of a claim.

I should be quick to point out that *The Debating Game*, by itself, cannot take credit for creating the epistemology of professional historians. The game was part of a curriculum that systematically reinforced the message that history is about trying to understand what happened in the past by sorting through evidence and evaluating arguments based on that evidence. But by giving players roles whose rules of behavior emphasized the importance of competing interpretations of events supported by specific evidence, the game helped students develop a more authentic view of history.

In this sense, then, epistemology is at the heart of what school is about. The intellectual and historical justification for the traditional disciplines—mathematics, science, history, language arts, and so on—are that these are the ways of thinking that are fundamental in anything students will do when they finish school.

The idea of fundamental disciplines of knowledge goes back to the ancient Greeks, who divided knowledge about the world into the quadrivium of arithmetic, music, geometry, and astronomy and the trivium of rhetoric, grammar, and logic. If the details have changed (logic, arithmetic, and geometry now go together in the mathematics curriculum, for example), the idea that some ways of understanding the world are basic to all the things we do remains the same.

The liberal arts curriculum of our schools, with classes in the basic disciplines of mathematics, science, and history or social studies, English, art, and foreign languages, is based on the idea that each of these disciplines represent ways of thinking that students need no matter what they will do in life. But what the example here and Wineburg's work suggest is that school classes are not doing such a good job of teaching kids these fundamental ways of knowing.

And the reason they are not is that school classes weren't really designed to do that in the first place.

What's in a Game?

The Debating Game is a particular kind of game: a role-playing game in which the roles players take on require them to think and act in ways that matter in the world. To play *The Debating Game*, you have to accept a particular epistemology: a particular way of deciding when something or someone is right, of justifying what you do, of explaining and arguing for a particular point of view, course of action, or decision. In this sense, *The Debating Game* is an *epistemic* game: It requires you to think in a particular way about the world.

KNEES AND TOES

By this definition, of course, *School* is an epistemic game. The players take on particular roles: most are Students, a smaller number are Teachers, and still fewer are Administrators. There are clear rules—whether implicit or explicit—about how to play these roles, and the role of Student in particular carries certain expectations about how you have to think to succeed in the game.

The modern game of *School* as we know it was invented during the Industrial Revolution, at about the same time as the modern game of *Baseball*, in fact. And some of the same historical forces—urbanization, industrialization, and immigration and migration—formalized and spread both games across the United States.

Historian David Tyack describes the roots of our modern school system as beginning in the years leading up to the Civil War, when hundreds of thousands of Americans moved from the farms and countryside to cities where they were joined by new immigrants to form a workforce for urban factories.[27] In 1820 there were fewer than five urban areas in the United States that had more than 25,000 residents. By 1860 there were over thirty-five, including nine cities with a population over 100,000. With this concentration of relatively poor people in closely packed urban areas came urban problems: crime, poor sanitation, riots. Urbanization brought the challenge of socializing new immigrants to life in America and making everyone accustomed to new ways of life in the chaotic landscape of the industrial city.

Mob violence in Massachusetts in 1834 and Louisville in 1855, draft riots in New York during the Civil War, and violent strikes in cities across the country in the years that followed convinced civic leaders that something had to be done. Then, as so often happens now, education was offered as a solution to social problems. In the wake of widespread strikes in 1877, the U.S. Commissioner of Education argued that the country "should weigh the cost of the mob and tramp against the cost of universal and sufficient education." Author and school administrator John Philbrick argued: "The future of our cities will be largely what education makes it." School reformer William T. Harris suggested: "The industrial community cannot exist without free popular education carried out in a system of schools ascending from primary grade to the university."[28]

The existing system of small village schools was not up to the task of educating multitudes of city children. In 1850 Chicago had only twenty-one teachers struggling to teach nearly two thousand students; another eleven thousand school-age children in the city received no formal instruction at all. In the late nineteenth century, school leaders like Harris, Horace Mann, and Samuel Howe began to build what we now know as the modern school system. These reformers developed standardized tests that systematically showed that the decentralized village schools, each run by its own board of overseers, were not educating students adequately. They used these data to argue for the development of centralized and standardized school systems across the country.

It is in this period—the middle and late 1800s—that most of what we think of as the structure of *School* was developed: the so-called egg crate school, with identical isolated classrooms, each with individual desks for individual students;

age-graded classrooms filled with similarly aged students; the nine-month school year and 5-day school week; the 45-minute school period; and the Carnegie unit, or standardized class of 130 hours of instruction in a single subject.

In developing this basic framework—what Tyack and his colleague William Tobin have called the *grammar of schooling*—school leaders in the 1800s deliberately used the factory as a model for the orderly delivery of instruction.[29] Just as theologians in the Enlightenment described God as a divine watchmaker and cognitive scientists today write about the mind as a computer, so factories in the late 1800s were a dominant model for explaining and organizing activity.[30] While superintendent of schools in St. Louis, William Harris wrote: "The first requisite of the school is *Order*: each pupil must be taught first and foremost to conform his behavior to a general standard . . . to the time of the train, to the starting of work in the manufactory. . . . The pupil must have his lessons ready at the appointed time, must rise at the tap of the bell, move to the line, return; in short, go through all the evolutions with equal precision."[31]

Students were asked to literally "toe the line," standing motionless and erect with their knees together and their toes against the edge of a board on the floor. After all, as one enthusiastic teacher asked: "How can you learn anything with your knees and toes out of order?"[32] But if the factory model was embraced with enthusiasm, it was also a matter of necessity. As one critic wrote in the 1860s: "To manage successfully a hundred children, or even half that number, the teacher must reduce them as nearly as possible to a unit."[33]

THE GAME OF SCHOOL

The rules of the game of *School* are well documented.[34] The grammar of schooling creates what Philip Jackson and others have called a *hidden curriculum*—the lessons that students take away from school about how they should act in the world and about what it means to think and to learn.[35] The hidden curriculum is what makes math class and history class and science class all seem so similar, even though the subjects are so different. The hidden curriculum is what makes the textbook's multiple-choice questions about the Spanish-American War seem so familiar—we've all seen questions just like these before. Because the hidden curriculum pervades our schools, wherever and whenever we went to school, we played more or less the same game.

When *School* was invented, though, this curriculum was anything but hidden. Quite the contrary, in fact. *School* was deliberately, explicitly, openly designed to impose a new urban discipline as a means to avert social strife in rapidly expanding industrial cities. As Tyack suggests, it was a means to industrialize humanity. And that matters, because the hidden curriculum of *School* is still very much with us. We tend to think of *School* as we know it as something necessary and inevitable. But it is not. It is just one particular game, invented in a particular time and place to achieve certain goals.

Not surprisingly, the epistemology of *School* is the epistemology of the Industrial Revolution—of creating wealth through mass production of standardized goods. *School* is a game about thinking like a factory worker. It is a game with an epistemology of right and wrong answers in which Students are supposed to follow instructions, whether they make sense in the moment or not. Truth is whatever the teacher says is the right answer, and actions are justified based on appeal to authority. *School* is a game in which what it means to know something is to be able to answer specific kinds of questions on specific kinds of tests.[36]

Now, not every school or every classroom is like this, of course, and the hidden curriculum of *School* is about more than what happens in the classroom. There are sports teams and playgrounds and a host of other interactions that Students have in the game of *School* that shape what they learn about the world from playing. But in the era of No Child Left Behind—the federal law that links school funding to how well students perform on high-stakes standardized tests—it would be hard for any child in a public school to conclude that learning in any subject means more than learning how to identify the answer that someone else has already determined is right.

BETTER GAMES

In other words, our sons and daughters go to school in factories. They are not working on a shop floor operating heavy machinery, but from the building, to the curriculum, to the schedule for the day, almost everything about *School* was designed—*deliberately* designed—in and for life in industrial America.

The problem, however, is that industrial schools don't particularly encourage innovative thinking. We live in an era where global competition is sending overseas any job that relies on standardized skills and knowledge. When information can travel overseas with the click of a mouse, and barriers to trade in goods and services have been lowered to create a global economy, work flows to where it can be done for less money. As business writers John Seely Brown and Paul Duguid explain, the jobs in high-wage economies will be in "areas where making sense, interpreting, and understanding are both problematic and highly valued—areas where, above all, meaning and knowledge are at a premium."[37] In his book *Thinking for a Living*, Thomas Davenport suggests: "It's not clear exactly what workers in the United States, Western Europe, and Japan are going to do for a living in the future . . . but it is clear that if these economies are to prosper, the jobs of many of the workers must be particularly knowledge-intensive."[38] Already today nearly a third of the jobs in the workforce in the United States require complex thinking skills, and barely a quarter of all workers are up to the challenge.[39] In a postindustrial world, we need to build better educational games than industrial *School*.

Better educational games don't necessarily require new technology. *The Debating Game* helps players to think about issues the way historians do: to understand complex situations and develop and defend their own point of view on controversial issues. It is a game about finding creative solutions to problems rather than looking for right and wrong answers. But whether new technologies are *required* to build better educational games or not, it is clear that we need to ask: Can we use computers to build games in which players learn to think creatively—games in which young people can learn the epistemologies of innovation they need to succeed in a digital age of global competition?

The next chapter looks at one such game and at how computers make it possible for players to learn in new and powerful ways.

For Parents, Teachers, and Mentors

The Debating Game I have described is not available in any pre-packaged form, but is certainly the kind of game that teachers and mentors can create for students.[40] There are also commercially available computer games that give players a chance to think with a more realistic epistemology of social science than is available in a traditional history class.

One example is *Civilization*, a strategy game that lets players build an empire throughout human history. Players choose a civilization to lead, and beginning with a Stone Age settlement they make strategic decisions to invest in technological development or trade, to use diplomacy or cultural exchange, religious conversion, or open warfare to help their civilization grow and thrive. The game is based on a historically accurate model of advances in technology, religion, and the arts, and as players master the game system, they can begin to ask and play out historical experiments. While "experiments" are not the usual activity of historians, simulations are a growing part of other social sciences. Many world history textbooks, particularly at the middle school level, tell a story about Western progress—history as the story of the growth and development of European Civilization. In contrast, as game researcher Kurt Squire argues, *Civilization* gives players an opportunity to think in terms of a materialist-determinist approach to history, not unlike the one presented by Jared Diamond in his Pulitzer Prize-winning *Guns, Germs, and Steel*.[41] In this view of history, geographical location, ease of trade, and access to raw materials create structural conditions that shape historical developments.

But whether *Civilization* is the best example of a game about a way of thinking that matters in the world is less important than recognizing that the epistemology of any game matters. For example:

→ Parents, teachers, and mentors who want to help children learn from games need to think carefully not just about what kinds of things players do in a game but about what justifies those actions. How do you know in the game when you have made a good decision or a bad one? What kind of evidence is available to base your decision on, and how are you supposed to evaluate that evidence? What makes something "true" in the sense that you can use it to guide your choices in the game?

→ These questions are not the things that most game reviews focus on—although they should. The best way to find out what a game could be teaching your children is to play it yourself, and ideally play it with your kids. Remember, Max's mother played a key role in developing his island of expertise in dinosaurs. Help players figure out (or figure out with them) how they need to think in order to play the game well—and choose games where those ways of thinking matter in the world outside the game too.

→ If you haven't played many games before, playing games and thinking about their epistemology may seem intimidating. Taking risks is part of innovative thinking, and you can't help children learn to do that if you won't do it yourself. Use your kids as a resource. Ask them the questions you hope they will ask about the game, and let them teach themselves by teaching you.

CHAPTER TWO

Knowledge:
Digital Zoo

This chapter looks at how computers change what it means to think and thus what it means to learn. It begins by looking at *Digital Zoo*, a game developed by researcher Gina Svarovsky at the University of Wisconsin.[1] In the game, players become biomechanical engineers and design virtual creatures. Along the way, they learn about science and engineering. The computer plays a central role in this process, as players learn fundamental physics concepts in collaboration with the machine.

After a brief overview of the scientific principles that players encounter in the game, the chapter looks at two different groups of middle school players that Svarovsky studied. Her studies analyzed both what the players learned and how they learned it. As a result, the game illustrates how the simulated worlds of computer and video games change what is worth knowing—and thus what is worth learning—in the digital age.

Walking

Plato once famously defined man as a *featherless biped*—to which Diogenes the Cynic waved about a plucked chicken saying: "*Ecce homo!* Behold Plato's man!"

Bipedalism—standing, walking, and running upright on two legs—was a critical step in human evolution. Standing and moving upright made it easier for early humans to use tools with their hands. Upright posture is still one of the things that distinguishes us from apes, chimpanzees, and other primates. Almost all humans who are physically able learn to walk, and almost all do so before their second birthday.

But walking is actually an incredibly complex process of constantly adjusting balance: tipping forward and to one side and then extending a leg to correct the imbalance with just the right timing. Lean too little or too far, move the leg a little too soon or too late, and the walk becomes a trip and a sprawl to the ground. Running is even more difficult: a kind of continuous falling, made smooth by repeatedly and very precisely pushing disaster farther off with one leg after the other. From the point of view of an engineer, we move through carefully interrupted collapse—something that is far easier to do than to explain or describe.

SODACONSTRUCTOR

If you want to see how much physics and engineering you need in order to understand how creatures walk, take a look at *SodaConstructor*, a fascinating example of a computer program that lets kids of all ages do things that once only computer scientists and engineers could do. You can find the program, last time I checked, at http://sodaplay.com, and if you have a chance it is worth exploring for yourself. Like many computer tools, *SodaConstructor* is more interesting and compelling on screen than it is explained in print.

SodaConstructor is a free, Java-based spring-mass modeling system—and when described that way it sounds like it might be about as interesting as a simulation of growing grass. But start up the program and the first thing you will see is a little creature, The Dainty Walker, strolling across the screen. (See the illustration.) The Dainty Walker, the mascot for *SodaConstructor*, is an impressive piece of engineering. But it is just one of the literally thousands of monsters that you can find wandering, jumping, slithering, bouncing, cavorting, jiggling, and otherwise traipsing around in the SodaZoo, a Web site devoted to creatures made by people across the globe using *SodaConstructor*.

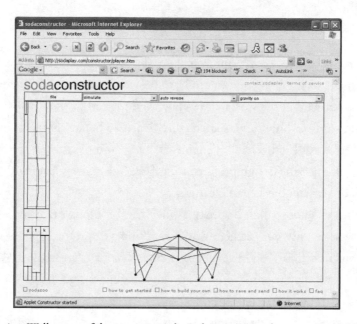

The Dainty Walker, one of the creatures in the SodaZoo. (Image from www.sodaplay.com)

Creatures in SodaZoo are all made by putting springs and masses—little slinkys and virtual marbles—into *SodaConstructor* and connecting some of the springs to a muscle wave. The wave makes the springs expand and contract in rhythm. Time the expansions and contractions just right, and the little creature moves across the screen.

The program has two modes: *construct* and *simulate*. Construct mode freezes the design, turning off gravity and the muscle wave, making it possible to add new masses and springs (new marbles and slinkys) to a creature. Simulate mode makes the creatures come alive, showing how they work when gravity, friction, and muscles are all in play.

Of course, more often than not the first time around—and the second and third and through many more tries—a creature will jiggle and wiggle without going anywhere. Or even more likely, just collapse in a heap under the effects of simulated gravity. Designing a creature that can move realistically is hard work, as any animation designer, robotics scientist, or biomechanical engineer can tell you.

DIGITAL ZOO

An old proverb says: "If you want to make a perfect painting, make yourself perfect and then paint." So if you want to learn how to do something interesting but hard, find out who in the world knows how to do it and learn to be like them.

If you want to build a virtual creature, learn to be an engineer. In *Digital Zoo*, players act as biomechanical engineers. They join design teams to work on a series of engineering design projects using *SodaConstructor*, leading to the construction of virtual objects and creatures.

The teams choose their own names, like the Fabulous Engineers. They get design specifications from a client who wants to develop prototypes of creatures for an animated film—say, a sequel to *A Bug's Life* or *Monsters, Inc.* Along the way, players follow the roles and rules of engineering design, based on how real engineers in training learn to design.

As in real engineering design, the projects are open ended, with no right answer and no guarantee that every team will be able to solve every problem. The teams develop innovative solutions by repeating the basic steps of engineering: designing, building, and testing alternative solutions to problems. Like real engineers, players optimize their designs in terms of cost and performance and identify the cost/benefit trade-offs of their creations. Just as real engineers do, teams document their designs and tests in design notebooks. Just like real engineers in training, teams meet with advisors while developing and implementing their ideas, and present their work to clients for review. In fact, the game's designer, Gina Svarovsky, was trained as an engineer before she became a teacher and educational game designer, and the game is based on her careful study of how engineers are trained at the University of Wisconsin.[2]

MECH-E

Before the players in *Digital Zoo* can make their creatures walk, of course, they have to get them to stand up. And among the many things an engineer needs to understand in order to do that are two fundamental concepts from physics and engineering: *center of mass* and *cross bracing*.

Technically, the center of mass is the point in an object where the sum of all torques is equal to zero and rotational equilibrium is achieved. It is an abstraction that physicists use to talk about the place where something balances in all directions. In a regularly shaped object—a beam in a building or one of the triangles we all played as a musical instrument in elementary school or a weightlifter's dumbbell—the center of mass is in the center of the object. A weightlifter holds a dumbbell in the middle so the unbalanced weight doesn't twist in his or her hand. You can find the center of mass of an irregular object—a lump of clay or a backhoe or a person—by suspending it from a string. Actually, you have to suspend it a few different times from different places on the object and each time mark the line down from where the string is attached. Where all the lines meet will be the center of mass, since that will always line up directly under the point from which an object is hanging. Of course, that technique works better for lumps of clay than it does for people or backhoes. But the principle is the same: Any object has a place where it balances, called the center of mass.

Center of mass is one of the key concepts in the branch of physics known as mechanics, which studies the behavior of objects interacting in space, and in the field of mechanical engineering (Mech-E). It is a key concept because nearly all of the calculations in mechanics are based on an object's center of mass. In fact, for a physicist, a rigid object (one that keeps its shape) is defined by its edge or boundary, its total mass, and its center of mass.

This is why understanding the center of mass is so important to a mechanical engineer figuring out how to make something stand up or walk. If the object's center of mass is too far to one side, it will tip over. How far is too far? Well, an object will stand up as long as its center of mass is over its base—the boundary defined by connecting the edges of where it touches the ground (or whatever it is balancing on). Walking is a matter of moving your center of mass beyond the edge of that base—the area beneath and between your feet—and then moving your feet so that your base is back under your center of mass before you fall over.

All of this depends, though, on the fact that people (and backhoes and beams in a building and barbells) are rigid objects—that is, that they more or less keep their shape. And the key to building things that keep their shape in the world of a mechanical or structural engineer is the concept of cross bracing.

Although many buildings and other large structures are rectangular, rectangles are actually not very stable. They don't hold their shape well because there is nothing to stop joints at the corners from twisting under the structure's weight—much less the weight of something placed on top of it. But the corner joints in a triangle are stable. Placing a rigid brace along the diagonal of a rectangle—a cross brace—divides it into two triangles, making the rectangle more stable. Of course, adding more cross braces makes something even more likely to hold its shape, but adds to the cost and weight. That's why if you look at many bridges, boat docks, or barn doors—structures that either hold a lot of weight or weigh a lot themselves—you'll see X-shaped supports connected to the main posts, floors, or walls. Two cross braces keep the structure stable without increasing the weight or cost too much.

Making something walk in *SodaConstructor*, in other words, means using cross bracing to make it stable and rigid and then attaching springs to a muscle wave to shift its center of mass so that it moves across the screen without falling over.

Walk the Walk

To find out what happens when players in *Digital Zoo* try to build stable structures and moving creatures using these principles, Svarovsky tested the game with different groups of middle school students. Twelve students—volunteers from local schools—played the game for about ten hours over a weekend during the school year. Another group of thirteen players (this time all girls) spent nearly forty-five hours with the game: three hours each morning for three weeks during the summer. These summer players were from the PEOPLE program at the University of Wisconsin, a program designed for students "who are African American, American Indian, Asian American (with an emphasis on Southeast Asian American), Chicano/a, Puerto Rican, Latino/a and disadvantaged students with strong academic potential," and priority is given to those eligible for the free and reduced hot lunch program. The program seeks to increase college enrollment and graduation of low-income students.[3] In other words, Svarovsky's tests included players from local schools who had expressed prior interest in the game and players who were playing only as part of a larger program designed for at-risk youth.

Svarovsky interviewed players before and after the game and recorded their game play on audio- and videotape. In the interviews she asked questions about physics and engineering. She asked about whether and why players had decided to play the game and what they thought of it after it was over. Svarovsky's studies thus give us a thorough record of what the game was like for the players and what they learned from the experience. They make it possible to use the game as a monument—a point on the map of educational games whose position we understand in great detail.

YOU CAN BUILD ANYTHING!

Let's look first at Rick and Carl, two of the weekend players in Svarovsky's studies. Soon after the game started, Rick and Carl were using *SodaConstructor* for the first time. They opened a design window and began rapidly placing masses on the screen.

"Wow, you can build anything! This is so cool!" exclaimed Carl.

But when the design was finished and he simulated it, the structure collapsed. This was the first of many errors in the boys' design process. But it was a process marked, for both players, by a sense of excitement rather than failure. Building in the game focused their attention on how they could make things that they thought were interesting, rather than on whether they could find the right answer to the question on a test.

After spending some time figuring out how to make a design that stood up, Carl and Rick started working on their team's first project: building a multistory structure, a tower made by stacking the same shape on top of itself several times. Their first design looked good but sagged to the ground as soon as they were finished.

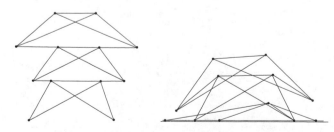

Rick and Carl's initial multistory tower as built (left) and after it was tested in simulated gravity (right). (Images made with www.sodaplay.com)

Rick and Carl reloaded the saved design. Then, like real engineers, they repeatedly redesigned and tested their structure.

Rick: This is cool. . . . I want to do this all the time. . . . I could do this all day!

Carl: This is amazingly better. Tell me when you simulate it.

Rick: All right.

Carl: Oh, that's not going to work.

Rick: It might not work because I made the top triangle too big.

Carl: Simulate it!

Rick: I have to save it first—

Carl: (louder) SIMULATE IT!

Rick: Woo! It works!

The text of their conversation doesn't do justice to the enthusiasm in their voices as they worked on this hard problem. Designing and testing their structure as engineers was exciting for them, and their repeated interactions with the computer were progressively linking that excitement with understanding about engineering and physics.

The second design did not collapse as much as the first—the upper stories were smaller now—but Rick wanted to minimize the "droop" of the structure, so he added additional supports to the top and sides of the structure. He created more triangles, which braced the loose ends of each story by linking it to the levels above and below. When they went into simulate mode, the structure did not move. It was rigid and stable.

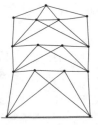

With added cross bracing, Rick and Carl's final multistory structure was stable. (Image made with www.sodaplay.com)

Later in the game, Rick and Carl were working on an "Overturn" project to design a stable cantilever—a structure that extends outward from its foundation, like a streetlight, diving board, or construction crane. They loaded a predesigned but half-completed structure and tried to build a base for it by connecting to the two lowest points on the object. Once again, their first attempts failed:

> *Carl*: This won't work.
>
> *Rick*: Try it!
>
> *Carl*: (pause) Okay, I'll try it. Oh wait, I should save it first. I still don't think this will work. Let's try it.
>
> *Carl*: Grrr. . . . Oh, I know! I should . . . widen the base!

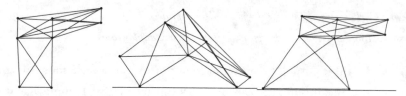

Rick and Carl's first design in the "Overturn" project, which fell over when simulated. Their final design (right) stood because its center of mass is over the base. (Images made with www.sodaplay.com)

Rick and Carl went through a number of design trials to move from a design with a narrow base to one with a base wide enough to prevent tipping. The process was a series of experiments, each of which was by itself fairly unremarkable. But these short experiments accumulated over time into understanding about how to use cross bracing to keep a structure rigid and how to balance a rigid structure by controlling the placement of its center of mass relative to its base.

COMPETITION

At the end of the game, Rick and Carl were working on the final design project: a competition to build a cantilever with the widest span and narrowest base possible.

They started by trying to balance a long beam on top of a narrow pillar. The beam and pillar were stable on their own—notice the crossbraces in the center of each piece to keep them rigid. But the structure collapsed when they simulated it.

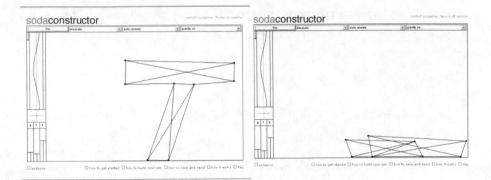

Rick and Carl's initial design for the "Cantilever" project (left) and the results of their first simulation test (right). (Images made with www.sodaplay.com)

Rick said, "I think it fell because the center of mass is a little more on this side when I was making it. . . . Yeah, now it's further out, so I think that was probably it."

They went back to a previous design that stood up but sagged too much, added more braces, and placed counterweights on the back half of the cantilever (on the left) to balance the structure. They saved and tested nineteen different versions before they came up with the winning design—one that had a span six times longer than the width of the base.

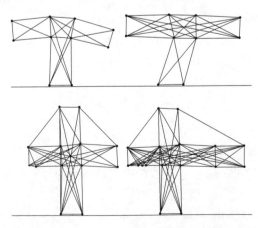

Some of the nineteen design stages of Rick and Carl's "Cantilever" project. (Images made with www.sodaplay.com)

As was the case in Rick and Carl's earlier game play, the nineteen experiments it took to finish the level each represented a small improvement in their design. Each experiment reflected a relatively small change in understanding about the underlying problem. But over time—across the levels of the game and through the designs and tests at each level—these interactions with *SodaConstructor* led to a sophisticated understanding of fundamental concepts in physics and engineering.

Based on these experiments, Svarovsky has suggested that repeated interactions with a computer built Rick and Carl's understanding in the same way that short interactions with his mother helped Max understand physiology and evolution.[4]

WHAT WOULD AN ENGINEER DO?

When players in the summer got to the more advanced levels of the game, it became clear that the islands of expertise they were developing were about more than just players' interactions with the computer.

The girls who played the longer and more advanced game in the summer went through the same first levels of the game as Rick and Carl.[5] In the higher levels, they moved from building structures that stand up and balance to designing creatures that move about. One player, for example, started with a robotlike figure—notice the cross bracing she used to help the figure hold its shape. She recorded in her design notebook that she found it "very confusing."

A page from one player's design notebook in Digital Zoo. (Image made with www.sodaplay.com)

"It is very hard to make it stay," she wrote. "At first I thought that it was easy but when it collapsed I had to think harder than before and I felt really confused but I thought carefully what would an engineer do so I thought very hard for a sec and it kind of started to turn easy."

In *Digital Zoo*, players advance from one level of the game to another by producing designs for clients. They build rigid forms and animate them, producing creatures that are both functional and expressive. But at each level, the client's requirements become more complex, and to meet those needs, players have to do more than simply interact with the computer: They have to learn to do what engineers do by thinking the way engineers think.

Let's look at how one player, Wanda, designed one of her first walking creatures. Like a practicing engineer, she recorded her work in a design notebook, making explicit the tests she performed while working out how to use cross bracing for support—what she refers to as "an experiment":

The arms and legs didn't work. The joints at the arms and legs kept falling in. I did an experiment by changing the last legs into two big x's instead of two little x's in the front arms. The back legs worked well now and it was very strong.

I made a trapezoid. Put braces with x in the middle, then I added 4 rectangles with big x's as braces. Next I added a head, in this picture it doesn't have braces but in my next structures it is braced with an x.

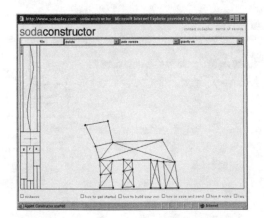

An early design for Wanda's first walking creature. (Image made with www.sodaplay.com)

The final level of the game is to design a prototype creature for a computer-animated film. One player, Kris, decided to make a "happy ballerina," Lindsey, who would be the sister of Heimlich, one of the characters from the film *A Bug's Life*. Kris started, as an engineer would, by making a sketch of her design idea. To build a prototype, she started by making the outline of the creature in *SodaConstructor*. She added cross bracing to make the butterfly rigid. "I have to add springs in the wings," she wrote in her design notebook, "so that they stay up." Then she added legs, "but," she wrote, "it doesn't balance so it doesn't walk."

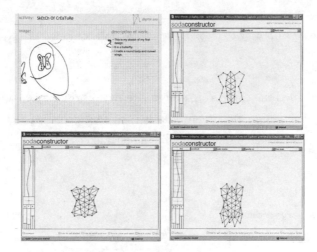

Kris's first butterfly design. (Images made with www.sodaplay.com)

In her second attempt to design a butterfly—like real engineers, players in *Digital Zoo* create and evaluate several design alternatives—Kris made the wings triangles instead of rounded forms. This had the advantage of requiring less bracing to keep the wings stable and thus less weight and a lower initial cost.[6] She added legs to make it stand and then extra braces to support the wings. Then she added two extra legs to help keep the design balanced and connected the legs to the muscle wave to make the creature walk.

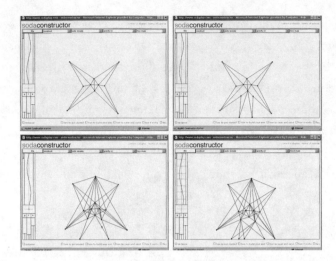

Kris's second butterfly design. (Image made with www.sodaplay.com)

Kris then evaluated the competing design alternatives the way engineers do and prepared a final design document for her client, including detailed design specifications and a sketch biography for the character.

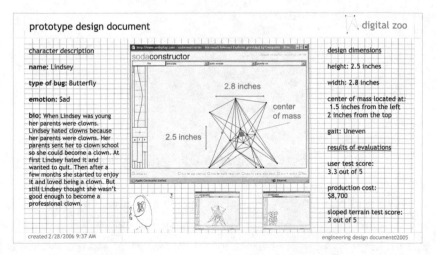

The poster from Kris's final design presentation shows the design specifications for her character, Lindsay the Butterfly. (Image made with www.sodaplay.com)

WHAT CAN A PLAYER DO?

It's easy to see that these players in *Digital Zoo* were able to make buildings that stand up and creatures that move about—and that doing so was a complicated process. It is also easy to see that as they learned to build these creatures, they came to understand concepts—such as center of mass and cross bracing—that gave them control over the design process. The things they built didn't just work by chance. The players Svarovsky studied were developing knowledge that they used to create innovative solutions to complex design problems.

But what good did that knowledge do them outside the game? After all, learning to design virtual creatures in *SodaConstructor* is fun but is not that important by itself. Svarovsky's interviews with players before and after the game—and in the case of the summer players in the fall, after they had played the game and been back in school for a few months—show that the impact of the game goes beyond learning to design in the program itself.

For example, these players learned to define the center of mass and could use the term to describe objects and physical situations. When they were asked to give a definition of the center of mass before the game, one player said:

Maybe where it's like the strongest of gravity?

After the game, the same player said:

Center of mass is like not the middle, but the point where weight is divided evenly. The weight is distributed on both sides. . . . Center of mass is like where most weight is equal. Kind of like the place where you put your finger and balance something on it without falling. Pretty much where all the weight is equaled out and you can balance. . . . It doesn't have to be in the middle. It can be a side. It depends I guess what the object looks like. The shape of it. . . . Where there's more weight.

Svarovsky also gave players problems from a physics textbook before and after the game. She found that players used scientific justifications, on average, five times as often after the game than they did before.

For example, one problem asked:

A man balances on his two hands with his feet in the air. Then he lifts his right hand off the floor and stands on the left one alone. How must his body shift if he is to keep from falling?

Before the game, one player answered:

I don't know what to say. He just picks up his hand and maybe leans over . . . ? I'm not sure why, that's just what I think—he will fall over to this side.

After playing the game, the same player responded:

He'd have to shift over to the left side to make sure that his center of mass is over his arm and hand and lines up. He'd fall over if he didn't do any shifting because the center of mass would still be over here. I think he would fall over. I think he would have to even out [his weight] by moving to the left side.

In other words, through the game, these players developed an understanding of the same phenomena that they study in physics class in school. But more important than that is the way they were able to use the knowledge they developed in *Digital Zoo* to think about all kinds of other things. Players talked about understanding why cranes don't topple over at construction sites or how they thought about the game when they went on rides at a carnival.

As part of the interviews, Svarovsky asked players to look at things with legs—real things and things on a computer screen—and analyze how they move about. After the game one player said:

I liked thinking about a way they walk. Like you had to put [things] in certain places—like the walking cycle; like the gait cycle and the stance cycle. . . . You have to have them even otherwise . . . the two legs or four whatever will cross each other and it will fall over.

Among the summer players who played the full version of the game, 86 percent said they think about science and engineering differently. As one explained:

Science I thought before was like blowing stuff up and experimenting, and now it's like you have to do exact measurements and then you have to build stuff the right way otherwise it could all just collapse in front of you.

After the game one player took apart a cell phone to try to build a video game controller. The controller didn't work, but the player said about the experience:

> I think about how stuff works now. Like now I'm like "I want to dissect this or I want to dissect that," like radios or whatever, and now I actually do it, like I don't just think about it. I'm like: "Can I dissect this?" And then I'll just take it apart and look at everything and I'll try to put it back together.

Svarovsky also tested players' engineering design ability by asking them to make flowcharts showing how they would design a tower out of toothpicks and marshmallows. Their design plans became, on average, 55 percent more complex after playing the game. As part of her interviews she asked players to choose seats for the Chicago Transportation Authority's new buses based on a matrix of alternative products—a matrix similar to the product comparisons you see when shopping for electronics or other goods online. Players considered 47 percent more features in making a decision, on average, after playing the game than they did before.

After playing the game, many of the players Svarovsky studied said that they were considering engineering as a career. More than 40 percent of the summer group had the poster from their final client presentation hanging on their wall at home. Many said that playing the game made them feel smarter. Others said that keeping a design notebook and presenting it to clients made them feel more confident in school. Still others said they use knowledge from the game in math, science, or art class in school. And like this player, many came away thinking that engineering is an important field:

> Engineers are like scientists or something. They like find out lots of things that we didn't know, and so they're important for like getting more advanced in like technology and medicine and stuff like that.

Or, like this player, who came to see engineering as a diverse and interesting profession:

> I found out a lot of people do engineering not just a couple guys. It's kind of like a stereotype: Only guys can do [it]. But lots of girls, I see, and lots of people [can do it].

In other words, these players came away from *Digital Zoo* understanding important concepts in physics and engineering design. More impressive, though, they were able to use these ideas to think in innovative, insightful, and motivating ways about the world around them.

Before we turn to the broader lessons about games and learning that we can draw from *Digital Zoo*, notice that the players Svarovsky studied developed islands of expertise in physics and engineering. They were learning things that matter in school and that will potentially be useful later in their careers. The game made them more interested in technology and more willing to consider a career in a technical field. A game about becoming an engineer, in other words, did many of the same things for these players that Max's mother was doing for him in the museum. It started them on the road to technical expertise and innovative thinking.

But what matters more, though, than understanding that players learned these things from *Digital Zoo* is understanding *how* and *why* the game made that learning possible.

Thinking Digital

Understanding how players learned from *Digital Zoo* gives us a glimpse of what learning can—and should—be like in the digital age. In the process of making creatures that stand, walk, and even dance, players learned to use specialized language: technical terms and concepts from physics and engineering. They used concepts like "center of mass" and "gait cycle"—terminology they didn't know before playing the game. Indeed, these were concepts they wouldn't be seeing until high school physics, and perhaps ideas they would not encounter unless they decided to become undergraduate engineering majors. Players in *Digital Zoo* thus develop the concepts and language of an important form of innovation. Even if they don't one day become physicists or engineers, this kind of knowledge can help them work on what business analysts call *cross-functional teams:* groups of people with different backgrounds and skills who can work together to develop innovative solutions to complex problems that require multiple forms of complementary expertise.[7]

Some people might say that a familiarity with technical terms isn't particularly important or impressive. Just using a bunch of jargon—pretentious, complex, and overly technical words—doesn't mean that you are smart. Game and media scholar Marc Prensky, for example, argues that it is actually counterproductive to "drape sets of confusing jargon around . . . commonsense things."[8] Just knowing words doesn't get you very far.

That, of course, is part of the problem with tests in school, which are mostly about jargon, testing how well students can substitute one set of words for another. For example, tests of physics knowledge ask students to identify the meaning of the word "force" on a multiple choice test. This is why there is so much research showing that even students who do well on school tests cannot apply their knowledge to real-world problem solving. For example, one classic set of studies shows that students who have passed a physics course and can write Newton's Laws of Motion down on a piece of paper still can't answer even simple problems like "If you flip a coin into the air, how many forces are acting on it at the top of its trajectory?" Which is, of course, a problem that can be solved using Newton's Laws.[9]

In *Digital Zoo*, though, the players don't just learn new words for old ideas, and they don't learn these new terms for their own sake. Any profession, any area of expertise, any group of people who do things that matter in the world have their own specialized language. We have words that we use in particular and distinct ways—*terms of art* that have specific meanings in and for the work we all do.

The specialized vocabulary that players develop in *Digital Zoo* is *knowledge* rather than mere jargon because it is not a set of unrelated terms or isolated facts. By themselves, the concepts (and terms) *center of mass, cross bracing*, and *gait cycle* are useless. But in *Digital Zoo* players don't experience them as unrelated or isolated ideas. They learn these terms to be able to analyze and solve problems. They learn these terms of art as part of thinking like, and acting like, engineers.

Put another way—in a different technical language, this time the technical language of professionals who study learning—the concepts that players learn in *Digital Zoo* stick with them because the knowledge they develop is tied to a particular epistemology. Players in the game are trying to do what engineers do, and to see the world as an engineer sees it, you need to understand complex and fundamental aspects of science and technology—things like the center of mass and cross bracing.

Anthropologist Charles Goodwin describes this process as the development of a *professional vision*.[10] Seeing the world as a professional requires using a particular vocabulary. A professional's knowledge serves at least two functions. First, it codes the world, providing the labels that he or she uses to talk about problems and issues and to search for solutions. Second, and equally important, the act of labeling highlights some things as being important and not others. It frames the problem by defining what matters in the situation and by excluding from consideration the things that don't. The process is similar to the work that Max's mother was doing in drawing his attention to features of the fossil in the museum. Instead of being knowledge in an informal island of expertise, though, in *Digital Zoo* players develop knowledge as part of a particular professional vision.

Professional knowledge of the kind players develop in *Digital Zoo* matters beyond the game itself, and not just because the concepts learned will come up again in school. The ability to use specialized language—technical language from a professional field—is one of the biggest predictors of success in school.

Traditional academic literacy has two components: decoding—that is, matching sounds with letters—and vocabulary. Both are essential to academic success. A child who does not learn to decode by first grade has an 80 percent chance of being behind in school by eighth grade. But the biggest predictor of school success from first grade on is a child's vocabulary before starting school—not the child's everyday language, but preparation for "academic language" tied to school-based, technical content like math and science. Preparation for complex academic language is becoming a more pressing task than ever as globalization makes mastery of technical fields a key to future success. Children who can't read academic language well by middle school face a daunting struggle in school, in the workplace, and for the rest of their lives.[11]

In other words, knowledge matters—but not if it is just a list of words to learn, as in E. D. Hirsch Jr.'s list of "what every American needs to know,"[12] or like too many vocabulary tests in too many classes in school. When children learn important concepts—and the words that go with them—to solve problems that are meaningful to them and in the world around them, the words go from empty jargon to solid preparation for future learning. Technical language matters when it is part of coming to see the world through the eyes of innovative professionals. In fact, it matters because it is an essential part of coming to see the world the way professionals do.

Knowledge and epistemology go hand in hand.

If knowledge and epistemology do go hand in hand, what it means *to know* has changed over time because what it means *to think* has changed over time. In his book *Origins of the Modern Mind*, Merlin Donald looks at anatomical evidence of human evolution and argues that the mental development of our species took place in several stages.[13]

To our closest evolutionary relatives—apes, chimpanzees, and other primates—to "know" is to remember. Apes can remember details of a social interaction and can even recall those details in context. An ape might remember that a larger male is dominant because he can recall a fight when the dominant male won. But apes do not attach labels to events, meanings to events, or generalize from events. They simply store their images to recall later. Even apes who have learned rudimentary sign language, Donald argues, are just storing and using the signs as conditioned responses. Like remembering a fight won by the dominant male, an ape recalls that the last time she gave a sign in some situation, it led to pleasure or pain, so she either repeats or avoids making the sign again.

Distinctly human thinking, Donald argues, began when our evolutionary ancestors developed the ability to *represent* events with gesture or mime. For example: Children quickly learn that when someone points their finger at a cookie, they are not asking you to look at their finger but at the cookie.[14] Following someone's finger means understanding that they are trying to point out something interesting. Gestures are about communication, and understanding them requires realizing that the gesture is *about* something important rather than *being* something important. When a child scolds a doll after getting a scolding herself, she is reenacting or re-presenting events, communicating about them to herself and to others in the process.

Donald argues that this ability to represent events doesn't require language as we think of it today. The changes needed in an ape's neck and throat to make speech possible are quite dramatic—and actually dangerous. The human larynx is located low in the throat, which makes it possible to create a wide range of sounds, but it also means that we are more likely to choke than any other animals. Our throats were redesigned for making sounds rather than eating safely, and it is unlikely that these changes would have occurred without the evolutionary advantage of some already-established ability to communicate using symbolic representation.

A *symbol* is one thing that stands for another without necessarily sharing any features in common with the original. Thus the word "ball" is a symbol for a real ball: I can describe things happening to a ball using the words rather than the ball itself even though the word is not round, does not bounce, and so on. Donald argues that standardized or ritualized gestures developed as the first symbols—things that represent something else in a standardized, fixed code, the way that holding up a thumb indicates "Everything is okay" or twirling your finger around your ear indicates that someone is crazy in many parts of the United States.

Words evolved as extremely efficient symbols for representing (and communicating) complex ideas. In most cases it is easier to form words than gestures, so we can communicate more precise ideas more quickly using words.[15] The ability to communicate more complex ideas ultimately made it possible to organize more complex societies, farm crops and raise livestock, raise more food, and thus support larger settlements.[16]

Donald argues that our modern world, in turn, is based on our ability to write down ideas expressed in words: to produce written symbols and generate scientific theories based on what we've recorded. Managing the activities of thousands of people in complex agrarian societies meant keeping track of business information—who owed what to whom—and the record-keeping needs of commerce drove the creation of external symbol systems, notably mathematical notations for counting goods and recording debts. Pictures were used to represent goods being traded, then other ideas that needed to be recorded, and those pictograms were gradually transformed into alphabets (like Greek and Roman letters or Hindu's Devinagri script) and ideographs (like Chinese characters). Once ideas could be written down, they could be studied systematically, and from that systematic study came scientific theory.[17]

It is no accident that the scientific revolution was based on the careful collection and analysis of data. Tycho Brahe, the Danish astronomer, spent a lifetime making and recording precise measurements of the positions of the planets in the sky. After his death in 1601, his assistant, Johannes Kepler, used this body of work to formulate his laws of planetary motion. Kepler's laws, in turn, became the base upon which Sir Isaac Newton developed the theory of gravity.[18]

The history of modern medicine similarly begins with systematic dissections of human cadavers beginning in the 1500s and recorded in printed atlases by Vesalius and his followers: Eustachi, Falloppio, and de Graaf—after whom the Eustachian canals, fallopian tubes and Graafian follicles are named. This research on the structure of the human body led to William Harvey's *Theory of Circulation* in 1628. The development of medical science over the next two centuries can be charted in the titles of books published about the body: *Treatise on the heart* (1669), *On animal motion* (1681), *On fevers* (1750), *On electrical powers in the movement of muscles* (1792), and *Morbid anatomy* (1793). Today the science of medicine depends on the printed word. The PubMed database of articles on the life sciences has cataloged over 16 million citations since 1950 alone.[19]

The development of medicine depends on the existence of external records for storing and disseminating information, and the same is true for much of science, engineering, democratic capitalism, vernacular literature, and the rest of the culture, society, economy, and technology of the modern world. As a result, much of schooling is about learning to access parts of this cultural record: learning to read, and write, and work with mathematical symbols.[20]

Writing and mathematics are, of course, static representation systems: The symbols don't change on their own. They just sit there until some person comes along to erase, alter, recombine, or otherwise work with them. Modern, literate culture is a kind of partnership in which the biological brain evaluates and transforms information stored in books and other records to make decisions.

In other words, memory was once the only method we had to keep track of important information. Now we don't have to rely on keeping track of things ourselves because we can write things down. We can record symbolic information—words and numbers—to refer to later, or to pass on to others. But we still have to know a lot, because while the tools for storing symbolic information developed in the last two millennia are incredibly powerful, we have never had tools that will actually transform symbols for us. Words on a printed page are inert. Someone has to be there to read them, to interpret them, to use them. To do anything with written words, first you have to know a lot about what you are doing. Until now, that is.

If gestures are *shared* representations of the world and words are *symbolic* representations—that is, they take a particular abstract symbol and tie it to a particular idea—then what writing does is let us *store* those symbols. It lets us put them down in a permanent way so that they can be shared with others. Once information is written down, we can return to reflect on it later and create theories, just as Newton and Harvey examined data collected across Europe over hundreds of years to develop theories about gravity and the circulation of blood: theories that changed the way we understand our world and ourselves. In the same way, an engineer uses reference and code books full of information about the design specifications of beams and materials in designing a building. The ideas in this book build on the work of scholars of education over the last century. And online game FAQs and guidebooks with information and cheat codes help players explore the more advanced and complex features of a game world.[21]

What makes computers so special—so transformative—is that they make it possible to *process* information externally. Writing "off-loads" or outsources memory. I don't have to worry about remembering things when I make a list—as long as I remember where I put the list. The list keeps track of the details for me, which is good because a list is much better at keeping track of things than I am.

What computation does, in contrast, is outsource thinking and acting. As I write this page, there is a little red squiggly line under the word "outsources" in the last paragraph. Ironically, it seems, Microsoft Word doesn't recognize "outsources" as a correctly spelled English word. It is not in the dictionary that Microsoft's spell-checker refers to. So the computer is telling me that the word is misspelled and asking if I want to correct the mistake. Many common mistakes it doesn't even ask me about. In that last sentence, for example, I forgot to type the "e" in "mistakes." The program automatically replaced what I typed, "mistaks," with the correctly spelled word, "mistakes."

While these may seem like small and commonplace features of a word processing program, they actually matter a great deal. I am a terrible speller, but I don't have to fix these simple mistakes myself because I can rely on the computer to correct them. That doesn't mean that the machine is ready to write a

Shakespearean sonnet. But it does mean it is able to do an important part of what, in the past, without a computer, I would otherwise have had to do or would have had to pay an editor to do for me.

Obviously there are many other examples. Computer controlled robots routinely replace factory workers throughout the industrialized world. Computers fly airplanes—both as automatic pilots and by translating the general directives of a human pilot into specific adjustments of the flaps, engine, and rudder, depending on flight conditions. Computers help us drive our cars by controlling fuel mixture and gear ratios; in luxury models, they even give us directions based on our current location. Computers search for information on the Internet and can bid for merchandise on our behalf. Computers can generate anatomical models from X-rays (as in a CT scan), perform statistical analyses, and test complex mathematical models in ways that human beings alone cannot.

A computer can perform almost any task for which we can write down a set of explicit rules. Not just *remember*, but actually *do*. That is, computers make it possible to create artifacts that take a particular form of thinking (understanding that can be expressed in the form of a finite state algorithm) and allow it to be carried out independent of any person. Computation makes it possible to develop simulations that dynamically enact and reenact parts of the way we understand our world.

As the late Jim Kaput and I have argued, if written symbols led to a theoretic culture based on external symbolic storage, then computers are in the process of creating a digital or virtual culture based on the externalization of symbolic processing.[22] This is the kind of change that has happened three or four times in the course of human evolution—a change of similar magnitude to the development of the printing press and the development of writing and language itself. What it means is that being "literate" in the digital age is not about reading and writing but about solving problems using simulations. What matters in the digital age is not learning to do things a computer can do for you but learning to use the computer to do things that neither you nor it could do alone.

Digital Education

You probably know that the square root of 16 is 4. But could you compute, with a pencil and paper, the square root of 17? As it turns out, there is an algorithm for extracting a square root by hand: a set of steps to take to find the square root of any number. It is a lot like long division, actually, only harder, but it is quite unlikely that you have ever seen how to do it, much less learned it in school. It hasn't been in most mathematics textbooks in the United States for a very long time, although it was once, and still is in some other parts of the world. I first saw it in a textbook, in fact, when I was teaching in Nepal.

The reason the algorithm for extracting square roots was removed from textbooks in the United States is that slide rules came into wide use beginning in the late 1800s. Slide rules are much better at extracting square roots (and doing a lot of other calculations) than the hand algorithm. However, in order to use a slide rule, you have to understand logarithms and know how to read a log table. If you are as old as I am, then very likely when you went to school you spent time in a high school trigonometry class learning how to read a log table. One of the key skills in reading a log table is interpolating values—figuring out numbers that lie between entries on the table. You also need to know how to interpolate to read a table of values of sine and cosine, which is why the skill was usually taught in trigonometry class.

These days most students don't spend much time in math class on interpolation. Why? Because pocket calculators are widely available, and for 99 cents you can buy little solar-powered computers that compute square roots quicker and more accurately than a slide rule—and actually do just about everything else a slide rule does too, only better and faster. Computers can now perform calculations that students once had to learn to do by hand.

Some people, such as cognitive scientist Gavriel Salomon, argue that we still should learn to do things by hand because only then do we really understand them.[23] But here's the problem with that: By definition, the things that a computer can do are things that can be represented by a well-formed algorithm. That is, they can do things that can be standardized. So learning to do what a computer can do by definition means learning some standardized skill. In an age of global competition, the high-paying jobs are the ones that can't be standardized. Innovative thinking is what counts, and education for the digital age shouldn't be about learning to do what a computer can do. If we are going to survive as a nation, education needs to be about learning to use computers to do things that neither person nor machine can do alone.[24]

SIMULATIONS

Learning to use a computer means learning to work with simulations because every computer program is a simulation: it represents some part of the world—real or imagined—in bits of code and memory. The program moves those bits around in ways that we can use to tell us something about the real or imagined world on which the simulation is based. Every computer program creates a world: what Seymour Papert and others have called a *microworld*.[25]

A microworld is a little universe that you can explore—a universe that, like the one we inhabit with our physical bodies, responds differently depending on what we do in it. It is *interactive* in the sense that when we act, the simulation reacts, and then we react to the reaction, and then it reacts again, and so on.

Decades of research have shown that interacting with simulations is a great way to learn complex topics. One of the seminal concepts that has emerged from this body of research is the idea of *autoexpressivity*. Users come to a microworld with a set of beliefs (usually implicit) about how that simulated world works. As they act in the microworld, the responses they get depend on the choices they make—choices that are based on their underlying assumptions. Acting in the microworld thus helps bring to the surface and challenge those assumptions, and ultimately refine understanding. Mathematics researchers Richard Noss and Celia Hoyles describe how one student came to understand ratios in a mathematics microworld while trying to design a house. The student started with a small version and enlarged the dimensions by adding the same amount to each part of the house. The result was a house that looked quite distorted, since preserving proportions requires multiplication rather than addition. To get it to look right, the student had to figure out that multiplication by a constant preserves proportion while addition by a constant does not.[26] In other words, every action in the simulation contains an explicit or implicit hypothesis. Whatever you do, you do based on assumptions about how the world works. By working with a simulation, users explore the domain being simulated—and build their understanding of that world—through cycles of action and reaction.

Over the years, this process of learning by making mistakes and figuring out how to correct them—and doing that over and over—has been documented in a wide range of computer tools in a variety of subjects: mathematics and science in *LOGO*, *StarLogo*, *Boxer*, and the *Geometer's Sketchpad;* civics, economics, and urban planning in *Stella*, *StarLogo*, and *SimCity;* history in the *Oregon Trail* and *Civilization*. Collectively, this work has shown the educational value of computer simulations: They make it safe to make mistakes, and thus people can learn by making mistakes and fixing them rather than having to always get everything right.[27]

This is what was happening for players in *Digital Zoo*. Rick and Carl designed structures, watched them fall down, and reevaluated the problem—at least nineteen different times for their final design. Wanda deliberately "experimented" with cross bracing. Kris struggled to make a butterfly with curved wings, adding springs, adding legs, rebalancing the design, only to simplify the design in a second attempt.

The *SodaConstructor* simulation makes it possible for players of *Digital Zoo* to make critical design mistakes. By fixing those mistakes, players figure out how to make their designs work—and in the process learn about the concepts in physics on which the simulation is based. They don't need to understand the center of mass and cross bracing before they make their first design. As in all good games, players can practice what game researcher James Gee calls *performance before competence*. They can learn by doing rather than learning first and doing later.[28]

As players in *Digital Zoo* test and revise their projects in the simulated microworld, in other words, they also test and revise their understanding of engineering and physics. However, they don't do this on their own, without any guidance. Wandering around in a rich computer environment without guidance is a bad way to learn. Learners are novices, and letting them work in a simulation without support leads to the very real human tendency to look for patterns and to develop creative but spurious generalizations.[29] The knowledge that matters in any domain is the knowledge that experts have—the knowledge they use to see the world, solve problems, and justify their answers. Any simulation for learning needs to be set in context if you want someone using it to develop professional vision about what is being simulated.

In *Digital Zoo*, the *SodaConstructor* simulation is set in the context of a game where players become biomechanical engineers consulting on the design of characters for an animated film. The game is modeled on the way engineers are trained, with the same activities, the same tools, the same kinds of conversations about the same kinds of mistakes. As players test and revise their knowledge of physics and engineering, they do so as part of a particular way of seeing the world.

The point is quite fundamental: A computer game can help players talk and think in ways that matter in the world.

Any game has, at its core, a simulation. It may be a computer simulation, as in the *Digital Zoo* or *Zoo Tycoon*, or it may be the cards in *Yu-Gi-Oh* or the board in *Chess*. All games create an alternate universe—a microworld—that operates by particular rules and that players can explore. The game may be collaborative, it may be competitive. Some of the things players do in the game may be fun, others may feel like drudgery. The rules of the game may be very close to the rules by which the real world operates—as when my daughters play *Family* or when millions of people play *The Sims*—or they may be quite fantastic—as in *World of Warcraft*.

A game is all of the things we do with, in, and around a simulation: the roles we play when interacting with a simulation, the norms we follow, the rules we obey. In fact, most of the things we call computer and video games—educational titles like *Math Blaster*, casual games like *Tetris*, sports games like *Madden Football*, and even controversial games like *Grand Theft Auto*—are actually simulations. Players bring a lot to the simulation to make it a game: They bring their own interests and desires. They bring their own experiences. More often than not, they bring their friends, and if they play long enough, the fun is as much in talking about what happens as it is in playing on the computer. Even when the simulation sets up goals—things you have to do to move from one level to another—players decide when and how to take up those goals. The game is always something more than the simulation by itself. The game provides the framework in which we make sense of what happens when we interact with the simulation.

This is why epistemic games can be so powerful. Epistemic games are based on simulations of interesting and important problems, where the framework for understanding what happens is based on the way that people who do innovative work see the world. In these games, the understanding that comes from acting in a microworld—the world of the simulation at the core of the game—is understanding that sticks, because it is developed in the context of analyzing and solving problems in the same way as a group of innovative and creative thinkers do. Of course, building such games means really understanding what innovators do, and how they learn to think about the problems they solve—which is the subject of the next chapter.

For Parents, Teachers, and Mentors

The *SodaConstructor* simulation is available free online and is a lot of fun to play with. Resources linked to the *SodaConstructor* Web site provide more information about how to work the simulation and how to start building wriggling, jiggling creatures. The *Digital Zoo* game is not as easily accessible, although Svarovsky and others are working on developing materials that would make the game available for classrooms or after-school programs.

In the meantime, some commercial games are similarly based on rich simulations of the real world. One example is *The Political Machine*, in which players become a campaign manager for a presidential candidate. The game uses real demographic data and models contemporary issues, including the War on Terror, current economic conditions, and U.S. policy in Iraq. The game Web site updates the issues to keep the game current. Players do many of the things that a real presidential campaign manager does: take out political ads, decide where and when to make speeches, set policy, raise money, and so on. Players can create their own candidates or use historical candidates. Playing the game well requires understanding quite a lot about American electoral politics, from the electoral college and its impact on campaigning to the constellations of policy issues that matter to voters in different regions. Players quickly learn the language of electoral votes, fundraising, spin, and advertising. They understand why some states get no attention in the general election and others are blanketed with advertisements, and why candidates are forced to equivocate and take centrist positions.

But whether *The Political Machine* is the best example of a game about a way of thinking that matters in the world is less important than recognizing the fact that the kinds of knowledge that players use in a game matters. For example:

→ When looking at a simulation, ask: What are the terms of art? What kinds of things do you have to know to use this microworld? When you play with children, be explicit about the underlying concepts. What are they? How do they work? Make the knowledge that is embedded in the simulation explicit.

→ Remember: what comes in the box is a simulation. Ultimately the players make the game. You can influence when and how the game is played—and, more important, how the game is discussed and evaluated.

→ Use the ideas in the simulation to create a professional vision. Describe elements of the game using terms of art that you know. If you know about cross bracing or media markets or probability theory, use those terms and ideas in talking about the game. Help children understand how you make sense of the game using your professional vision.

→ Help children see how the ideas in the game do and do not apply in the world outside the game. What do you see when you look at the world in the terms the game uses?

CHAPTER THREE

Skills:
Escher's World

Computers let us do more than we know how to do on our own—and thus let kids do things that innovative professionals do, and learn the ways of innovative thinking in the process. This chapter is about how professionals learn to be innovative thinkers.

The chapter looks at *Escher's World*, an epistemic game that I developed some years ago with help from colleagues at the Massachusetts Institute of Technology. The game is based on a study of a studio course in which architects in training were learning to think like designers.[1] In *Escher's World*, players become graphic artists and create an exhibit of mathematical art in the style of M. C. Escher. Along the way, they learn about geometry and design.

The chapter begins with an overview of the mathematical ideas that players encounter in the game and looks at how and why those concepts, as taught in traditional mathematics classes, are problematic for many students. We then turn to one group of players I studied, focusing particularly on how two young women experienced the game, on what they learned and, most important, on what they learned to do through playing the game. This shows how learning to *think* like a professional means learning to *act* like one—and thus how the training of professionals provides a model for learning in the digital age.

Melanie's Story

Here's a problem you might find in a standard geometry textbook—the kind of textbook that many math students still use in ninth or tenth grade:

> Point P is the center of arcs AB and CD. The length
> of arc AB = 1. If PC = 2 and AC = 1, what is
> the length of arc CD?

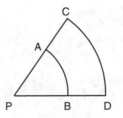

Spend a minute thinking about the answer before you read on—or if, like so many people, you hated math in ninth and tenth grade and only learned from your geometry class that you were no good at math and never wanted to study it again, spend a minute seeing if you can figure out what the problem is asking, and why.

Okay. Your minute is up. The answer, it turns out, is 2. Here's why: In the problem there are two *concentric arcs*. The smaller, inner arc (the curved section between A and B) and the larger, outer arc (the curved section between C and D) are pieces of two different circles that happen to have the same center, which is at point P. In fact, the bigger circle is exactly twice as far from the center as the smaller one. Now, it happens that the length around a circle—its *circumference*—is proportional to the *radius*, or the distance from the center of the circle. That is, if you make the distance from the center to the edge of the circle (the radius) ten times bigger, the distance around the circle (the circumference) gets ten times bigger also. If you halve the length of the radius, the circumference becomes half as long.

Since arcs are just a part of a circle defined by the angle they make at the center (the pie wedge at point P, which is called the *interior angle* or *arc angle*), the same proportionality applies to arcs with the same interior angle. That is, if you take the same size wedge from two different pies, the length of the edge of the wedge will vary directly with the size of the pie. Make the pie ten times as big, and the edge will be ten times as long—for a wedge with the same angle.

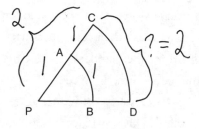

A diagrammatic solution to the problem.

The two arcs in the diagram both have the same angle at the center, so we can think of them as wedges of the same angle taken from two different-size pies. We know the radius of the outer pie is 2, since in the problem we're told the length of the line from P to C is 2. We can figure out that the radius of the inner pie. Since we know that the length of PC is 2 and the length of the line from A to C is 1, the radius of the inner pie (the line from P to A) must be 1. So the outer pie has a radius of 2 and the inner pie has a radius of 1.

Since the radius of the outer pie is twice as long as the radius of the inner pie, the edge of the outer pie is twice as big as the edge of the inner pie. We know the length of the edge of the inner pie is 1, since we're told the length of arc AB is 1. So the edge of the outer pie must be twice as big—that is, the length of arc CD is 2.

MORE OF THE SAME, ONLY WORSE

If you are like most people, you probably found that description of the answer hard to follow, even if you were actually able to solve the problem on your own. It's not hard to see why. Even if you understand the mathematics behind the problem, just keeping track of the letters and their positions on the diagram—not to mention what we know and what we are trying to find out—is a real chore.

The diagram with annotations helps to keep track of what we know and what we don't about the problem, but there is a deeper issue: The exercise doesn't seem particularly useful or meaningful in the first place. The problem, as presented, is completely abstract, disconnected from any particular situation, problem, or activity in the real world. Educational psychologist Mitchell Nathan and his colleagues have shown quite convincingly that although we know students learn mathematics better by starting with concrete examples and experiences, teachers tend to teach new concepts using abstract problems such as this one. In fact, their research shows that teachers who know more mathematics are more likely to start with abstract problems rather than concrete situations, even though that makes things harder to learn for their students.[2] Of course, we've known for a long time that when people learn something new—and particularly when children learn something new—they start with concrete experiences before they develop abstract understanding. This was Piaget's point in his work on the cognitive stages that people go through in the development of their thinking.[3]

So perhaps one way to make this problem better for students would be to put it in some real, concrete situation. For example:

Melanie's merry-go-round

One Sunday, Melanie took her little sister to ride the merry-go-round. Melanie sat on her favorite horse on the outer edge, 2 meters from the center of the merry-go-round. Her sister, Melody, sat in the inner ring of horses, 1 meter in from Melanie. As the ride was going around, Melanie found herself wondering how fast she was going. She noticed that in Melody's ring of horses, there was exactly 1 meter between the tip of the nose of one horse and the tip of the tail of the one in front of it. She counted slowly in her head, and found that in exactly one second, the nose of Melody's horse moved to the place where the tail of the horse in front had just been, so Melody's horse, Melanie realized, must be traveling at 1 meter per second (m/sec). Can you help Melanie figure out how fast her horse is going?

Fortunately, we don't need to go through the solution again, because this is *exactly the same problem*. The problem is now about a specific situation that most students already know something about (carousels or merry-go-rounds), but it turns out that translating the problem in this way actually makes it even *harder* to solve. In theory, we can now use our knowledge of carousels to make sense of what Melanie is doing and thinking. In the end, though, the problem is exactly the same, and so to solve it, we have to do the additional work of translating the information about horses and sisters into points and arcs, draw the same diagram as before, and then solve the problem in the same way. And . . . well, let's face it. This version of the problem still is not particularly interesting, and most students—perhaps even Melanie (or is it Melody?) herself—would probably feel similarly.

Now, we could imagine a whole curriculum of problems like this called *Melanie's Math Adventures*, and perhaps a flashy companion Web site with online problem-solving help, www.askmelanie.com. But this would still be the same problem in a new—and more complex—wrapping that makes it harder rather than easier to solve. Mathematics education researcher Jo Boaler has shown that, in general, making problems "real" by translating them into word problems makes them harder because students' understanding of the real world isn't much help in solving the problems.[4] An easy way to think about why understanding the real world isn't much help in solving realistic word problems is to ask yourself:

If a pencil costs 10 cents, how much does a pack of 10 pencils cost?

The correct answer is, of course, "something less than 1 dollar," because you always get a discount when you buy in bulk. But any math student knows you're supposed to ignore that fact when you solve a problem like this in math class. The way to solve word problems is to translate them out of the real world and back into their original form, which, Boaler's research shows, just adds more work rather than deeper understanding. Boaler argues that it is not the kind of problems that students do but the environment in which they solve them that makes mathematics meaningful.

So let's leave Melanie to her musings and look at what happens when this same problem came up in a much more authentic environment as part of an epistemic game.

Hallie's Story

Escher's World is a four-week-long game in which players become computer-aided designers. Players work in a design studio for four hours every morning, for a total of eighty hours.

My colleagues at MIT and I tested *Escher's World* some years ago. We recruited players by mailing flyers to local youth organizations and school district offices advertising a summer camp in computers, mathematics, and design. We chose the first fifteen middle school students who responded to be players. Our only requirement was that they had not yet taken a geometry course. The result was a mix of players from urban and suburban areas in and around Boston, including two African American, two Asian, and two Latino students. Three adults, all graduate students in the School of Architecture and Design at MIT, played the role of design mentors in the game.

We interviewed the players before and after the game and again three months later. In the interviews we asked questions about mathematics and design, and gave a short mathematics test of questions from geometry textbooks. Players described quilts and other designs. We asked questions about what they thought of the game, and whether it had any impact on their work in school. We made audio recordings of the game and kept records of players' designs, which made it possible to study both what they learned from the game and how they learned it.

The game was based on a study I conducted of an architecture studio course at MIT called the Oxford Studio. This study followed the work of the eleven students in the course and their three design mentors, a professor and two advanced doctoral students, and focused in detail on three students who were studying toward their Master of Architecture degree, a program structured to prepare students for professional registration as architects in the United States. For the study I observed the class meetings and interviewed students and teaching staff.

EXPLODING NEGATIVE SPACE

To tell the story of *Escher's World*, I'll focus first on the experience of one player, Hallie. She was a soft-spoken young woman: slight, shy, and somewhat awkward among her peers. It seemed as if that summer she was in transition: not quite comfortable with the kids who talked about Lego and going to the movies with their parents, not quite comfortable with those who were interested makeup and dating.

In the second week of the game, Hallie was working with another player when she discovered what she called "exploding negative space." She realized that if she took a pointy shape and repeatedly rotated it by a small angle, she could create an image where the negative space at the center—the white background in the empty area of the drawing—seemed to vibrate. (You can see what Hallie was referring to in the figure below.) Although she didn't know the technical term for it, Hallie had discovered an instance of the *Albers interaction*: a principle of color perception described by the famous artist and theorist Josef Albers, and an important concept in the design of computer interfaces.[5] Because our perception of a color changes depending on its context, the quick alternation of light and dark areas at the center of Hallie's image made the white space seem to have bright spots along the spokes of the design—so it looked like it was vibrating or exploding. This is why the Albers effect matters in interface design: If you choose colors that don't fit well together, you can produce distracting effects and make a computer display hard to read.

Hallie and the other players were excited by the effect, but she wasn't sure what to do next with the idea. So she asked one of the adults playing the role of a design expert for a desk crit.

Hallie discovered that it was possible to create an "exploding negative space" (the vibrating white space) at the center of a rotated image. The image on the right is a close-up of the center of the original design on the left.

DESK CRIT

Those familiar with design, particularly architectural design, will recognize the term *desk crit*. It is a design term of art: a part of the specialized language that design professionals use.[6] Desk crits are a particular form of critique in which designers discuss work in progress at the table or desk where the work is being done. When young designers are being trained in their studio courses, desk crits are the informal conversations that take place between student and expert— between designer and critic—that help students become better designers.

In the design studio, when a student runs into a problem in his or her emerging design or finishes some stage of the design process, he or she signs up for a desk crit with the professor or with a teaching assistant. The exact length, style, and form of desk crits naturally varies from student to student, professor to professor, and design studio to design studio. In the Oxford Studio, crits lasted somewhere between twenty and forty minutes and had a loose—but quite clear and quite consistent—structure. Crits began with a student explaining to the critic what she was trying to do with her design. That is, the student described a *design goal.* Then the student explained what she had done to try to accomplish that goal and the issue she was trying to deal with: some problem to be solved or decision to be made. For example, one student asked for a crit because she couldn't figure out how to design the roof line of the building she was working on.

After listening to the explanation—and often asking questions for clarification—the critic showed the student the problems he or she saw in the design, which may or may not have been the things that had originally concerned the student. Then critic and student worked together to design a possible solution to the problems they had identified together. In fact, they usually designed several possible solutions, discussing the advantages and disadvantages of each. The critic then left the student to decide how to proceed.

The goal of the critic in this process was to understand what the student was trying to do with the design and then to help her develop that design idea. The professor of the Oxford Studio described having a crit with students as "trying to get into their head" and "help them flesh out their own ideas, their own perceptions . . . [to] unlock the door to make the whole thing better [by] anticipating [problems] now before they complete their design."

In asking for a desk crit, in other words, Hallie was doing just what someone in a real design studio would do in the same situation. As she and the critic talked, they realized that neither of them knew exactly what conditions would produce the exploding negative space that Hallie was interested in. The Albers interaction—the change in the appearance of colors depending on their context—is a very important design concept, but how it plays out depends on the specific shape, color, and layout of the design as well as lighting conditions and the paper and ink (or the specific computer screen) being used. The Albers interaction tells you that you need to pay attention to the interaction between colors in close proximity; it doesn't tell you how to achieve any specific effect.

The outcome of this particular desk crit was that Hallie decided to try to figure out how to make the effect more dramatic using the software and printer she had available. She began a series of carefully conducted explorations into the workings of exploding negative spaces, making a set of designs—some twenty in all—to determine the factors that make a rotated shape look explosive. She concluded that you need "a nice pointy shape," "enough" points, and a dark color. As a result of these investigations, the idea of exploding negative space became a topic that Hallie would return to over and over in the game.

THE DESIGN STUDIO

In *Escher's World*, players take on the role of designers in training by doing more than just asking for desk crits, though, because in the Oxford Studio, learning to be a designer was about more than just participating in desk crits.[7]

The layout of the studio, for example, was quite different from most classrooms. The eleven students had more space for their own individual drafting areas than most K-12 schools provide for a class of twenty-five to thirty students. The studio had an additional meeting space the size of a seminar room and a large open space for formal presentations of student work. Class met from 2:00 to 6:00 P.M. three days a week, but this was more of a rough guideline than a fixed schedule. Students and teaching staff routinely came to studio before or after 2:00 P.M., depending on the work they had to do on a particular day, and the studio was busy through the night and on weekends as project deadlines approached. At any given time, students and teachers might be discussing projects around a seminar table or students might be working individually—or checking e-mail, or stepping out for a cup of coffee, or meeting with faculty or peers in a desk crit.

The Oxford Studio was thus, in one sense, a very unstructured environment. Students were free to do what they wanted to do when they wanted to do it. To a casual observer, it might even have looked downright chaotic. But the large blocks of unscheduled time and the flexibility of the routine made room for a different kind of structure: extended conversations about students' design projects. The Oxford Studio's lack of structure made desk crits possible.

In the Oxford Studio, students were working on the design of a new business school for Oxford University in Britain. Over the course of a semester, each student developed, presented, and defended his or her solution to this design challenge. To make that task more manageable, the semester was divided into six assignments, each focusing on a particular aspect of the design of the business school. Each assignment was about a specific task, such as making a sketch model of the site or designing one key part of the proposed building in detail as an example of the larger design concept.

For each assignment, the students and professor looked at examples of how other architects had addressed similar challenges for other buildings. Then students started working on their own designs. When questions came up or as they ran into problems, they met with the studio faculty in desk crits. Based on feedback from crits, students returned to their projects to prepare for the public presentation of their work. During each assignment, work was discussed publicly in pinups, with students literally pinning their work up on the wall and presenting it to the group for question, comment, and suggestions—in effect, a crit with the class acting collectively as critic. Finally, this process of design and critique was assessed in a formal *design review* or *jury:* a public event at which students displayed their work, presented their plans, and received feedback from professional designers from outside the studio.

A STUDIO GAME

What it means to say that *Escher's World* is based on the Oxford Studio, then, is that the game re-creates as much as possible the structure and activities of the studio on which it is modeled. As in the Oxford Studio, each player in *Escher's World* has his or her own desk with individual computers, and with the same ratio of players to master designers as the studio's ratio of students to teachers.

As in the Oxford Studio, the levels of the game are organized as a sequence of design tasks leading to a final project—in this case the design of a museum exhibit of art in the style of M. C. Escher rather than a new building. Each design task begins with a design goal, and players look at how other designers have addressed similar challenges. For example, the task in one of the early levels of the game is to make a straight-edged design using only curved lines, working from examples to create designs that build on, but are not the same as, the solutions that other designers have used for similar problems. Players work on designs on their own, with large blocks of free time in which they can schedule desk crits with master designers. Designs are discussed publicly in pinups and design challenges build on one another, leading to public presentations in two formal design reviews.

THE *GEOMETER'S SKETCHPAD*

Much of M. C. Escher's work is based on very sophisticated mathematics: complex combinations of the functions of transformational geometry (reflection, rotation, translation, and dilation), producing tessellations and fractal designs. However, the middle school students who played *Escher's World* in this test had never taken a class in geometry. They were unfamiliar with the basic concepts from Euclidean geometry, such as rays, arcs, or parallel and perpendicular lines, and advanced mathematical topics like the composition of functions.[8]

What made it possible for Hallie and her friends to play as graphic designers and work with sophisticated mathematical functions in *Escher's World* was a computer simulation tool called the *Geometer's Sketchpad*. *Sketchpad* is a software program designed by Nicholas Jackiw that lets the players in *Escher's World* create basic mathematical objects like points, lines, circles, arcs, and polygons, and define mathematical relationships between them.[9] Players can draw a point anywhere in the design, but they can also deliberately construct a point at the intersection of two lines or construct one line perpendicular to another line and passing through some other point in *Sketchpad*.

When any object in *Sketchpad* is moved (by clicking with a mouse and dragging), the other objects move as needed to preserve the mathematical relationships that the player constructed. The design changes in real time as points and lines are dragged about, and the effect can be very dramatic.

In *Digital Zoo*, the computer simulation *SodaConstructor* creates a microworld of springs and objects that respond to the force of gravity and the power of a muscle wave over time. In *Escher's World*, *Sketchpad* creates a different microworld—a world of points and lines and angles and polygons and the mathematical functions that can relate them to one another.[10]

What happens when you drag something around in *Sketchpad* depends on what mathematical concepts were used to make it. For example, the figure below shows two shapes (a1 and b1) that were made using *Sketchpad*. They both look like squares, but the first (a1) was only *drawn* as a square. It looked like a square when it was first made, but when its vertices are moved (a2, a3), it breaks down because it was *constructed* as an arbitrary quadrilateral—a four-sided figure with no mathematical constraints on its sides or angles. The second shape (b1), however, was *constructed* as a square.[11] Therefore, it stays a square in *Sketchpad* no matter what you do to it. Mathematical relationships define its parts so that all the angles are 90 degrees and all the sides are the same length. The square can get bigger or smaller, or get turned around, but it will always remain a square, no matter what else happens in the design. The square that was just drawn as a square may or may not keep its shape as the design changes.

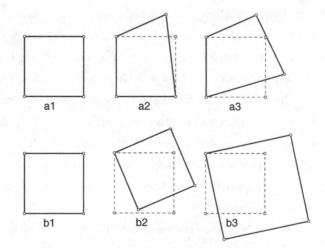

Square a1 was drawn *in* Sketchpad: *It looks like a square, but when its corners are moved (a2, a3), it does not hold its shape. Square b1 was* constructed *using parallel and perpendicular lines and a circle. When its corners are moved (b2, b3), it can change size and orientation, but it always remains a square.*

Of course, you can do more than build squares with *Sketchpad*. You can rotate shapes around in a circle, perhaps making exploding negative space, as Hallie did. You can make quiltlike designs by reflecting and translating objects to make a pattern. Or you can twist, shrink, and move objects using the mathematical functions of transformational geometry to make complex fractal designs.

Using *Sketchpad*, in other words, players in *Escher's World* can literally build designs using mathematical ideas. Just as players in *Digital Zoo* can learn about physics and engineering by trying to make creatures in SodaConstructor, players in *Escher's World* have to master fundamental mathematical principles to create beautiful images. To make the design below, for example, the player had to understand the mathematical transformations of rotation and dilation as well as the composition of functions to create fractal recursion: He had to make the fish twist and shrink by a constant rate toward a single point that serves as both the rotocenter and as the center of the dilation for the image.

An image created by an Escher's World *player.*

RINGS OF EXPLODING NEGATIVE SPACE

Let's fast forward to the final week of the game, when Hallie was working on the final level, creating an M. C. Escher-like poster of the kind that might hang in a museum exhibit. She had decided to make "rings of explosions" using the same shape in each ring—as if a real object were exploding, she explained, sending off shards in all directions.

As she began work on her final image, she ran into trouble. She was able to make an explosion in the inner ring of shapes or in the outer ring, but not in both. When the points of the shapes in the inner ring made an exploding negative space, the points on the outer shape were too far apart to create the visual effect she wanted. It didn't look like the outer ring was exploding. When Hallie moved the shapes so that the points on the outer ring gave the right effect, the points on the inner ring blurred into a continuous curve with no vibrating effect at all. So Hallie again asked for a desk crit.

Hallie's first explanation for the problem was that there was something wrong with the shape she had chosen—after all, she had conducted an extensive series of explorations, and she knew that the shape of the polygon used in the rotation is one of the important factors in creating exploding negative space.

The critic asked Hallie how she made the two rings. Hallie explained that she took a single shape and rotated it by 9 degrees repeatedly until it completed a circle. Then she translated the original shape to where she wanted the second ring to be and rotated the image of the translation by the same amount around the original rotocenter to make the second ring.

The critic suggested that they look at whether the shape of the polygon was the problem by changing the color of one of the polygons on each ring of the exploding design so they could watch carefully as they changed its shape.

As Hallie moved the points that determined the shape of the polygon she had translated and rotated to create her design, she saw that the problem was not with the shape. Seeing the two polygons—one in the inner ring and one in the outer ring—move relative to their rotated images (the polygons next to them in the rings), Hallie realized that the problem was in rotating the polygon by the same amount in both the inner and outer rings.

"Oh," she exclaimed, "you have to rotate the outside one more times—less degrees—[because] they're farther apart. . . . It's a bigger circle, [and] with a bigger circle you need to rotate it more times to keep it pointy."

In other words, in trying to make her rings of exploding negative space, Hallie solved the same problem that Melanie was struggling with on her merry-go-round. Hallie correctly concluded that if you have two concentric arcs and each has the same interior angle, then the length of the arcs depends on the distance of each arc from the center. Go farther from the center and for the same angle you get a larger arc. If you want the lengths of the arcs to be the same (so the points are the same distance apart), you need to use a smaller arc angle for the arc that is farther from the center.

There are two differences, of course. The not-so-important difference is that Hallie did not say explicitly that the ratio of the lengths of the arcs is exactly equal to the ratio of between the two radii—although there is little doubt that if she needed that information, she could have figured it out. The important difference is that problem was meaningful to her in a way that it never would have been to a student working on Melanie's Math Adventures. The problem had meaning because figuring out the relationship among the radius of a circle, the angle of rotation, and the distance between object and image (the arc or chord length) was the key to completing her design of a negative space explosion sending shapes flying off in all directions (see below).

Hallie Kraft: I am twelve years old and entering seventh grade. My picture grew out of the idea of exploding negative space. I discovered that by rotating a pointy shape, I could make the negative space seem to explode or move, almost pulsating or wiggling. I made rings of explosions and had them look like they were going off the page.

Natalie's Story

This study of *Escher's World* showed how in the game players have to figure out fundamental ideas about design, like the Albers interaction, and mathematics, like rotational symmetry, in order to make complex mathematical images. The players we studied learned about graphic arts in ways that might serve them well in their careers, and about some of the geometry concepts they would see in a year or two in their mathematics class in school.

As part of the study, my colleagues and I gave players a math test of questions taken from high school geometry textbooks. One question showed two congruent triangles placed in different positions and orientations on the page and asked: What rigid motions will move triangle P onto triangle Q in the drawing on the left? We gave players three versions of the same test, with different problems about the same mathematical topics. Their scores went up between the tests before and after the game—on average, scores were 14 percentage points higher after the game than they were before—and their scores stayed up when we tested them again three months later after they were back in school.[12] In other words, they learned school math, and their learning stuck with them later, even though none of them was studying geometry in school when they took the final test.

The players also learned to use mathematical ideas and design concepts to look at designs in a more sophisticated way. As part of the tests before and after the game, players looked at quilts and described what they saw. Before the game, one player we tested described a quilt (shown below) like this:

> A square with a square inside of it . . . and inside . . . there's some paint blotches or something. They almost look like chicken wings.

After playing Escher's World, *players were able to describe this picture in more sophisticated ways than before the game.*

After the game, the same player described the same quilt:

> A box with a red border, and then a smaller blue border around inside . . . and
> inside of that there's a yellow dot. And you're sort of drawn to that dot—
> meaning your eye is drawn to it. That's like the focus of the picture. And I guess
> I was going to say that it was symmetrical, but then I noticed these little blue
> lines coming out of these little red designs . . . and I realized that it was angu-
> lar symmetry. . . . Whoever made this . . . could have just started out with a
> block . . . and made four versions of it with different angles, and then just
> moved them together.

Notice that the player not only sees more detail in the design, he also uses
technical language. His description talks about the quilt the way a designer
might, thinking simultaneously about how the design could be made and how it
would affect a viewer. He uses mathematics and design knowledge as part of the
professional vision of a designer to see the world in a new way. These kinds of
changes were common in the players we tested. They gave longer and more
detailed answers, and used more technical vocabulary from mathematics and
design, after the game than before. During *Escher's World*, the players we tested
began to think like designers.

GETTING A'S

To understand how powerful learning to think like a designer can be, let's look
at what happened to another one of the *Escher's World* players we studied.
Playing the game in the summer, Natalie, like many middle schoolers, had been
shy around adults. She seemed more interested in flirting with the boys than cri-
tiquing graphic designs. She did not do particularly well on the math test before
the game started, and she said in her interview that she was an "okay" student in
school. Her test scores went up after the game, but not dramatically so.

Three months after the game, though, it was like she was a different person.
When I interviewed Natalie after she was back in school, she was still better at
solving problems in transformational geometry and graphic design than she had
been before the game. What was so striking, though, was how much more

confident she seemed overall. She was wearing a new pager, and when I asked her about it, she replied proudly that her parents had bought it for her because she was getting A's in all her subjects.

I knew that Natalie hadn't been an A student the previous year, so I asked what had changed in her schoolwork. She said: "I raise my hand at every single question. . . . Last year, I [was] like, 'No, please don't call on me!' Now my teacher doesn't want to call on me any more!"

She went on to describe in detail how her attitude had changed in each of her classes because of the game:

> I look at my [art] teacher's artwork . . . and she says, "What's your opinion, Natalie?" And I go, "You should put in more . . . symmetry in this. . . ." She was pretty amazed. . . .
>
> Some of my classmates, they don't [say much more than]: "Wow, it's a picture. It's colorful." But I tell my friends, "When you look at it carefully, it seems interesting." I tell them all these words I learned, like the mirror lines and patterns. . . . [My friends say] "Whoa, Natalie, where did you learn all this . . . ?" Now I'm teaching them art. . . . In music class . . . I brought up the symmetry, and the music is symmetry and balancing. They told me after school [that] now I have a different way of looking at music. . . .
>
> We're doing a lot of artwork in Spanish. . . . And I tell everybody, "But look at this. Just imagine like this, and how it balances out, and the colors. . . ."
>
> [In] math, I'm learning percents and degrees, angles we're supposed to be learning in math. That's helped me understand better. . . . And presenting, I had critics. So that's a big thing. . . . Now I'm loudspoken in public speaking, and pronouncing every single word, with no stumbles. Last year I was like "Uhhh" [makes a shivering sound].

We don't have specific data about how deep or long-lasting these effects were, but we know Natalie's grades were going up several months after the game was over. And even if there were other things involved, how students think about themselves and about their learning is an important part of how they do in school. The work of psychologist Albert Bandura shows that students who believe that they can achieve what they set out to do are more successful in school (and beyond) than students with low expectations about their ability to achieve their goals.[13] It isn't hard to imagine why this might be the case. Effective students believe that their performance in school is something they can control, so they are motivated to try to address problems in their learning. Students who don't think they are very effective tend to give up in the face of failure.[14] So if Natalie thought the game helped her in school, that matters.

What is interesting about Natalie's story, though, is not just that the game changed her in school but that it changed her in so many different ways. Natalie saw how the game had given her knowledge about mathematics and art that helped her in school. In math class, she felt more confident learning percents, degrees, and angles. Where she used to be "shaky," she started to feel "pretty stable." Natalie had been teaching her friends about art, telling them about symmetry and balance, mirror lines, patterns, and use of color. She was able to use some of the same concepts in music class.

This domain knowledge in mathematics and design wasn't just a collection of isolated pieces of information, however. It was a set of ideas that Natalie learned in the context of thinking like a designer. In school she started using symmetry and balance to show her friends how to look closely at works of art. Her "new way of looking at music" and thinking about art gave her a new and positive way to participate in Spanish class. In other words, knowledge learned in the context of a useful epistemology gave Natalie a powerful way of seeing the world—a professional vision as a designer that helped her do better in all of her classes at school.

SKILL

Knowledge and epistemology weren't the only reason Natalie was getting A's after playing *Escher's World*, however, because not everything that we know can be described in words. Most of us can ride a bicycle, but few of us could do a good job of explaining to someone how we are doing it or how they could do it themselves. Saying "push on the pedals, turn the handlebars, and don't lose your balance" doesn't count, since the trick isn't knowing *that* you have to do these things but in knowing *how* to do them.[15]

This difference between knowing that and knowing how—between *declarative knowledge* and *procedural knowledge*, or being able to explain something and being able to actually do it—is fundamental to education as we know it.[16] Most schools in the United States today celebrate declarative knowledge over procedural knowledge. Declarative knowledge is the knowledge that is tested on exams: facts like what country was annexed by the United States as a result of the Spanish American War, or what the definition of "center of mass" is. It is, for the most part, what standardized tests are about.[17] Procedural knowledge, however, is generally undervalued in school assessments. That is ironic, since in the world outside of school, knowing how to do things is generally more useful than knowing how to talk about things. But perhaps schools' bias toward declarative knowledge is understandable, since in the academic world, being able to talk about things (whether you can do them or not) is what counts. Schools emphasize knowledge over skills. This was part of John Dewey's critique of schools a hundred years ago. He complained that the traditional curriculum is based on the premise that "there is just so much desirable knowledge" and the goal of the school is to "give the children every year just the proportionate fraction of the total."[18] Critics of the No Child Left Behind Act and its regime of high-stakes standardized tests make a similar argument today.[19]

This emphasis on declarative knowledge is based on a particular view of learning, of course: the idea that you have to learn about something before you can actually do it. This idea, in turn, is based on a particular view of thinking: that we solve problems by figuring out which abstract rules to use and then applying those rules.

If we look at the experiences of the players in *Escher's World*, though, we see that was not really the case. As in *Digital Zoo*, players in *Escher's World* were trying things in a virtual world before they completely understood how to do them and learning from their mistakes. Hallie learned about the relationship between the radius of a circle, the size of an angle, and the length of an arc by trying—and at first failing—to make a design with exploding negative space. The result was that she was able to do better on math problems taken from a textbook—such as the problem Melanie was working on.

In order to make designs with exploding negative space, Hallie used a skill particular to the design world: participating in a desk crit. Over and over, we saw her turn to the master designers in the game. In desk crits, in pinups, and in design reviews, designers talk about their work with others. They look closely at designs and make constructive but critical comments on each other's work.

More important, though, than the fact that Hallie and Natalie learned how to do a desk crit is that the skills they learned in the game carried over in school. In explaining why she was getting A's in her courses after playing *Escher's World*, Natalie said part of the reason was the way she had learned to talk with teachers. She explained to her friends that if they pay attention to the details of a design, it becomes interesting. She had been afraid to speak in public, but in the game she gave presentations to critics, and as a result became "loudspoken in public speaking . . . pronouncing every single word, with no stumbles."

The skills Natalie learned playing as a designer helped her become an active participant in all her classes. In general, as developmental psychologists Barry Zimmerman and Timothy Cleary argue, experiences of personal mastery—times when you see that you can be good at something—are some of the best ways to develop a sense of personal efficacy. And that sense, when tied to skills that can be used to solve real problems, is an important component of academic achievement and later success in life.[20]

In *Digital Zoo*, we saw that knowledge stuck because it went hand in hand with a particular way of seeing the world and solving meaningful problems. In Natalie's story knowledge, skill, and epistemology were effective because they similarly went together. After playing the game, Natalie had a new way of participating in classes and a new way of talking with her friends and with her teachers about academic subjects. But this way of talking depended on having certain kinds of knowledge: concepts and terms of art of from mathematics and design.

The point is not that *knowing how* is better than *knowing that*. Natalie developed skills and knowledge together. Each depended on the other, and both depended on Natalie's growing ability to see the world as a designer. In the real world, skills, knowledge, and epistemology go together. Thinking like a designer (or in any innovative field) means linking ways of knowing and ways of doing in service of a particular way of framing problems and justifying solutions.

Schön's Story

PROFESSIONALS AND PROFESSIONALS

Innovation is by definition something that *cannot be standardized*. That's why standardized tests of isolated pieces of knowledge—and the school classes that prepare students for them—are not a good route to innovative thinking. We certainly know that what we are doing in the United States today is not maintaining our advantage in innovation. Over the last three decades, for example, the percentage of all scientific papers produced and patents filed in the United States has fallen.[21]

But while innovative work can't be standardized, the people who do innovative work are not simply "doing whatever they want." Educators from the philosopher John Dewey one hundred years ago to psychologist Howard Gardner today know that innovation doesn't happen in a vacuum.[22] As advertising executive Ernest Jones once said in an address to innovators in training at the Cranbrook Academy of Art: "Creativity not committed to public purpose is merely therapy or ego satisfaction."[23] Innovative and creative solutions to problems that matter in the world almost always come from working in and around a group of people working on similar problems in similar ways. Creativity is a conversation—a tension—between individuals working on individual problems and the professional communities they belong to.

Anthropologist Claude Lévi-Strauss argued that the Western idea of individual creativity is a myth, even in the arts itself.[24] Artists always work in relation to other work, and innovation cannot happen in isolation: It is by definition new and different; therefore it has to be new and different *from something*. But innovative ideas can't be so new and different as to be unrecognizable and therefore unusable. As inventor Jacob Rabinow explained, "You cannot only think of good ideas. . . . To say what is beautiful you have to take a sophisticated group of people, people who know that particular art and have seen a lot of it, and say this is good art, or this is good music, or this is a good invention. . . . A good creative person is well trained." Psychologist Mihaly Csikszentmihalyi argues more generally that "to be creative, a person has to internalize the entire system that makes creativity possible," including both knowledge of the domain in which he or she is working, and the professional judgment of the field of people who work in that domain.[25]

Gardner's work suggests that as children become more socially aware and develop critical acumen in adolescence, they become more judgmental about their own work. When you ask a group of kindergarteners who can dance, who can sing, or who can draw, they all raise their hands. By middle school, students become aware that their creativity is judged by external standards, and they begin to be critical of their work in new and more demanding ways; as a result, they often begin to feel inadequate and become discouraged about their creative abilities. The development of professional skills thus plays an important role in encouraging young people not to opt out of creative and technical fields.[26]

The word *professional* may seem a bit odd to use in a description of creativity. When we think of a professional, we usually think about one of the white-collar Professions: Medicine, Law, Architecture, Engineering, Accounting, and so on. But the reason that doctors, lawyers, architects, engineers, and accountants are professionals is not that they wear a jacket and tie to work, or that they belong to the American Medical Association, the Bar, or the Institute of Electrical and Electronics Engineers. A *professional* is anyone who does work that cannot be standardized easily and who continuously welcomes challenges at the cutting edge of his or her expertise. Professionals work on problems that involve uncertainty and that therefore require discretion and judgment. For a professional (in this sense of the word professional, which is the sense in which I will use it throughout this book), no two problems are ever quite the same, and no set of rules or routines tell a true professional what to do next. This is as much the case for a master carpenter as a transplant surgeon.[27]

By this definition, there are plenty of Professionals who are not particularly professional in their work because they are merely repeating the same routines over and over. At the same time, factory workers (whom we usually think of as the prime example of workers in a standardized job) can be professionals if they think in innovative ways about the work they do. The doctrine of total quality management, with its emphasis on constant improvement at every level of a company's operation, focuses on organizing quality circles of assembly-line workers, giving them time in their workday to identify problems in the manufacturing process and identify potential solutions.[28] Anthropologist Mike Rose has studied in depth what he calls the "intelligence of the waitress in motion, the reflective welder, the strategy of the guy on the assembly line."[29] Professionalism is a state of mind and a way of working, not a job title, degree, or dress code.

Put another way, innovation of the kind that is valued in a global economy always demands an understanding of how things work in the world. If being inventive means thinking outside the box, you have to understand something about the box to be an inventor. In our high-tech, global world, even thinking *inside* the box requires creativity.

REFLECTION-IN-ACTION

In the 1980s, Donald Schön studied in detail the way that professionals learn to do their jobs. He was looking primarily at Professionals in the traditional sense, but what he found is true of anyone who acts in complex situations where decisions need to be made without explicit guidelines—that is, anyone with professional ways of thinking and working.

Schön argued that professionalism is characterized by a particular way of thinking and acting that he described as *reflection-in-action*: "a capacity to combine reflection and action, on the spot . . . to examine understandings and appreciations while the train is running."[30] Reflection-in-action is the ability to think and work simultaneously—or, to be more precise, to reflect on what you're doing without pausing to do it. Schön contrasts reflection-in-action with *reflection-on-action*, which takes place when one looks back on a completed task or process to consider the implications and consequences of actions. Reflection-*on*-action occurs after the action is complete; reflection-*in*-action takes place within the span of time in which decisions and actions can still affect the situation at hand.

The distinction is subtle, of course, since the span of time in which decisions and actions can affect the situation at hand may last only minutes in a surgical procedure or a court trial but may stretch over weeks or months in an architectural design process or creation of a community redevelopment plan. The pace of reflection-in-action thus depends on the rhythms of a particular practice. But whether it takes place in minutes or months, what it means to say that professionals practice reflection-in-action is that acting as a professional means thinking like a professional, and vice versa. Reflection-in-action is the connection among the skills, knowledge, and epistemology of a profession, and Schön's work showed how this ability to reflect-in-action is developed in a *practicum*: a setting in which people have an opportunity to learn how to think and act in innovative ways—to simultaneously develop the skills, knowledge, and epistemology of a professional practice.[31]

PRACTICUM

The basic structure of a practicum is simple: Someone learning to be a professional does things he or she will do as a professional, and then discusses what happened with peers and mentors. Some practica are very formal, as are the design studios for architects and moot courts for lawyers. Some practica are very short: many certified nurse assistants receive only brief training; others are very extended: such as internship and residency for doctors. Some take place in school settings: capstone classes for journalists and engineers; others happen once a novice enters the workforce, as in the training of an apprentice or journeyman plumber or electrician. Whatever the specific context, a practicum is always an opportunity for a novice to act as a professional and get feedback on his or her actions from other novices and from experts in the field.

In a design studio—as we saw in the Oxford Studio and *Escher's World*—novices make a series of designs leading up to a final project. Throughout, work alternates with feedback in cycles of action and reflection-on-action. The primary mechanism, as we saw, is the desk crit, which is a formalized process, or a ritual if you prefer—the term of art in the study of learning is a *participant structure*—for reflection-on-action about design.[32] In a studio, designs are also presented to the class to be questioned and discussed by other novices and by experts in pinups and design reviews. Once again, these are formalized processes for reflection-on-action within the design practicum. In an engineering practicum, reflection-on-action happens in design advisor meetings and client presentations. During internship and residency for doctors, reflection-on-action happens during rounds and intake conferences.

These occasions for reflection-on-action in a practicum are the way that peers and mentors help novices by providing skills and knowledge that novices need but do not yet have. Reflecting-on-action lets them get help from more experienced others to do more sophisticated work than they could do alone. In this sense, reflection-on-action in a professional practicum creates what developmental psychologist Lev Vygotsky called a *zone of proximal development.*[33]

INTERNALIZATION

The idea of a zone of proximal development is not particularly complicated, but it is central to the process of learning to be a professional—and, in fact, to most kinds of learning that matter in the world. The zone of proximal development is all of the things that someone cannot do *alone* but can do *with help*. For example, at the moment, my older daughter can multiply a two-digit number times a one digit number (say, 21×7) by herself, but she can't multiply three-digit numbers (say, 621×434). She can solve simple number sentences with single unknowns ($4 + A = 8$), but she can't solve a complex polynomial ($x^2 + 4x + 4 = 0$). But the difference (for her) between 621×434 and $x^2 + 4x + 4 = 0$ is that she *can* do the three-digit multiplication with help. She gets lost keeping track of the intermediate products ($4 \times 600 + 4 \times 20 + 4 \times 1 + 30 \times 600$ and so on), but with some reminding— and perhaps a diagram—she can keep all of the steps straight and solve the problem. No matter how much help she gets, though, she can't yet factor a polynomial. She can write down whatever someone tells her to write, of course, but after the first step, she gets so confused that she has no idea what to do next without someone telling her exactly what to put on the paper. In other words, three-digit multiplication is in her zone of proximal development, but neither the simple problems (21×7) nor the polynomial are: The simple problem is too easy and she can do it herself; the polynomial is too hard and she can't do it even with help.

Vygotsky was making two related points in defining a zone of proximal development. First, and most distressingly, he was suggesting that zones of proximal development make traditional tests (such as the standardized tests that are so beloved these days) quite misleading. For example, let's say there were two high school seniors, both of whom got a score of 500 on the verbal portion of their SAT. Imagine for a moment that we could give these students the same test but let someone (perhaps a teacher) help them with their answers. Now one student gets an 800, while the other only gets a 600. Which student would you rather admit to college or hire for a job? You might object, of course, that both students would get an 800 with help, since the teacher could just tell them the answer. But that is precisely the point. This kind of test can't capture what is probably the most important thing to measure: What is the person capable of learning next?

Vygotsky argued that the zone of proximal development is the things we are ready to learn, and that the way we learn is by doing things with help and then progressively *internalizing* the process. We take what is first an external, social, and explicit process of solving a problem and gradually we do it on our own. First we may do it individually but still need to "talk through it"—and surely we all know what it is like to suddenly feel a little foolish talking to ourselves out loud while trying to figure something out. As an undergraduate I spent hours in the library pacing through the stacks and talking to myself while writing term papers, and my daughter still needs to talk out loud to add two-digit numbers. Later we talk through the steps but silently in our heads, which I can see my daughter doing when she adds a single-digit number to a two-digit number. And at some point, when we get really good at solving a problem, we aren't even aware of how we did it. My daughter no longer knows how she knows $2 + 3 = 5$. She just *knows* it.

The idea of internalization is that learning is always about bringing inside ourselves what once was help from someone else. We give ourselves the help we need—or to be more precise, we carry inside ourselves the people who helped us, which is why we all have moments of frozen horror when we realize we just said to our children exactly what our parents used to say to us. The little voices inside our head were once real voices outside our head, and we can understand how we do what we do by looking at what happened in the zones of proximal development that helped us get where we are.

ITERATION

Innovative professionals find creative solutions to complex problems by constantly working just beyond the boundary of what they can already do by themselves. That is why true professionals are constantly looking to push the envelope of what they can do. It is how they keep learning and growing in their work.[34] And they learn to do this originally in a professional practicum by working on problems and talking about them with peers and mentors. That is, professionals learn by repeatedly taking action and reflecting on that action. As these cycles of action and reflection-on-action repeat, each iteration of the loop brings action and reflection closer together, until the public reflection-*on*-action of the practicum is internalized as the individual reflection-*in*-action of an innovative professional.

That's why true professionals like to get stuck. They like challenging problems that expand the horizons of what they know and what they can do. It is the process of getting stuck and then getting unstuck that teaches professionals new things. They learn the skills and knowledge of innovative thinking in a practicum, by getting stuck and unstuck—over and over and over—and talking about why and how with the help of peers and mentors. This is what Hallie and Natalie and the other players were doing in *Escher's World* and what the design students were doing in the Oxford Studio, as public conversations *about* the design process turned into private and internal conversations *within* it.

But the skills and knowledge of innovation that professionals develop in a practicum are not some generalized or generic skills of innovation. The Oxford Studio was not training for innovation; it was training for a particular *kind* of innovation. The Oxford Studio—like any practicum—helped students become part of a community of people who think about problems in particular ways: in this case, a community of people who think about problems the way designers do.

ARCHITECTURAL IDEAS

In the Oxford Studio, as in most design studios, the iterative process of design guided by desk crits and public presentations of work was set up to help students learn the epistemology of architecture: that design ideas reflect an individual interpretation of an architectural problem. Mentors and critics spoke continually about the need to "develop an attitude," "develop an architectural idea," "find a valid architectural proposition," "decide on a strategy," "take a stand," "take a stance," "develop your criteria"—all expressions of the need to find an underlying idea or ideas to govern the development of a solution to the design problem.

Students were presented with design challenges that had an infinite number of potential resolutions. Their task was to develop a unique solution, to understand that solution, and to convey in words, diagrams, and models how the solution they chose met the demands of the original problem. The idea they developed was of their own choosing—as long as they could, with help from desk crits, develop a design based on that idea in a coherent way and defend their rationale to the larger community of architects in practice. As the professor explained to one student: "You're in control. Make it whatever size you want. Then I'll ask: 'Why is it that size?' And you'll say: 'Because it's doing this job.' And you'll develop your argument."

The action and reflection-on-action of the Oxford Studio were organized around building the skills and knowledge needed to create and articulate architectural ideas as innovative solutions to design problems. Players in *Escher's World* were able to develop the skills, knowledge, and epistemology of design—and carry them into their lives and schoolwork outside of the game—because they were playing a game based on a practicum that was designed to do just that.

GETTING STUCK

Now, of course, there are plenty of people in the world who respond to complex situations with pat answers: hack journalists, lawyers who draw up the same will for every client, engineers who stamp plans without reviewing them carefully, social workers who push the same forms at every client, carpenters who can only install one kind of cabinet and make a hash of it if there is anything irregular about the job, tech support people who can't do anything more than read from the manual, tollbooth attendants who don't know how to give directions to any of the nearby roads or landmarks for motorists who need help. And regardless of their job title, none of these people is a professional in the most meaningful and important sense of the word. True professionals are innovators, and epistemic games deliberately identify and copy the action and reflection that develop the skills, knowledge, and epistemology of some group of true professionals. An epistemic game copies the way professionals in training learn to find innovative solutions to complex problems by systematically getting stuck and unstuck with the help of peers and mentors.

Now, it may sound strange to say that professionals *like* to get stuck. But it is true, and raises the critical question: What makes someone want to get stuck and unstuck in this way? Which brings us to the question of values, to the next chapter, and to another epistemic game.

For Parents, Teachers, and Mentors

While *Escher's World* is not available as a prepackaged game, the *Geometer's Sketchpad* is a commercial product, and the publisher's Web site has curricula and workbooks that provide challenging and stimulating problems and activities that can be done with the software at home, in school, or in after-school settings.

Some commercial games similarly incorporate valuable real-world skills. One interesting example is *Roller Coaster Tycoon*, a game that lets players design and run an amusement park. (With add-on modules, they can also build water parks, theme parks, and so on.) The game incorporates several complex simulations, including a physics simulation of the rides, a social simulation of the patrons, and a business simulation of the finances of the park. To make a park successful, players have to exercise a number of complex skills. The interface for designing rides is fairly complex, and making the park look the way you want it to requires a fair amount of planning. The business simulation is also quite elaborate, and playing the game well requires following profit-and-loss sheets, interpreting graphs, and making sound business decisions about prices, investments, and staffing. The business simulation includes varying productivity for park staff (maintenance workers, concession operators, and so on). Good players have to develop management skills, deciding when to give raises or reprimands, when to send workers for more training and when to fire them.

But whether *Roller Coaster Tycoon* is the best example of a game that can develop real-world skills is less important than recognizing that the kind of skills that players develop in a game matter:

→ When you look at a game, ask: What are players learning to do? Are there other situations where those skills might be useful? Talk about other contexts where players might use similar skills to solve similar problems. Discuss whether there are situations in which those skills might *not* be appropriate to use. If they would not be appropriate, why not?

→ Decision making matters. Discuss and be explicit about strategy and tactics of the game. Find occasions in the game—or make occasions— to reflect on action. Talk about alternative choices and about how actions are justified and explained.

→ You are not an expert in everything, and different domains have different strategies for reflecting on action. Find games that build in teachable moments—which is not the not the same as expecting that the game will do the teaching for you.

→ In talking about the game, be explicit about how the skills in the game are tied to a particular way of thinking about the problems in it. What other skills or ways of thinking about the problem might help?

→ Remember, high performers take risks: Encourage risktaking and experimentation, but don't just take risks for the sake of it. Professionals learn innovative thinking by reflecting on success and failures and the reasons for them.

CHAPTER FOUR

Values:
The Pandora Project

This chapter focuses on the values of professional practices: on how thinking and working like a professional means caring about the things a professional cares about—and thus how learning to think like a professional means learning to value the things professionals think of as important, interesting, and meaningful.

The chapter begins by looking at *The Pandora Project*, an epistemic game I developed with a team of researchers at Harvard University, including Kris Scopinich, Chris Braiotta, and Victoria Martins.[1] In the game, players become high-powered negotiators, deciding the fate of a new biomedical breakthrough. Along the way, they learn about biology, international relations, and mediation.

The game is based on a real medical controversy: the ethics of transplanting organs from animals into humans. After a brief overview of science of xeno-transplantation, the chapter describes a study of what happened when a class of high school students played the game. The study shows how this epistemic game motivated adolescents to develop the kind of skills, knowledge, and values they need to succeed in the digital age.

Of Pigs and Men

X-Gen is a leading global pharmaceutical company with world headquarters in the Republic of Swindonia. Researchers at the company have been working for over a decade to make it possible to transplant organs from one species to another—a technique known as *xenotransplantation*. Yesterday, X-Gen's scientists announced that they are ready to begin clinical trials on humans at their research center in the capital city of Hoggopolis.

Their announcement created a firestorm within the scientific and medical community. Proponents argue that xenotransplantation might end the shortage of organs for patients suffering from late-stage organ failure who need transplants to survive. Opponents say there are too many potential problems associated with taking organs from one species—X-Gen plans to use pigs—and transplanting them into humans. Not least is the potential risk that a virus that flourishes in pigs could infect the human recipient and be transmitted from that patient to the general public, causing an epidemic. It is clear to the scientific community that this is a possible risk. But no one knows how likely such a scenario is.

Thus begins *The Pandora Project*. The scientists of Swindonia aren't sure how likely the dire scenario of global pandemic from xenotransplantation might be—and neither are scientists in the real world. X-Gen and Swindonia don't exist, but the organ donor shortage and the risk of diseases that migrate from one species to another are all too real. Each year more than six thousand people die in the United States waiting in vain for an organ transplant. Xenotransplantation offers the promise of being able to "grow" donor organs on demand, but there are obvious ethical concerns. Animal donors would be sacrificed to make organs available for human patients, and while alive, the animals would have to be kept in isolation and in sterile conditions—which some say would be cruel to the most likely donor species, primates and pigs, which are extremely social animals.[2]

We know that it is possible for a virus to migrate from animals to humans. It has happened in recent years with SARS (severe acute respiratory syndrome) and the avian flu even without transplanting animal organs into a human patient and suppressing the recipient's immune system with drugs to prevent organ rejection. The recent SARS epidemic caused over 750 deaths, with cases reported in over 20 countries worldwide. As of January 2006, the more recent avian flu had only 85 deaths in five countries—but more than half of the people who contracted the disease died as a result. And, of course, it is now widely believed that HIV, the virus that causes AIDS and has claimed some 25 million lives since 1981, came from a similar virus in chimpanzees.[3] Whatever happens, decisions about xenotransplantation are decisions about life and death on a large scale.

Despite these very real concerns, development of the science of xenotransplantation continues. In 2001 the Pontifical Academy for Life in the Vatican announced that it does not object to the transplantation of animal organs into humans. The US Food and Drug Administration (FDA), which has regulatory oversight in the United States for xenotransplantation, has developed guidelines for clinical trials using the procedure. In 2004 the World Health Organization Resolution on Human Organ and Tissue Transplantation urged member states to allow xenotransplantation "when effective national regulatory control and surveillance mechanisms overseen by national health authorities are in place."[4]

Globalization isn't only about trade in goods and services, and in the era of AIDS and SARS and avian flu, part of being an informed citizen means learning to make decisions about complex, science-based public health issues. Part of thinking in innovative ways in a global economy is learning to assess the risks and rewards of new inventions and innovative solutions—solutions to old problems and new ones.[5] And *The Pandora Project* is an epistemic game designed to help players do just that.

The Science of Xenotransplantation

To understand the potential risks and potential benefits of xenotransplantation, you have to know something about genetics, epidemiology, and immunobiology. You have to understand that the human immune system protects the body from potentially harmful microorganisms and cancerous cells using antigens: proteins that identify cells as belonging to the body. When foreign antigens are detected, the body's immune response begins. Phagocytic cells—more commonly known as white blood cells—aided by antimicrobial proteins, try to surround, absorb, and destroy the foreign cells.

The human immune response system matters in understanding xenotransplantation because any transplanted organ—whether from a human or animal donor—is by definition a foreign substance to the body, and the body's natural defenses work to reject it. Before transplantation, donor organs are typed—that is, their antigens are matched as closely as possible to the antigens of the potential recipient—but drugs are still needed to prevent the recipient's immune system from attacking the transplanted tissue. These immunosuppressive drugs make transplant recipients more likely to catch colds, flus, and other diseases that pass from person to person. More alarmingly, though, if the donor organ carries an undetected virus or bacteria, the recipient's suppressed immune system is less able to fight it off.

So, on one hand, it might seem that xenotransplantation, if feasible, would be safer than human organ donation. After all, the animals could be raised in completely sterile conditions. The genetics of their organs could be matched as closely as possible to the recipients by breeding them for particular combinations of antigens on their cells that would match the host. And perhaps best of all, because different species have different genes, they often are affected by different viruses. The things that would make a pig sick often have little or no effect on a human, and vice versa.

Ah, but there's the rub. The particular danger of xenotransplantation is that a virus or bacteria that is harmless to pigs (or other donor animals) could be introduced into a human host. The immunosuppressive drugs would make that host a perfect breeding ground: The person would have little ability to fight off the new bacteria or virus, and it would be free to multiply, perhaps mutating into a form that can cause human disease. In fact, it could mutate into a form that would not only infect a human host, but could also pass directly from one person to another without having to be introduced through a transplant. The result could be a worldwide epidemic.

Understanding the costs, benefits, and risks of xenotransplantation thus depends on understanding the science behind it. But assessing xenotransplantation means grappling with the moral dilemmas that this new technology raises.

The procedure would require careful breeding and maintenance of genetically altered animals raised in sterile conditions, which would be extremely expensive. Every dollar spent on xenotransplantation would be money not spent on less expensive procedures, or on investment in public health measures more generally. The money spent researching the technique would be money not spent trying to develop other solutions to the organ donor shortage or cures for other diseases. If the procedure works, most of the patients who benefit would be from wealthy countries. If an epidemic breaks out, the victims who suffer most would be from countries without adequate healthcare or the infrastructure to support a massive public health effort to prevent the spread of a new disease. Even within wealthy countries, the benefits of the procedure would accrue to individuals, but the risks would be borne by everyone. Who should decide whether the risk is worthwhile?

MUTUAL GAINS NEGOTIATION

If and when xenotransplantation researchers want to work with human patients, science will play an important role in deciding whether and how to proceed, but in the end any decision will be reached through some process of negotiation. Decisions will be made by interested parties working together—and against one another—to influence regulators at the FDA and its equivalents in other countries. Central to that process will be people representing the interests of biotechnology companies developing the procedure, the World Health Organization and other nongovernmental organizations, animal welfare groups, patients' rights advocates, medical associations, and others. And these different interest groups will be represented by people skilled in the ways of negotiation, mediation, and dispute resolution.

In *The Pandora Project*, players take on the role of negotiators for groups in Swindonia interested in xenotransplantation, and the game they play in these roles is modeled on the training of professional negotiators as developed by the Harvard Program on Negotiation.

The Program on Negotiation emphasizes a particular way of thinking about negotiating known as the *mutual gains approach*, described in the book *Getting to Yes* by Roger Fisher and William Ury.[6] Unlike some theories of negotiation, which emphasize things like making your adversaries in the negotiation physically uncomfortable (perhaps by seating them with the light shining in the faces) or playing "good cop/bad cop" with a member of your negotiating team, the mutual gains approach is based on the idea that different stakeholders in a dispute have legitimate but conflicting interests. In this approach, no side is necessarily in the right or in the wrong. Rather, the goal of a negotiation is to reconcile different interests in a way that satisfies the groups in the dispute.

The approach is called "mutual gains" because the idea is to find ways for the parties to *trade across differences*—that is, for each side to give up something that does not mean much to it in order to get something that it cares about more. To do that, a mutual gains negotiator has to focus on the parties involved in a problem, understanding their needs and analyzing how different solutions impact their legitimate interests. The negotiator constructs a *conflict assessment:* a matrix that systematically identifies the different issues in a dispute and the positions of the different stakeholders on those issues. Part of the conflict assessment is identifying each group's BATNA, or *best alternative to a negotiated agreement*. A group's BATNA represents what the outcome would be for it if the negotiation fails. For any party in a dispute, a negotiated agreement has to be better than its BATNA to make the agreement acceptable. Otherwise the group would be better off walking away from the negotiation.

In this way, the conflict assessment prepares the negotiator to trade across issues with different values to different stakeholders, looking for an outcome that is better than the BATNA of enough groups in the dispute to produce a negotiated settlement. And, of course, if more than one resolution is possible, the mutual gains negotiator tries to find the arrangement that will get the most for his or her side.

In other words, mutual gains negotiators are professionals who specialize in finding innovative solutions to complex social, economic, and interpersonal conflicts. Theirs is a valued profession, with the skills and knowledge needed to deal with contentious issues like clinical trials of xenotransplantation.

GETTING TO GETTING TO YES

To learn about xenotransplantation in *The Pandora Project*, players need to think like mediators. They need to learn about BATNAs and conflict assessments and the other concepts of mutual gains negotiation: the knowledge of the profession. They need to use these tools to trade across differences: the key skill of mutual gains negotiation. And they need to develop the mutual gains perspective of thinking about conflict in terms of legitimate conflicting interests and resolution as a means to reconcile those different interests in a way that satisfies the groups in the dispute: that is, they need to think like negotiators.

Like most professionals, negotiators learn though a practicum. The practicum for mutual gains negotiation is based on simulated negotiations in which negotiators in training take on the roles of the stakeholders in fictitious disputes and then debrief about their experiences. A simulated negotiation identifies key issues in a dispute and for each issue specifies a set of possible outcomes. For example, in a contract negotiation between a mine workers' union and the owners of a coal mine, the issues might be retirement benefits and layoffs. For layoffs, the possibilities might include laying off workers whenever the company wants, laying off only the most recently hired workers, or not laying off any workers. For retirement benefits, the possibilities might include continuing the current pension plan, continuing it only for existing employees, or divesting the pension plan entirely.

The players representing stakeholders in the dispute receive a confidential point score for each option, representing the value of that outcome to their stakeholder. These *utility points* vary for each stakeholder. In the mine workers' contract negotiation, the company might receive 100 points if it can lay off workers at will and lose 100 points if it bargains away the right to lay off workers, because temporary layoffs are one of the ways that this company responds to seasonal fluctuations in the price of coal. The union might receive 75 points if the contract protects workers from layoffs, but lose only 20 points if the company can lay off workers as long as the newest hires get laid off first because the union's primary interest is to protect its most senior members. In other words, the company, in this example, cares more about layoffs than the union does, and this is reflected in the fact that the company's utility point scores are larger (both positive and negative) than the union's on this issue.

At the same time, the union may care more about pension benefits than the company does. This would be reflected in more extreme utility point scores on the pension options for the union than for the company, and would make it possible for the two sides to trade across differences. If the union accedes to the company's wishes on layoffs and the company accommodates the union's interests on pensions, each side gains more than it loses, and it may be possible to find a mutually acceptable contract.

In other words, each stakeholder gets a high score in utility points for a different set of outcomes to the issues in dispute. The negotiation takes place as the stakeholders trade across the issues in dispute, trying to find a set of options that will satisfy the needs of all participants—that is, negotiators try to find an agreement that will get enough of the stakeholders a score higher than their BATNA (which is also represented with a utility point score) to be mutually acceptable.

Of course, this process is intensely competitive, since the goal for each side is to get a negotiated settlement that maximizes its own utility points, even if that means (as it usually does) lowering other participants' scores.

Negotiators in training prepare by constructing a conflict analysis. While each participant knows the utility point scores for his or her own side, the scores of other stakeholders are confidential, so planning a negotiating strategy requires investigating the wants and needs of the other groups involved in the dispute. When the negotiation is concluded, the negotiators debrief with experts, discussing their strategies, what worked and what didn't, and trying to understand the process of the negotiation from a mutual gains perspective.

SWINDONIA CODE OF MEDICAL REGULATIONS, PART 227

The Pandora Project, then, is modeled on a practicum for mutual gains negotiation using a simulated negotiation about xenotransplantation. The premise is that the X-Gen company has submitted a 227(e) application to the National Government of the Republic of Swindonia for permission to begin clinical trials in xenotransplantation as a Class V medical procedure, which Swindonia's regulations define as "any device or procedure that is of substantial importance in preventing impairment of human health, but which presents a potential, unreasonable risk of illness or injury." Concerns about the safety of xenotransplantation place it in this category.

The national government would like to see research on xenotransplantation go forward, but has significant concerns about safety, public perception, and international reaction, should it approve the procedure for clinical trials. The government asked representatives from interested groups to meet and decide on a set of conditions under which it would be appropriate for clinical trials to proceed. Negotiations went on for several months with no resolution. X-Gen, concerned about the time the process was taking, threatened to file a lawsuit against the government for delaying regulatory approval. The government wants the issue settled, but will not grant approval without resolving the outstanding concerns, so its representatives have asked the chief negotiators from each party to meet one last time to try to reach a compromise. If these talks fail, the government will deny approval for the technology, and X-Gen will have to decide whether to bring suit in court.

Five participants are at the table:

1. X-GEN: Medical experts and researchers at X-Gen are convinced that the decade they devoted to conscientious research provides a solid foundation to move forward into clinical trials of xenotransplantation.

2. PATIENTS' RIGHTS ORGANIZATION (PRO): PRO is interested in patient welfare. It understands that advances in the field of xenotransplantation will bring significant benefits to patients who are currently being treated by dialysis or respirators as well as patients on transplant waiting lists.

3. WORLD HEALTH ORGANIZATION (WHO): WHO is particularly concerned with the question of international equity. Exposure to the risk of an epidemic is global, but access to the benefits of xenotransplantation will be restricted to countries that can afford the procedure.

4. NATIONAL GOVERNMENT: New drugs and medical procedures in Swindonia are authorized by government regulators based on health and safety. But xenotransplantation raises concerns about safety that are hard to evaluate. The government would like to see the benefits of xenotransplantation realized but not at the cost of compromising public welfare.

5. ANIMAL RIGHTS COALITION (ARC): ARC is a coalition of animal rights groups that is opposed to research done on animals. It recognizes that

in the current national climate, it is impossible to ban animal research entirely, but it wants to limit the impact of research on animal subjects.

The issues being considered cover many of the key questions and concerns about xenotransplantation: Should recipients be subject to quarantines or a life-time of monitoring by regular physical examinations and tissue sampling? If something does go wrong, what outcomes will indicate that the procedures should stop? Should X-Gen be responsible for paying for a response to possible outbreak? Under what conditions will donor animals be kept? Will X-Gen or the government fund public health initiatives in developing countries to provide a response in case of an epidemic? Will the cost of xenotransplantation for citizens in developing countries be subsidized? Should X-Gen or the government pro-vide research funds for less expensive solutions to the organ donor shortage or more general public health initiatives to reduce the incidence of more widespread diseases?

The government is eager to see the proceedings resolved, and hopes that the meeting results in a unanimous consensus. However, it is willing to accept a set of options that four of the five stakeholders sitting at the table agree on, as long as both X-Gen and the government are in agreement with the proposal.

And so the negotiation begins.

"Pigs, Pigs, Pigs"

To find out what happens when young people play a game based on the training of professional mediators, we studied one class of fourteen high school students who played the game over two weeks of class time: a total of nine hours of game play. The students were enrolled in an ethics class at an independent school in Massachusetts, and it was the teacher's decision to play the game as part of the curriculum.[7]

For the study, we interviewed players before and after the game, and players wrote daily in an online journal. In the interviews players described their views on xenotransplantation and biotechnology. They completed concept maps about xenotransplantation, representing diagrammatically their understanding of the issues and interest groups relevant to the procedure. They responded to *transfer scenarios*: problems designed to see whether they were using ideas learned in the game to solve problems outside the game. And we asked them what they thought of the game, what worked well and what did not.

The game began with a multimedia introduction to the issues of xenotransplantation: a cut-scene that gave an overview of the game to come. Players took on stakeholder roles in groups of three and spent several class periods conducting a conflict assessment, using Internet links in the game to research their positions on xenotransplantation and the positions of the other stakeholders. They gathered information on genetics, epidemiology, and cell biology they needed to argue for their position. Based on their research, each stakeholder group prioritized the issues in the dispute and the various options for each one. Using these priorities, the game computed utility points for each role. Players then divided into groups of five, with each player representing a stakeholder in one of three separate negotiations. The negotiations themselves took place over three days, and the game ended with the same kind of debriefing that takes place in a negotiation practicum.

In other words, the game was modeled explicitly on the kinds of action and the kinds of reflection-on-action that negotiators in training go through in their practicum.

SKILLS AND KNOWLEDGE

It hardly comes as a surprise to learn that a game based on the training of professional negotiators helped players develop their skills in negotiation. Players needed to conduct conflict assessments to understand the positions of the various sides in the dispute, which meant gathering, reading, and making sense of detailed information about the dispute. As one player explained:

> [I found] a whole bunch of legal documents that I read through about patients in terms of xenotransplantation and the government [and] where they stand on it.

Once they found information, players needed to figure out where their stakeholder stood on the issues—and equally important, what players representing other stakeholders were likely to do. Said one player:

> We met every night before a negotiation day. We had to get everything
> straight—get the issues straight and figure out what we thought about every-
> thing—and we ended up meeting for like two hours that first night and talk-
> ing about it and reasoning it out, like every argument with every option, and
> hypothesizing about who was going to support what.

Of course, skill in negotiation is not just about preparation. A mutual gains
negotiator focuses on issues rather than tactics: on staying calm and negotiating
based on interests rather than emotions. As in the negotiation simulations that
train real negotiators, the negotiation simulation at the heart of *The Pandora
Project* demanded the same kind of discipline. As one player said:

> Our group got pretty heated sometimes . . . [but] when people were upsetting
> me I tried to remain calm. . . . And I think that was really important
> because . . . when people's voices start to raise and people get irritated and stuff
> like that then people get defensive. And then once you're on the defense you're
> not looking to compromise, you're looking to save yourself. And that's not
> effective.

In other words, players began to develop some of the skills of a mutual gains
negotiator—which necessarily meant developing the knowledge about the professional practice, and in this case about xenotransplantation as well.

In explaining what she learned from playing *The Pandora Project*, one student remarked that she knew very little about xenotransplantation before the
game—and, more than that, before playing the game she had naively assumed
that scientific and technological advances were always good:

> I had no idea what xenotransplantation was or how it could affect people in
> this way. So I think [the game] definitely created a better sense of awareness
> about "the public versus technology" and how that could affect us. I guess I
> always assumed that whatever [scientists] were doing to make things better was
> great. But I never really thought about how it was affecting us as a globe or a
> huge group of people. So I think [the game] made me more aware.

Overall, 91 percent of the players we studied said they had changed their opinion about xenotransplantation during the game. The same proportion reported that they understood the process better after playing the game.

We were able to measure whether players' thinking about xenotransplantation became more complex by asking them to complete concept maps showing the people and issues involved, and how they were connected. Players completed one map before the game and another two weeks later, after the game had ended. The maps made after the game included more people and issues and 45 percent more connections among them.[8]

Describing the difference in his maps before and after the game, one player explained how he was thinking more deeply about the implications of xeno-transplantation:

> When I first did it . . . I sort of just pointed out the obvious [connections] like patients, government subsidies. . . . I wasn't really looking [for] more involved relationships that some groups might have with one another, or how one thing might be related to another.

In *The Pandora Project*, players learned about the process of negotiation, and about the science and bioethics of xenotransplantation. And as we've seen in the other epistemic games, players' new knowledge stuck because they were, as one player explained, actually using what they knew:

> Through books I would probably learn the definition of xenotransplantation, what are the risks and benefits and the procedures and all these numbers. But the negotiation I actually had to live as a person that is directly interested or in, that is, deciding on an issue. . . . You can read all the procedures and the expected results, but you have to actually use it to realize what it is and how it works.

EPISTEMOLOGY

What tied skills as a negotiator to knowledge about negotiation and xenotrans-plantation in *The Pandora Project* was the epistemology of negotiation: the perspective that one takes as a negotiator, the kinds of questions a negotiator brings to a new situation, the kinds of answers a negotiator accepts, the way a negotiator justifies his or her actions.

To understand whether and how players began to think like negotiators after playing *The Pandora Project*, we gave them transfer scenarios: questions about issues like the differential impact of technologies in developed and developing countries, the relative importance of individual and social risks in evaluating new technologies, and the cost/benefit trade-offs of expensive technologies.[9] These transfer scenarios asked players to make recommendations about fictional technological breakthroughs based on complex scientific topics that raise difficult ethical issues. For example, one scenario described a new surgical technique used in treating cancer. The procedure has a 5 percent success rate with patients for whom all other techniques have failed, but it is extremely expensive, and some people have raised concerns that it will divert resources from less expensive and more effective treatments for other diseases. The scenario asks players to describe what conditions, if any, they think should be imposed on the use of this new technique.

Before the game, one player suggested that the technique should "definitely" be developed because "diverting resources from less expensive and more effective treatments is definitely important." The player went on to explain: "It definitely says hope. . . . I think it should be developed more, and . . . maybe they should be working on a technique that would be, you know, more cost effective, or I don't know." Notice that this answer is vague. What is the "it" that "says hope"? Also, the solution proposed—"working on a technique that would be, you know, more cost effective"—is essentially that the problem should be addressed by coming up with something better.

Both of these characteristics changed when the same student responded to a similar scenario after the game:

> I think that the doctors are right . . . to be concerned that money is going to go to this research. But I would almost be inclined to allow this treatment to continue only if [the company that is developing it is] paying for everything but no money is taken away from other techniques. Since it only has a 5 percent success rate I would be more inclined to not even mention it to

patients. . . . [because] at the very end people would be really willing to do things that if they were more conscious of what was happening they might not have agreed to.

Here we see the response is more specific: The player identifies particular stake-holders (doctors, the company, patients) and the concerns they have regarding the problem. Moreover, the solution proposed is not merely to make the technique better, but one that tries to address the concerns of these stakeholders simultaneously.

Answers to these transfer scenarios showed that the game helped the players we studied think about ethical dilemmas raised by new technologies using the epistemology of professional negotiation. Players began to analyze disputes in terms of legitimate conflicting interests of stakeholders, focusing on understanding the needs of the parties affected by a problem.

In other words, the skills, knowledge, and epistemology developed in a negotiation practicum about xenotransplantation helped these players think like negotiators about other technological dilemmas.

BRIAR

Players got a lot out of *The Pandora Project:* skills, knowledge, and a new way of seeing the world in which to use them. Part of the reason they gained so much was that the game was fun to play. As part of the interviews, we asked what the players liked and didn't like about the game. As one player put it: "I think this really got us engaged. It really got us motivated." Another said:

> Meeting before the negotiation was kind of like this intense period of five minutes, we'd be like: "OK. You make sure you got this." "Are you all set on this? And what if they do this? Do you know what our alternative is?" And: "Make sure you don't give into this!"

And a third: "I didn't want to sit at the table and have somebody be, like: 'So how do you know that?' And be, like: 'I don't really know.' "

But what made the game powerful is that the "fun" of the game was directly related to the things that players were learning. When they finished playing,

82 percent of the players we studied said they were interested in learning more about xenotransplantation and questions about ethics and technology. As one player said:

> I think I definitely want to follow up on everything that we've done. Because it's really interesting. And it's really so powerful and so permanent in the science world that I think it would be a shame to just drop it.

In other words, this game motivated players because it made them care about what they were doing.

Now in some ways, that is not very surprising. After all, this was a game based on a professional practicum, and one of the things that a practicum has to do is help novices learn to care about the kinds of things that matter to some group of professionals. Being a professional is always hard work, and learning to think and act like a professional always means learning to care about the things you are doing. Otherwise no one would bother, and the profession would die out.

One of the ways we tested how well *The Pandora Project* helped players think like professional negotiators was to ask them about Briar Lockhart, a teenage girl suffering from liver disease and waiting for a donor organ. She is introduced to players as part of the opening of the game through an excerpt from a Canadian news broadcast that describes her plight. At the beginning and end of the game, we asked players whether Briar should consider accepting a xenotransplant if one were available.

Most of the players we tested changed their mind about Briar during the game. At the beginning, 82 percent said Briar should take the transplant with relatively few reservations. At the end, 45 percent recommended the transplant but only if certain conditions were met; 36 percent recommended against the transplant; the rest felt that they did not know enough to make a recommendation.

What is more dramatic, though, about the change in players' responses to Briar is the extent to which they came to value her perspective rather than their own. For example, at the beginning of the game, one player wrote:

> I think that Briar should accept the transplantation. As I see it she has two options: 1. Not get the transplantation, and turn yellower and then die. Or 2. Take a risk and get the transplantation. . . . There is a possibility that it

would work out, and she would be fine, plus one pig liver. Whatever. I wouldn't get xenotransplanted for fun. But what has she got to lose? Her life . . . ? She should give this a chance.

According to this player, Briar should accept a donor organ raised in a genetically altered animal because that's what he (the player) would do. The key phrase was "as I see it," and this player's response to Briar's dilemma was to see the problem from his own point of view.

After playing the game, the same player became far less certain. But the dramatic change was in the extent to which he came to care about what Briar herself thought:

I cannot make that judgment without a lot more information on the procedure and its accompanying issues. . . . But I can come up with the questions I think she would need to have answered:

1. Is there a quarantine? How long? How strict? Can I see my family? How long am I going to be restricted to a hospital bed for . . . ? What kind of a life would I have saved myself for?

2. What happens if the transplant works, but I get even sicker from a disease I get from the pig . . . ? Is this something no one will know how to deal with? What kind of a life will that be . . . ?

3. How much do I want to be a part of this procedure which is an experiment, when I know that the results are so unpredictable and I am so aware of the risks . . . ?

I guess part of me is still pretty skeptical about the whole thing. However, I think the answers to the above questions are key to the eventual decision of whether or not the transplant is a good idea. Not only do they ask for more information on the details of the operation, they also pose personal questions which are essential to the question of whether or not she should do this that can only be answered by Briar.

In other words, this player came to value someone else's perspective as much as (and in this particular case, more than) his own.

VALUES

One of the critical values of a mutual gains negotiation is respecting the needs of different parties in a dispute. A mutul gains negotiator believes that different groups can have conflicting but nevertheless legitimate goals and objectives, and that negotiating is more effective—for the group as a whole and for the particular side he or she represents—when the problem is seen based on that respect. This is what takes what one player called the "heat" out of difficult negotiations and lets the different sides in the conflict find ways to trade across differences to find a workable solution. In the professional practice of negotiation—and in any profession—the skills, knowledge, and epistemology of the profession go hand in hand with its values.

As a result of the game, players in *The Pandora Project* began to respect multiple perspectives. For example, one player described why she was analyzing the transfer problems differently after the game by explaining that she now cared more about the questions of equity—about making sure that everyone involved in a decision gets treated fairly. In one of the problems, a company has genetically engineered grain that is inexpensive but infertile. So if farmers buy it (because it is cheap), they cannot save seeds from one year to plant the next. They have to keep buying seed each year. After the game, this player said:

> I'm think I'm thinking a little bit . . . more fairly. When I first read [this problem] . . . I was like: "If they [the biotech company] made it up [i.e., invented it], they should get to do what they want with it. And the poor countries should not buy it if they don't think they're going to be able to buy it in the future." But [now I] realize, you know, in the short run, they might think: "Oh, it's a great, a great way to improve our economy . . . !" And after that they could be in trouble, especially because it's a monopoly. So, I think [now] you sort of realize what can happen, and you're sort of like looking to make sure that everything is okay in the end, I guess, for everyone.

To learn to be a good negotiator, you also have to develop the values of the profession. As one player said:

> I had a sense for where each of the different groups would be coming from, but I think hearing them say what they believed . . . made me rethink it in a way. Animal rights always sticks in my mind because I thought she was

going to come to the table being like: "Pigs, pigs, pigs." And then they were really about taxes and issues that I didn't really think that animal rights would be concerned about. So I think in that sense it definitely made me reevaluate everybody's position. . . . Listening to each one, you put yourself in their shoes.

Another player said: "In order to do it right, you had to look at everything from everybody's point of view."

Postprogressivism

Any game is about values because playing a game always means playing a role and following the rules that role implies. In this sense, all games are ideological: They all emphasize some things as being more important than other things. Any game utilizes certain skills and not others, develops and uses some kinds of knowledge and not others. You need to know and do different things to play Chess than you do to play Tag, for example, or to play *Digital Zoo* than to play *The Pandora Project*. Every game is about some kinds of situations in some kind of simulated world and therefore not about others. And thus to play any game well, you have to learn to care about the kinds of things that matter in the game. A game may start out being about something you like, but any good game ends up by making you value what you are doing and how you are doing it. Any game that you are willing to keep playing has to do that.

In other words, games begin with players' interests—some thing or things they value—but transform those interests, making them stronger, or weaker, or more narrow, or more focused, or somehow more complex as players take on the values needed to master the game. Games thus embody some of the ideas about learning popularized by one of the giants of progressive education, John Dewey.

JOHN DEWEY

John Dewey founded the Chicago Laboratory School in 1896 as a response to problems he saw in the industrial school system that had been developed in the

United States in the last half of the nineteenth century. By 1904 the school was the most innovative experiment in education in the country, and the ideas of progressive education Dewey explored there would inspire educational innovation, policy, and theory for the next century.

The typical caricature of progressive education is that progressives believe children should be free to learn by exploring their own interests. Dewey agreed that children are full of what he called "ideas, impulses, and interests." Indeed, Dewey argued that finding interests is easy. "The child," he wrote in *School and Society*, "is already intensely active, and the question of education is the question of taking hold of his activities, of giving them direction." The challenge, Dewey claimed, was to take these impulses and use them to lead the child "to larger fields of investigation and to the intellectual discipline that is the accompaniment of such research."[10]

The process of moving from interest to understanding, according to Dewey, was learning by doing—or, to be more precise, learning by trying to do something, making mistakes, and then figuring out how to fix them. "If the [child's] impulse is exercised, utilized," Dewey wrote, "it runs up against the actual world of hard conditions to which it must accommodate itself; and there again come in the factors of discipline and knowledge." For example:

> Take . . . the little child who wants to make a box. If he stops short with the
> imagination or wish, he certainly will not get discipline. But when he attempts
> to realize his impulse, it is a question of making his idea definite, making it into
> a plan, of taking the wood, measuring the parts needed, giving them the nec-
> essary proportions, etc. There is involved the preparation of materials, the saw-
> ing, planning, the sandpapering, making all the edges and corners to fit.
> Knowledge of tools and processes is inevitable.[11]

If this process sounds familiar—perhaps recalling Rick and Carl in *Digital Zoo* or Hallie in *Escher's World*—it is because this kind of learning by overcoming obstacles is the foundation of all of learning by doing. Summarizing the process in *Art as Experience*, Dewey wrote:

> Impulsion from need starts an experience that does not know where
> it is going; resistance and check bring about the conversion of direct forward

action into re-flection; what is turned back upon is the relation of hindering conditions to what the self possesses as working capital in virtue of prior experiences. As the energies thus involved re-enforce the original impulsion, this operates more circumspectly with insight into end and method. Such is the outline of every experience that is clothed with meaning.[12]

Dewey's point is an important one, and the center of any progressive view of education: We learn by trying to accomplish some goal in the face of obstacles. When we bump into an obstacle, we have to step back and try to figure out what we know—and what else we need to know—to help us get past it. Of course, if there is nothing we are trying to do, then when we bump into an obstacle, we just give up, which is why we have to be doing something we care about.

PUSH BACK

The result is a somewhat curious state of affairs. We learn best when working on things that are neither too easy nor too hard—a psychological state that researcher Mihaly Csikszentmihalyi describes as *flow*.[13] If there are no obstacles, we don't learn much. If there are too many, we don't get anywhere, and give up. But this balance works only if, as Dewey put it, "the adverse conditions bear intrinsic relation to what they obstruct instead of being arbitrary and extraneous."[14] That is, the obstacles have to be relevant to the thing you are trying to do: They have to push back on issues that are related to the task at hand, rather than being something irrelevant or extraneous that you have to overcome in order to keep working.

Dewey was not talking about learning math by playing a board game where you have to answer questions about math facts in order to move your piece. He was talking about the kind of learning we see in *The Pandora Project*, when players have to conduct research about immunology and learn to conduct a mutual gains conflict assessment in order to find a negotiated settlement for clinical trials in xenotransplantation. The obstacles are the needs, desires, and objections of the other players, and in the game those obstacles are overcome by thinking and acting like a negotiator trying to get the best settlement for a client. One player summed up quite nicely how Dewey's model of learning by overcoming obstacles in pursuit of a meaningful goal applied in the game: "In order to do it right, you had to look at everything from everybody's point of view—but you had a very definite angle on it."

The fact that people learn this way makes it clear why it is so important that educational experiences develop values as well as skills and knowledge: This kind of learning *requires* that you care about what you are doing. You have to care enough to persist in doing it in the face of obstacles significant enough that overcoming them leads to real learning.

Dewey's ideas about learning have been influential for a long time, so perhaps it comes as no surprise that some educators are interested in games because they can be used to create progressive learning environments where young people learn by doing things they are interested in. But it is not clear that doing so by copying Dewey's ideas directly would work so well. After years of trying, his model of learning has been implemented in only in a relatively limited way. Only the rarest of classrooms is modeled on Dewey's Laboratory School, where cooking was the basis for much of the science taught and children built their own miniature iron smelters.[15] While epistemic games do build on Dewey's ideas, they go beyond his vision of progressive education in at least two significant ways.

IT'S A HARD KNOCK (VIRTUAL) LIFE

Dewey's model of learning through active engagement in meaningful activity (and all of progressive pedagogy that follows his work) depends on the *medium* in which activity takes place—that is, on the tools and materials with which the student is working. The "obstructions" that a student encounters in trying to achieve some goal lead to learning only if, in Dewey's inimitable turn of phrase, they "bear intrinsic relation to what they obstruct instead of being arbitrary and extraneous." This matters because using traditional materials, such as Cuisenaire Rods, it is relatively easy to capture essential properties of objects in the world, such as shape, number, or color.[16] Complex social and technical concepts, however—ratio, feedback, or social justice—are harder to "build" into traditional media. Put another way, traditional materials do a good job of representing elements of children's mental universe when they are in Piaget's stage of concrete operations, thinking about the observable properties of objects. It is harder to represent abstract ideas of Piaget's more advanced, formal operational stage of thinking without a computer.

But complex social and scientific concepts are quite easy to build into the simulated world of a computer or video game. The virtual worlds of *Digital Zoo, Escher's World, The Debating Game*, and *The Pandora Project* are worlds in which players act using complex concepts of locomotion, mathematics, historical interpretation, biotechnology, and ethics using the tools and practices of engineering, graphic design, parliamentary debate, and negotiation. Computer-based games expand the range of what players can realistically do—and thus the worlds they can inhabit and obstacles they can overcome.

As players express their intentions in the virtual world of the game, their understanding runs up against a *simulated* "world of hard conditions" of the kind that the Dewey suggested was essential to learning. While the scope of virtual worlds is certainly not endless—at least with current technologies—games make it possible for players to participate in activities that are hard, or even impossible, to do with traditional materials.

We know, for example, that in the virtual and cyber worlds that computers make possible, young people can develop new mathematical proofs, collect and analyze scientific data, publish work on the Internet, run a political campaign, or manage a city—not to mention reenact world history or steal a car.[17]

Of course, virtual worlds are not necessarily better than activities in the real world. It might be more effective to participate in a real election for student body president instead of a simulation of an election. The issues being debated would be those that directly affect students' lives. But working in the real world has disadvantages too. Compare, for example, an election for student body president to a simulation of an election for President of the United States in the game *The Political Machine*. Student elections take longer. They address a narrower range of issues. Not as many students can run a real campaign as can play the game. And in the case of *The Political Machine*, the knowledge gained in the game (about the electoral college, fundraising, and advertising) applies more directly to conditions that students will encounter outside of school than what happens in most student government elections.

Computer and video games make it possible for more people to learn about the world by participating in a wider range of meaningful activities than is possible with traditional materials alone. Epistemic games thus go beyond traditional progressive education because they make it possible to extend progressive pedagogies into new realms. But epistemic games also go beyond traditional progressive education because they are *epistemic:* That is, they are explicitly about epistemology.

SCIENCE, SCIENCE EVERYWHERE

For Dewey, the result of overcoming obstacles in the pursuit of valued ends was a particular kind of knowledge: It was *scientific*. It was knowledge that, as Dewey explained, "replaces the repeated conjunction or coincidence of separate facts by discovery of a single comprehensive fact" based on "observations formed by variation of conditions on the basis of some idea or theory."[18] For example, Dewey explained at great length how cooking an egg (an activity designed to make "a transition from the cooking of vegetables to that of meats") could be a point of departure for such systematic "experimental work":

> In order to get a basis of comparison they first summarized the constituent food elements in the vegetables and made a preliminary comparison with those found in meat. . . . They found that starch and starchy products were characteristic of the vegetables . . . and that there was fat in both—a small quantity in vegetable food and a large amount in animal. They were prepared then to take up the study of albumen as the characteristic feature of animal food, corresponding to starch in the vegetables. . . . They experimented first by taking water at various temperatures . . . and ascertained the effect of the various degrees of temperature on the white of the egg. That worked out, they were prepared not simply to cook eggs, but to understand the principle involved in cooking eggs.[19]

Dewey was not suggesting that everything we do follows the "Scientific Method" that most children learn about in school: the steps that scientists supposedly follow in advancing formal hypotheses, designing experiments, and drawing conclusions based on the results. Nor did he think that children should learn only science. For Dewey, disciplines such as history, geography, and literature were critical to the process of education. They were "tools which society has evolved in the past as the instruments of its intellectual pursuits."[20] But he believed they are all *scientific* in the sense that they are all based on propositional understanding—discovering general laws or principles—from conducting experiments. For example, Dewey explained the value of studying the history of "primitive life" primarily as a kind of scientific experiment:

> Recourse to the primitive may furnish the fundamental elements of the present situation in immensely simplified form. . . . We cannot simplify the present situations by deliberate experiment, but resort to primitive life presents us with the sort of results we should desire from an experiment. Social relationships and modes of organized action are reduced to their lowest terms.[21]

Leaving aside the outdated idea that life in the past was a simplified version of modern societies, Dewey was describing historical inquiry as a process of formal experimentation: history as a form of social *science* rather than a distinct way of knowing. Compare his description of history, for example, to Wineburg's:

> A detail is first remembered, but the historian cannot remember its source. This recognition sends the historian searching for the sources of this detail, and, when reunited with its author, the detail is rejected. The reason is that the historian knows that there are no free-floating details, only details tied to witnesses.[22]

For Dewey, when we try to accomplish goals, obstacles push back on us. Overcoming these obstacles pushes us toward scientific understanding of the work we are doing. Or, as Dewey wrote: the "scientific method is the only authentic means at our command for getting at the significance of our everyday experiences of the world in which we live."[23]

NOT JUST SCIENCE EVERYWHERE

It is certainly true that innovators always conduct experiments of one form or another: the cycles of action and reflection that Schön describes in his studies of professional practice. But as Schön points out, this general process of thinking tells us little about how professionals understand the world unless we look more closely at the epistemology that guides that experimentation. It may be true in principle that all knowledge comes from experience, but the pedagogical issue is that different kinds of knowledge are created through different kinds of experiences.

My point is not to suggest that Dewey was wrong or mistaken. But computer and video games let young people think and act in more ways than were possible before. They make it possible for people of all ages to act in virtual worlds whose obstacles push back on social, technological, and conceptual issues far more complex than those that can be simulated using traditional materials alone.

In an epistemic game, those obstacles can push players toward scientific thinking, to be sure. But they can also push players toward other kinds of innovative thinking: into the arms of a professional community and into the kinds of reflection that structure professional learning.

We know a lot about how people become innovative thinkers because we know a lot about how professionals develop their ways of thinking and acting. Epistemic games create virtual worlds that push players into dilemmas that can be resolved only by developing the skills, knowledge, epistemology, and values that guide innovative thinking.

Not all innovative thinking, in other words, is most effectively characterized as *scientific*. There are a many ways of knowing—many epistemologies—that characterize meaningful, socially, culturally, and economically valuable ways of acting in the world.

MOTIVATION

In postprogressive epistemic games, players learn to care about the kind of problems that face doctors, lawyers, architects, engineers, journalists, and other innovative professionals and to develop the skills, knowledge, and ways of thinking that are used to solve such problems. That process means hard work, and a lot of it. It is rigorous, because the professions that shape innovative thinking demand rigorous thinking. There are high standards, and rightly so, because by definition a professional works in complex situations: situations that require judgment and autonomy—and thus trust. The training of professionals, when it is done well, is about standards of behavior and expectations for results. It is about sophisticated skills, specialized knowledge, guiding norms, and the epistemology that ties them together.

But as we've seen, games based on the training of professionals—high standards, hard work, and all—are fun, for two reasons. First, part of the fun of any game is playing by the rules, and the rules of many games are even more complex and demanding than the norms and practices of a profession. The rules of many games children like, such as *Yu-Gi-Oh*, are extremely complex—too complex, in fact, for many adults to play. And, of course, we know that many games require a lot of hard work. In fact, all of the best ones do.

But more than that, adolescents in middle and high school are trying to find their place in the world. They are trying to understand who they are, who they want to be, and how the world works as they move outside of the protective arms of their parents and families. Developmental psychologist Robert Kegan describes the process as developing a "capacity for independence; self-definition; assumption of authority; [and] exercise of personal enhancement, ambition, or achievement."[24] Studies by Csikszentmihalyi and his colleagues show that adolescence is a period when young people are learning the patterns of participation in society. Csikszentmihalyi's work demonstrates that this learning process requires developing a sense of discipline, and that adolescents are willing to participate in activities when they believe that goals are worthwhile and their actions have meaning. Csikszentmihalyi argues that "intrinsically rewarding learning produces an experience of growth and of mastery, a feeling that the person has succeeded in expanding her or his skills."[25]

In other words, adolescents are fascinated by efficacy: the things they can do in the world and the sense of their own power that comes from being able to make things happen. An epistemic game gives players a chance to see how the world—or at least some piece of it—works. It gives them a chance to experience their own efficacy in the face of complex problems by showing them what it is like to be one of the people who makes decisions that shape the world around them. An epistemic game pulls back the curtain and shows players some of the mechanisms of power.

If efficacy is the hook, the thing that gets players to start the game—if players enjoy an epistemic game at first because they are being taken seriously and given a chance to do the kinds of things that really matter in the world—then what keeps them in the game is the structure of the practicum itself. Part of what any professional practicum has to do is help create the values of the profession. You can't be a professional unless you care about the things that a professional cares about, and thus professional training has to develop professional skills, knowledge, and epistemology in the context of professional values.

Epistemic games are thus a potentially important part of children's development. Based on his extensive investigations of knowledge work and knowledge workers, business analyst Thomas Davenport argues that personal commitment is an essential part of all innovative thinking. You can do standardized work as an automaton, but innovation requires engagement with the tasks at hand. You have to *care* about what you are doing.[26] And in most professions, caring about what you are doing means stepping outside yourself and seeing things as others see them: stakeholders, the public at large, or some specific client. It means shifting focus away from what is interesting to you and toward what matters to others.

This kind of decentering is an essential part of growing up. Children need to shift from thinking exclusively about their own needs and interests to reflecting on and respecting the needs and interests of others. As developmental psychologist Erik Erikson explains, becoming an adult means "taking a place in society at large and *caring*."[27]

Epistemic games thus fulfill young people's basic need to make things happen in a positive and constructive way. In this sense they go beyond what Max's mother was doing in creating an island of expertise. These games are fun because they let players think and act like professionals who care about doing things that matter not just to themselves, but to others in the world.

To be clear: these games are not about *becoming* professionals, no more than the chores students were doing at the farm school in Vermont were about becoming organic farmers. The goal of epistemic games is not to train players to be doctors, nurses, therapists, lawyers, architects, graphic designers, engineers, negotiators, debaters, urban planners, business leaders, plumbers, carpenters, contractors, or any of a host of socially valued and socially valuable professions. Rather, by playing a game based on the things professionals do in training, players can learn to think in innovative ways—and to care—about a wide range of complex and important problems and situations.

But if players in an epistemic game don't become professionals, then what do they become? To answer that question, the next chapter looks at the profession of journalism, and at an epistemic game based on the training of journalists.

For Parents, Teachers, and Mentors

The Pandora Project is not readily available for use in classrooms, but there are some commercial games that can help players develop professional values in important ways. One such game is *A Force More Powerful*, which was designed as a teaching tool for nonviolent activists. In the role of chief strategist in a nonviolent movement, players direct the movement's resources, recruit members, and build and break alliances. In the process, they learn about strategic planning, the formulation of objectives, and the development of tactics to meet those objectives. They also come to understand how nonviolent conflict works: the mechanisms and functions of disruptive actions such as strikes, boycotts and mass protests. The game models more than 80 different forms of nonviolent action. Through these scenarios based on real grassroots movements around the world, players learn how fear and enthusiasm work to suppress and motivate recruiting and the value of mobilizing ordinary people to take action.

But whether *A Force More Powerful* is the best example of a game that can develop professional values is less important than recognizing that the values that players develop in a game matter:

→ Values matter more than interests. Try to find games that transform existing interests into some form of lasting values rather than just reinforce them.

→ It may seem like an obvious point, but seek out games about things that matter in the world and that focus on understanding and dealing with the perspective of others.

→ Be explicit about the values in a game. Talk about the ethical implications of decisions in the game—and about how those values would or would not be appropriate in situations outside the game.

→ Perhaps most important, especially with younger children: Don't be afraid to stand up for the values you believe in. Just as there are books that are not appropriate for young children to read, the same is true of games. Make informed decisions about what games your kids play. Once again, one of the best ways to do that is to play them yourself.

CHAPTER FIVE

Identity:
science.net

This chapter is about what it means to be an innovative professional: how thinking and working like a professional means seeing oneself as a professional, and vice versa. It is about how professional training helps people learn to identify themselves as professionals, and why playing a game based on that process is so powerful for adolescents as they are making a developmental transition from childhood into the adult world.

The chapter focuses on *science.net*, an epistemic game developed by researchers David Hatfield and Alecia Magnifico at the University of Wisconsin. In *science.net*, players become journalists, reporting on scientific and technological breakthroughs for an online newsmagazine. Along the way they learn about science and its impact on society, become better writers, and come to see themselves as innovative professionals. The game is based on a study of a journalism practicum, and the chapter begins with a description of that study to make clear the parallels between the experiences of these journalism students and the middle school students who played *science.net*.

The game and the study on which it is based show how skills, knowledge, values, epistemology, and identity come together in the work of one group of innovative professionals; how an epistemic game can make the same ways of thinking, working, caring, knowing, and being available to adolescents; and how seeing the world through a lens of professional innovation helps young people prepare for life in the digital age.

Profession

No profession is monolithic. In journalism, there are feature writers and straight news reporters. Print journalism is different from television news, and attracts different kinds of people as reporters, editors, and producers. So any detailed description of journalism is really about the practices of some group of journalists—and thus an epistemic game based on the training of journalists is necessarily based on the training of some group of journalists as it happened in some place and at some point in time. This only reemphasizes the important point that a game based on how people learn in the real world will be only as good as the example it is modeled on.

Journalism is by its very nature filled with writers, but surprisingly little has been written about how journalists learn their profession. A few writers have looked at the kinds of personal changes that a cub reporter goes through in becoming a professional journalist, but most research on journalism education is much more specialized, focusing on such things as the role of ethical theory in textbooks, how survey research can help students learn journalism, or whether Web-based tools can help teach basic writing skills.[1]

One reason that there is little information on how journalism courses develop professional skills is that school is only the beginning of a journalist's training. Many practicing journalists believe they learned their craft through "osmosis," by watching more experienced reporters at work and (often) through talking with them late into the night over drinks. Still, new reporters have to have some preparation to work in a newsroom, and journalism schools play an important role in helping many new reporters prepare for entry level work in the profession.[2]

In the genre of investigative news reporting, there are three critical things a novice reporter needs to be able to do: write *to formula*, write *as a watchdog*, and write *for story*.

WRITING TO FORMULA

Journalism has its roots in the Enlightenment. The First Amendment to the U.S. Constitution is based on the idea that comparison of information from multiple sources leads to greater understanding, and Enlightenment concepts of accuracy and verification are at the core of journalism's values—however imperfectly they may be understood or practiced by some journalists today. Journalists pursue understanding through accuracy and verification by focusing on the *method* of their work. Journalism's claim to fairness is not that reporters manage the superhuman feat of being unbiased; rather it is that the methods of reporting and writing are systematic: They produce stories by a uniform set of rules.[3]

Small wonder, then, that the methods of journalism are codified with almost compulsive precision. A single book on the craft of writing offers eighteen different lists to guide the reporter, including eight tips on writing to deadline, fourteen ways to "see the obvious," eight ways to write without writing, thirty questions to ask to produce effective leads, four ways to get organized, eleven ways to develop a draft, and thirty-six questions to ask when editing your own copy, nine elements of craft of writing, the writer's ten senses, the reader's five questions, seven qualities of a good story, six conditions that encourage writing, six qualities of an effective lead, nineteen forms of effective leads, fifteen elements of lively writing, twenty things I wish I had known before I started at a paper, twelve notes on narrative, and fourteen elements of voice.[4]

Journalists must adhere to the requirements of Associated Press (AP) style: rules about capitalization, punctuation, and reference to sources. But the rules also extend to things that we might imagine would be left to the writer to decide. One guidebook gives eight different lists of words and phrases that should not be used by journalists.[5] Another lists fifty-six words that reporters should use in place of the word "said."[6] Yet another tells novice journalists to "quote from the best representative of the parties involved by the fourth or fifth paragraph" and to "give the last word to the side [you] personally disagree with." It warns them not to "end your best quotes with an attribution" but instead to "put it within the quote, set off with commas." And it includes the helpful explanation: "A feature about people needs descriptive detail . . . [but] reference to blonde hair is almost always sexist . . . [and] mention of high cheek bones only proves you wasted too much time reading Ian Fleming."[7]

Journalists, in other words, write within a tightly prescribed genre. How-to books repeatedly emphasize that news stories—and thus good reporters—follow the formula of journalistic prose. The goal of this formula is to produce stories that appear to have no writer: stories written not in the distinctive voice of a reporter but in the generic voice of the newspaper. There is a very practical reason for this, since writing in a generic voice makes it easier for teams of reporters and copy editors to work on the same story without worrying about preserving the distinctive voice of one or another writer. But a story without a writer also appears more truthful. It is impossible to ever be completely objective, but the formula of news reporting is designed to make stories *sound* objective.

WRITING AS A WATCHDOG

Of course, writing to formula is about *how* journalists write. The reason *why* they write to formula is to present information that readers need as citizens in a democratic society. One study found that half of the journalists interviewed saw their primary role as informing the public about important information and events. One-third said that their role was to support democracy by reporting news needed for informed public debate.[8]

To fulfill their responsibility to help the public make good decisions, reporters use the formula of journalism writing to give readers information and help them make sense of it. In interviews, journalists describe their role as "transforming data into information—by presenting objective facts so that they will have subjective meaning and, thereby, empowering the public to make adaptive choices."[9] Studies of journalism emphasize how the press can make public debate possible. An important part of making public debate possible is, of course, making people aware of problems: As one overview of modern journalism described it, to "monitor power and offer voice to the voiceless."[10] Journalists write to formula to put facts on the record and help the public make sense of them, and investigative journalists focus on bringing to light facts about forces and institutions of society that might otherwise remain hidden. A journalist—particularly an investigative journalist—writes to formula as a watchdog for the public trust.

WRITING FOR STORY

In order to use the journalistic formula and fulfill their role as investigators, informers, and explainers, journalists have to write about something in particular. As one introductory text explains, in the end, the job of any media writer is to "tell stories."[11] The term *writing for story* comes from a book of the same name by journalism professor and two-time Pulitzer Prize-winning journalist Jon Franklin. Franklin's focus is on feature stories: articles, such as investigative reports, that are not necessarily linked directly to a specific event (in contrast with straight news stories that report on current events). Franklin argues that any feature story is, in the end, about specific people. "A story," he writes, "consists of a sequence of actions that occur when a sympathetic character encounters a complicating situation that he confronts and solves."[12]

Franklin explains that the conflict or complication at the heart of a story must be "significant to the human condition"—that is, it must be important to a wide audience of readers. But he also argues that any journalistic story "must be told in terms of unique individuals and their specific actions and thoughts." The goal of journalism is to tell readers about issues that matter in their lives. But to do so, journalists write about the stories of particular people and the things that happened to them. Franklin suggests that in journalism, "the universal is finally achieved by focusing down, tightly, even microscopically, on specific events and the details that surround them."[13]

COMMUNITIES AND SCHEMATA

Journalism, in other words, is an innovative profession in which reporters write to formula to produce stories that serve the public interest. While some news reporting is formulaic—perhaps too much so these days—for a good journalist, no two stories are exactly alike, and a good journalist's job is to seek out and report things that are new and interesting. Journalism thus exemplifies the way in which innovation always takes place within some larger system of practice.

Current theories of learning have at least two different ways to account for how a journalist becomes an innovative thinker by learning to write to formula, write as a watchdog, and write for story.

The older and more traditional view (where *traditional* in this case means for the last half-century) focuses on what happens to individuals when they solve problems and when they learn to solve them. This research on *symbolic thinking* or *information processing* looks at how knowledge and beliefs developed in solving one problem can be used to solve other analogous problems. This is one way of thinking about how solving the problem with Melanie's merry-go-round in math class might have helped Hallie with her design problem—and how solving a problem in the *Escher's World* game might help her solve problems on a math test or in math class. The idea is that the knowledge and beliefs used to solve problems are organized as *schemata*: the declarative and procedural knowledge, or facts and the problem-solving rules and strategies that go with them. Thinking is a matter of finding the right schema for a problem and then using the information and rules it contains to produce a solution.[14]

This schema-based view of thinking is at the core of many descriptions of learning, including both current school practices and more informal islands of expertise: Learn the right facts and rules and beliefs, and then apply them in the right places. From this point of view, we would expect that the training of journalists would be primarily about knowledge and values: the things a journalist needs to know and the beliefs that would guide the use of that knowledge.

More recently (where *recently* in this case means in the last two decades), researchers have suggested that this information processing view of "thinking as problem solving using abstract rules" is misleading. In contrast, research on *situated cognition* studies how all human activity is part of *communities of practice*: groups of people who share similar ways of solving the same kinds of problems.[15] Naval quartermasters, meatpackers, and members of Alcoholics Anonymous (groups studied early in this research) are all members of different communities of practice. Each of these groups has a common identity: rank and military occupational skill for quartermasters, membership in a union for meatpackers, or belonging to a local chapter for the recovering alcoholics. Each group also has shared practices: recording bearings while standing watch, trimming standard cuts of beef, or following the 12-step program.

Communities of practice include Professional communities (in the sense of the traditional white-collar Professions) as well as professional communities of innovation. In the situated view, newcomers learn a community's common ways of solving problems through *legitimate peripheral participation*. That is, they learn by doing things that members of the community do. At first newcomers do less important and less complicated tasks, but they move gradually toward things that are more difficult and more central to the activities of the community—and in the process come to see themselves more and more as legitimate members.

From this point of view, we would expect that the training of journalists is primarily about letting novices act like journalists and as a result come to see themselves as journalists.

Practicum

Each of these views of learning highlights an important part of what happens when novice reporters learn to think and act like journalists, but neither tells enough of the story on its own. Even when the two views are put together, the picture is not quite complete—and it turns out that filling in some of the missing pieces is the key to rethinking thinking for the digital age.

To see what I mean, let's look at a snapshot of how one group of journalists learned to think and act in the ways of the profession. The snapshot comes from a study Hatfield, Magnifico, and I conducted of a journalism practicum: Journalism 828 (J-828), a capstone course on in-depth reporting at the University of Wisconsin.[16] In the class, twelve advanced undergraduate and beginning graduate journalism students worked in teams of four over the course of a semester to produce investigative news reports suitable for publication in a local newspaper. The students were guided in this endeavor by a nationally known reporter on the faculty of the school, Kate, with help from five local editors and reporters.

During the semester, the novice reporters in J-828 filed three news stories. First, the reporters spent a day at the county courthouse and filed a story about one trial. Next they wrote a follow-up story, reporting in more depth on an issue raised at the trial. For the final project, they selected three topics from the twelve follow-up stories and divided into teams of four reporters. Each team produced a feature package, including a main story and related sidebars.

While writing these stories, the reporters reflected on their work with each other and with more experienced journalists in three ways: through *war stories*, *news meetings*, and *copy editing*. Since the reflection-on-action of the practicum gets internalized as professional reflection-in-action, looking at each of these kinds of reflection tells us what innovative thinking looked like for these journalists and how it was developed.

REFLECTION-ON-ACTION

In war stories, experienced journalists described events from their careers and talked about the lessons they learned. In the middle of the semester, for example, a local journalist, Brian, told the class about his newspaper and his own style of journalism. "The key question for many journalists," he explained, "is: What are the credentials of a person who wants to raise an issue or concern?" Brian explained that he tries to have a "lower standard . . . that includes ordinary people. . . . I like to be there in those rare instances where something happens and someone says: 'I need a reporter.' " But he also said that talking to a reporter is not always in an individual's best interests, so he is careful to explain to potential sources why it might be a mistake to talk with him.

Brian illustrated the problem by describing a story he had reported about a woman who had been raped and robbed at knifepoint. The police did not believe her story, and under pressure she recanted. The district attorney brought charges for lying to the police, although later the woman was exonerated and the charges against her were dropped.

"Did your reporting make a difference?" asked Kate.

"Yes. A negative difference," replied Brian. "They [the police] dug in their heels to prove they didn't make a mistake." The police wanted "to prove they were right" and in the process "demonized" the victim. Brian went on to explain that the criminal justice system "scares the hell out of me. [The police have] so much power and so little accountability. They feel they can get away with anything—and they can. They never say they're sorry. They're unwilling to accept their terrible capacity for error. And that makes them the most dangerous people on the planet."

In this war story, Brian showed the cub reporters a particular set of values: enabling those who would not otherwise be able to have their story (or their side of the story) heard, and doing so to make the police—who "feel they can get away with anything"—accountable for their actions. These values were tied to a set of skills: explaining possible negative consequences to potential sources so they can make an informed choice about whether to talk to the reporter. These skills required specific knowledge about journalism: that the police have "so much power and so little accountability," and thus talking to a reporter is not always in a person's best interests. This set of values, skills, and knowledge were principally about *writing as a watchdog*: the things a journalist needs to know, do, and care about to draw attention to inequities, monitor people and institutions in positions of power, and offer a voice to those without power.

Later in the same class, Brian led a news meeting. By this time in the semester, the class had chosen topics and divided into investigative teams, and each group presented its reporting-in-progress and got feedback.

Brian liked the story one group was working on about how difficult it is to get a lawyer if you are poor. "Too many people," he said, "face the justice system without an attorney." He suggested that the group "quantify the problem" by finding out how often it happens. But he added that the reporters should also "keep the focus on a person and situation . . . [on] what happened at the trial . . . [and] jam the information in between. Tell it as an organic story around a single case."

He gave similar advice to the team working on a story about drunk drivers: Talk with the assistant district attorney to find someone convicted of drunk driving. "Find someone for whom it's too late," he explained. "Anyone facing the system will not want to talk." As an example of such a story, Brian described a recent headline about a middle-age man who killed a teenager in a drunk driving accident.

One of the novice reporters asked: "How do you get in touch with these people?"

"Write a letter to them in prison," Brian replied.

Another reporter added: "I can put you in touch with the mother [of the girl who was killed]."

"There," said Brian, "you have everyone: the mother, the DA, the offender."

When the news meeting ended, Brian reminded reporters: "Be mindful of finding the story, not the topic. Drunk driving is too much. . . . But you can find a person's story."

In this news meeting, we see Brian talking with the novice reporters about a particular set of journalistic values: to be "mindful of finding the story, not the topic." These values were put into action with a set of skills: focusing "on a person and situation" so as to tell "an organic story around a single case." These skills required specific knowledge about journalism: how to contact a person in prison, or that "anyone facing the system will not want to talk." And this set of values, skills, and knowledge were about *writing for story*: the things a journalist needs to know, do, and care about to tell stories about particular people encountering problems or conflict, the specific events that happened, and the unique details surrounding them.

We are all familiar with the term *copy editing*, but because the formulas of news and feature writing are so detailed, in J-828 (and in journalism more generally) copy editing was a more exacting process than most of us are used to. In J-828, each story went through a peer copy editing session, where groups of four or five reporters exchanged papers for comments and feedback. The reporters then revised their stories for submission to Kate, who provided written comments, corrections, and suggestions, after which she led a copy-edit session with the whole class for the rough drafts of the final project stories.

Kate said she liked the rough draft of the story about the difficulties poor defendants have in getting a lawyer, but she was "concerned about organization and focus. . . . What is the 'so what'? Why do I care about this as a middle-class reader?"

One of the reporters on the team, Bill, replied: "I don't know how you can make middle-class people care about poor people—especially poor criminals."

Kate explained that the story has "great shock value because people assume [they'll get a] lawyer." It is an "outrage story" that needs to "invoke outrage in people not affected."

"So go from the anecdotal lead," Bill suggested, "to 'he's not guaranteed [a lawyer]'—that's the nut."

Kate gave a detailed description of how to reorganize the piece as an outrage story: Start with an anecdotal lead to energize the reader. Then put the so-what. Explain *why* this matters. Convey the big picture: What is this country about? Some day you're not going to have a lawyer. After the so-what, ask, "What is the crisis here?" Then explain that this state used to be number one in providing public defenders, but has been sliding down for a decade. Then list the contributing factors. In the so-what section, include a graf [a paragraph] on the key issues: an underfunded public defender, out-of-date scale for costs, a bizarre system for court appointments. Be sure to use subheadings to be clear for the readers, and close with an anecdote that ties back in to the lead.

"I thought the story was pretty clear," she concluded, "[but] this needs a powerful focus. You're going to have to be ruthless."

In this copy editing session, we see Kate talking about a particular set of journalistic values: to energize the reader, to make the story matter to middle-class readers. She talked about how to put these values into practice using particular skills: use subheadings, tie the end of the story back to the lead. These skills, in turn, use specific knowledge about journalism: concepts like an "anecdotal lead," a "nut," and an "outrage story." Moreover, this set of values, skills, and knowledge were principally about *writing to formula*: the things a journalist needs to know, do, and care about to write in the forms traditional journalism.

SCHEMATA

In his authoritative study of the current state of the professions and professional education, researcher William Sullivan describes professional training in terms of "three apprenticeships": an intellectual or cognitive apprenticeship, an apprenticeship in the tacit skills of the profession, and an apprenticeship in attitudes and values.[17] What we see in this brief description of J-828 is how Brian and Kate were using war stories, news meetings, and copy editing to carry out these apprenticeships in the knowledge, skills, and values of the profession.

Each of the different kinds of reflection-on-action in the practicum was focused on a different aspect of thinking like a journalist: a different set of knowledge, skills, and values that a journalist uses in reporting stories. War stories emphasized writing as a watchdog. News meetings emphasized writing for story. Copy editing emphasized writing to formula. In a sense, each kind of reflection-on-action was building a different schema: how to decide what is worth reporting, how to find a specific example to illustrate a topic, and how to write an engaging story. In this view, learning to be a journalist is about learning to do all of the different parts of reporting and then putting them together to produce stories for the newspaper: innovation as a collection of professional schemata.

It seems quite natural to think about what was happening in J-828 in this way because the schema view of learning is pervasive in our current education system. It is why we teach isolated facts and problem-solving strategies and test whether students have retained them, assuming that what it means to be educated is to have a collection of problem-solving skills and the knowledge that goes with them. The schema view of learning suggests that teaching in this way is worthwhile because these collections of facts and rules, taught in classroom settings, will be available for students to use in other places.

The problem is that nearly a half-century of research has shown that things don't work that way. Facts, rules, and problem-solving strategies learned in isolation do not carry over to other problems encountered later on. Transfer in this sense is rare, difficult to achieve, and limited to problems that are very similar to the original context in which a solution is developed—which is described in the field as *near-transfer*.[18] You can train someone to do a particular task, but skills, knowledge, and values learned in isolation don't account for innovative thinking that is developed in J-828 and other professional practica.

The schema view tells only part of the story.

COMMUNITY

To begin to understand why problem-solving schemata are not enough to explain what happened in J-828, let's look at what one of the novice reporters on the indigent defense story, Alecia, said in summing up her experiences in the practicum:

> You learn quickly that news writing is fairly formulaic: how to present both
> sides, leads, an orientation graf. I'm a straight news person: not very creative.
> This [gave me] inspiration that you can make a difference. . . . Nobody had said
> before: "This is not just about what you're covering, but [about] why this affects
> the average person." No one made that connection before.

Alecia talked about knowledge, skills and values, to be sure. But she did two
other things. First, she linked *across* the different practices of writing to formula
("news writing is fairly formulaic") and writing as a watchdog ("you can make a
difference"). Second, she spoke about how, in the process of linking these different aspects of journalism, she came to see herself as more than just "a straight
news person." For Alecia, the practicum was about more than just the knowledge she learned, the skills she developed, and things she came to value: It was
about a particular way of seeing the world and about a particular way of seeing
herself. I'll say more about seeing the world in the next section. But first I'd like
to focus on how she was seeing herself—that is, on the question of *identity*.

Kate spoke repeatedly in J-828 about what she called "good journalism: critical, skeptical, knowledgeable, smart, and—we hope—beautifully written." But
with that, she talked not just about doing smart reporting, but *being* a "smart
reporter." She contrasted being a smart reporter with someone who is still a
"police reporter" or a "beat reporter" who covers the same formulaic stories day
after day. War stories, news meetings, and copy editing in J-828 were not just
about the knowledge, skills, and values of writing as a watchdog, writing for story,
and writing to formula. They were about being journalists and what that means.

In his war story, for example, Brian pointed out that part of his identity as a
journalist is being someone who is "there in those rare instances where something happens and someone says: 'I need a reporter.' " In explaining the role of
a reporter as a watchdog, another visiting journalist said: "Eventually word of
scandal leaks to someone honest—they're looking for someone to talk to. If
you're a reporter, you want to be the person they think of." In one war story,
Kate suggested that politics is "a manipulated system: you need to be the one
person not manipulated." At another point she described being a journalist as

being "a professional pest." In copy editing, Kate told the novice reporters that they had to be "ruthless."

The particular kind of professional, innovative thinking that a journalist does is not just about schemata of knowledge, skills, and beliefs. It is also about seeing yourself as a particular kind of person: as a journalist who knows, does, and cares in these ways. Being a journalist means not just writing as a watchdog, writing for story, and writing to formula; it means seeing yourself as a watchdog, as a writer, and as a "news person." As a situated view of learning suggests, novice journalists in J-828 learned by becoming members of a community, and they came to see themselves as members of the community by learning to do things that members of the community do.

In other words, J-828 was a kind of road map showing how the skills, values, knowledge, and identity of investigative journalism are linked together. As novices worked on producing an investigative report, they talked about their work with each other and with more experienced journalists. Like the desk crits and reviews in the architectural design studio, the conversations about reporting in the journalism practicum were opportunities for novices to reflect on their action. The mostly private, personal, and internal process of reflection-*in*-action of an experienced journalist was created as novices internalized public, extended, and distributed opportunities for reflection-*on*-action.

Nearly a decade ago, Edwin Hutchins conducted a landmark study of how quartermasters in the navy learn to navigate large naval vessels coming in to port.[19] His study focused on how in that process thinking was spread out, or distributed, over people and tools. What Hutchins showed was that different novice quartermasters working on different parts of the task of navigation worked in a shared space. Because each person worked on a small part of the bigger problem, the mechanics of a complex task became explicit. Each person could see the whole process at work, even if he or she was doing only part of the job. There was a link, in other words, between the problem space (the things to be done) and the social space (the things each person was doing). This link turned a process that for expert quartermasters can be done mostly alone into a public process that the novices could see. And of course, it also made smaller pieces of a large and complex process easier for novices to do.

In this view, a practicum is about learning by doing, but the learning takes place because experts have divided the task into the right chunks for novices to be able to do. While novices are working, experts are available to talk with them about the skills, knowledge, values, and identity that they need to get the job done.

The problem is that in this view, skills do not transfer between settings; rather, individuals learn to do particular tasks within particular settings. The students in J-828 learned to be investigative reporters. Perhaps some of them learned to be *good* investigative reporters. All of them surely would need more training to be excellent ones. But merely saying that these novice reporters learned a particular set of skills—and learned to see themselves as people who have those skills—does not explain how this learning might change them in other ways. It does not explain how they might think differently, see the world differently, or act differently when they are not actually doing the work of preparing an investigative news story. That is, the situated view explains how we might train people to do a particular kind of work. It doesn't explain how someone might come to think in a new way in the process.

To understand how and why that happens, we need one other concept that is not included in either the schema view of learning or the situated view.

We need epistemology.

EPISTEMOLOGY

The goal of J-828 as a practicum in investigative reporting was not just to teach novice journalists to write as watchdogs, write for story, and write to formula. Nor was the goal just to help them *be* investigative reporters. The goal was also to help them *think* like investigative reporters.

In an investigative news story, Kate explained, "the important question [is]: What is the story behind the story . . . ? Cops and courts are about changes in people's lives, [but] pattern recognition will define a reporter who really goes somewhere and one who is still a police reporter." This pattern—what Kate called "the story behind the story"—is the larger social or political problem that is the cause of some specific event. As Kate explained in an interview: "Telling the story behind the story can win you awards. . . . [My goal is] to produce smart reporters [who] practice smart journalism, [and] think like journalists."

Learning to think like a "smart" journalist in J-828 meant learning to simultaneously reflect from three perspectives. It meant understanding that a good investigative report takes a specific set of events (*the story*) and represents them in the formula of journalism (*a story*) to shed light on problems of the larger systems that organize society (*the story behind the story*). The epistemology of a practice is the means by which actions are justified, and in J-828, that meant using *the* story to create *a* story about the *story behind* the story.

By the end of the practicum, the novice reporters had internalized this way of thinking about journalism. In explaining why he thought their final project was a success, one student explained:

> We had facts and figures—we had our indictment of the system—but people don't really care about the system, numbers. We had to find a person who could be an anecdotal lead—show how the system had impacted him. Just be able to relate it to a person and say: "This happened to him and here's why. . . ." You need to capture attention . . . [to] find a way to give story a face, [and then] without editorializing show how the system is not living up to its end of the bargain.

It is not enough to simply have the rules for what to *do* as a reporter. It is not enough to be able to put these rules into practice, or to have the values to do so. It is not enough to see oneself as a journalist with this set of knowledge, skills, and values. Like any professional, a journalist needs to understand what actions are justified and how to justify actions within the profession. Knowledge, skills, values, and identity go hand in hand with epistemology. They come together—in J-828 and in professional practica more generally—into a very important and very powerful way of seeing the world and acting in it.

Game

If identity is central to a journalism practicum—that is, if part of learning to think like a journalist is learning to think of yourself as a journalist—then what happens when young people go through a game based on a journalism practicum without actually intending to become journalists? Will they still learn to think like journalists?

To answer these questions, let's look more closely at what it means to say that a practicum develops skills, knowledge, identity, values, and epistemology—which you can remember with the most unfortunate acronym SKIVE—by focusing on an epistemic game based on J-828. In *science.net*, middle school students play the role of novice science journalists, reporting on the impact of new scientific developments for an online science newsmagazine.

SCIENCE.NET

In J-828, twelve undergraduate and graduate journalism students spent a semester—about forty-five hours of class time—producing investigative news reports. In *science.net*, ten to fifteen players spend their mornings for three to four weeks in the summer—about forty-five hours of time in a summer outreach program—producing stories for an online science newsmagazine. But more important, *science.net* re-creates essential elements of J-828: the action and reflection-on-action that were central to the development of the skills, knowledge, identities, values, and epistemology of journalism.

In J-828, students worked on three news stories. For each story, they received a general story assignment, pitched their stories, did background research, conducted interviews, wrote draft stories, copy edited each other's stories, revised their drafts based on copy edits, and submitted their stories to the professor. They reflected on their reporting and writing in news meetings, copy-edit sessions, and through war stories from practicing journalists.

In *science.net*, players work on three stories. They pitch stories for the health and medicine, technology, and environment sections of the magazine. Working with desk editors for each section, players interview sources, submit stories for copy editing, and copy edit each other's work. Visiting journalists hold news meetings where they tell war stories and talk about stories in progress. To produce finished stories, players learn to write leads and headlines, to use the neutral voice of the newspaper, to source their stories using AP style, to include art and captions, to format their work for distribution on the Web, and to prioritize copy on the section front. And by the end of the game, the players of *science.net* collectively produce some fifty news articles about science and technology.

VIRTUAL WORLD

Fifty publishable news stories is a lot of work for middle school students, even for ten to fifteen players working for forty-five hours. What makes this possible are features of the game that help players focus on the key elements of the practicum and distribute the rest of the work to the people and technologies of the game's virtual world.

As in J-828, players in *science.net* interview real scientists and engineers. Real journalists tell war stories. And real people playing the role of desk editors run copy editing and news meetings. Players do original research online. But the particular topics from which they develop stories have been identified in advance, and appropriate interviews are scheduled to help them write to story.

As in J-828, players write and copy edit stories. But in *science.net*, they write using a journalism microworld whose features push back on specific elements of writing to formula and writing as a watchdog. This microworld, called *Byline*, gives reporters a set of *journalism tags* that correspond to key elements of the formula of journalism writing. Text marked by these tags—such as lead{ }, body{ }, and jump_line{ }—is interpreted by the microworld and presented according to news conventions to produce realistic-looking Internet news stories. The tags handle graphic and layout issues to help players produce a newsmagazine. But to do so, players have to mark the journalistic elements of their stories. The tags thus make explicit the organization and structure of writing to formula. Likewise, *Byline*'s preview panel, which displays how readers see the finished stories, helps players focus on why the story is important to someone else as a reader rather than to themselves as writers—that is, why they have to write as a watchdog about things that matter to the public.[20]

The virtual world of the game—which is constructed partly by a computer tool and partly by the people and activities organized around it—makes it possible for middle school students to play a very complex and demanding role in a game based on a very complex and demanding set of real-world activities.

SKIVE

Science.net has been studied by Hatfield and Magnifico in some depth. I'll describe the results from two studies here. One was part of an after-school enrichment program at the University of Wisconsin, in which fourteen middle school students (five female, nine male) from the Madison metropolitan area played for twelve hours over four consecutive Saturday afternoons. In a second study, ten middle school students (four female, six male) from the PEOPLE Program—the same program designed for at-risk youth that the summer players came from for the *Digital Zoo*—played for forty-five hours: three hours each morning for three weeks.[21] Thus these studies look at players with different backgrounds and different motivations for playing the game.

Hatfield and Magnifico recorded players in the game using audio- and video-tape, and kept copies of all the work that they did in *Byline*. They also interviewed players before and after the game—and, in the case of the summer players, again in the fall after they had returned to school. They also interviewed players before and after the game—and, in the case of summer players, again in the fall after they had returned to school. Hatfield and Magnifico asked the players questions about journalism and science. They asked players why they had decided to play the game and what they thought of the game after it was over. And they gave players a set of carefully constructed transfer scenarios about science and its impact on society similar to those used to study The Pandora Project.

In both of these studies, players began to develop the skills, knowledge, identities, values, and epistemology of the profession. In the after-school outreach program, players used more journalism skills in their final stories than in their first stories. They gave more balanced information and attributed more information to specific sources—both important techniques of journalistic writing. They used more of the journalism tags in *Byline* to structure their story and used them earlier in the story-writing process at the end of the game than at the beginning. They learned how to format stories using important elements of AP style and organize their stories with leads and inverted pyramids, putting the most important information first, as in many straight-news stories.

Players knew and used more journalistic terms of art after the game than before the game: almost three times as many, on average. Players could use this knowledge to talk about journalism stories with considerable insight. For example, we can compare players' copy edits of each other's stories from early and late in the game. Commenting on another player's draft of the first story of the game, one player said: "I liked everything, especially I liked his lead because he had everything in there, all of the 5 W's and an H [who, what, when, where, why, and how]." This comment uses terms of art (a lead, 5 W's and an H), but it has very little to say about the story and nothing about how to improve it. In contrast, talking about another player's draft of the final story, the same player used journalistic terms of art to dissect the workings of the story and offer suggestions to make it better:

> Okay, the first [suggestion] is in the first sentence . . . where she introduces the Waisman Center, but she doesn't tell us where it is—and I don't know where it is, and I never heard of it before. And after that it's in the same sentence . . . she starts talking about . . . stem cell research . . . but then she introduces it in the second paragraph instead. . . . [I]f she puts it there, people might be like: "What is that?" And then they keep reading on, and then they find out. . . . She should introduce it in the lead. . . . [In the second paragraph] I think you should be a lot more specific here because I didn't know what you mean when you say disabilities—like, what kind of disabilities?

Her comments continued at the same level of detail throughout the text of the story, showing a dramatic difference in her knowledge and skill about journalism after playing *science.net*.

The players that Hatfield and Magnifico interviewed began to develop the values of journalistic writing. When asked "What does it mean to be a journalist?" before the game, nearly four-fifths of players talked about writing without any mention of readers or writing for the public. Before the game, for example, one player said: "A journalist is someone who would write because they want to but they get paid to do it." After the game more than three-fifths of the players talked about journalists as people who write to inform other people about important events: "To be a journalist," said the same player after the game, "[is] to inform people about current events by writing them."

Players came to understand the epistemology of journalism. For example, before and after the game Hatfield and Magnifico gave players a *tip*—some information that could potentially form the basis of a news story—and asked them: "If you were a reporter given this information, what would you do with it?" Before the game, a typical answer focused on getting more information: "I'd get more information on it, because there isn't very much here, and I'd probably, like, ask some people what they thought."

After the game, players talked specifically what kind of people they would talk with and why, justifying the choices in terms of the structure of a balanced news story:

> I would go and interview whatever scientist that discovered this. And then I would interview a few environmentalists about what's happening. It would give me all the information of the story and would give me opposing sides of view. . . . Because it could be biased if you just include the scientist or the environmentalist point of view. . . . You want both sides of view to be included in the story.

Or, as one player explained, "if you support both sides and tell [the reader] what's good about each one and what's bad about each one, they can decide for themselves."

Finally, while developing the skills, knowledge, values, and epistemology of journalism, players came to see themselves as journalists. As one player explained at the end of the game:

> [The game] put . . . us in a journalist's view. So then once I was in the journalist's view, I was like doing a journalist's work, me being a journalist. I started to like it myself because, you know, this is what a journalist does every single day.

In other words, even though these middle school students who played *science.net* didn't plan to be journalists when they started the game, they still developed the skills, knowledge, identity, values, and epistemology of journalism.

IMPACT

Along the way to learning about journalism by working on science news stories as part of a journalism practicum, players also learned quite a lot about science. To be sure, they learned scientific facts and theories related to their stories, whether about nanotechnology ("Small Technology Goes to War"), ecology ("Study: Phosphorus Threatens Mendota"), or information technology ("Can games really help children?"). But what is more striking is how the game changed their understanding of what science is and why it matters.

Players learned about science in the game by writing about science as reporters, in the context of informing the public about events that impact their lives—that is, as part of the way a journalist thinks about events, issues, and problems. As a result, they came to see science through this journalistic perspective. For example, when asked "What is science?" before the game, one player saw science as a list of topics—the kind of topics that one studies in science class: "I think science is . . . things that include electricity or the human body . . . . I just, like, do science . . . I don't really think about what science is."

After the game, the same player talked about science as a broad field of inquiry, touching on a wide range of issues that matter to people in the world:

> I think science can be a lot of different things. Science can be technology, environment, health and medicine. Football fields can be considered science . . . How to grow the grass . . . I didn't know science could be health and medicine. Things like environment: . . . before I just thought they were what they were . . . [but I think about them differently after] picking the articles and finding stories about them and writing about them.

Before the game, players described science in terms of school subjects and topics ("electricity or the human body") nearly eight times more often, on average, than they talked about it in terms of the impact of science on society. After the game, they spoke about it more in terms if its social impact than its place in the curriculum.[22] Players came to see science and scientific issues the way a journalist does: as something that matters not because science is a subject in school but because it has an impact on the public.

But Hatfield and Magnifico found that the experience of playing *science.net* changed players in other ways too. When interviewed once they were back in school, some players said the game had helped them with current events assignments. Others said that after the game, they "care a lot more about science than I did last year" because it showed them that "science can be fun." Some talked about how copy editing as a journalist helped them in language arts class: "When we do persuasive essays, [other students] will read me their essay, and I will say what things I liked and didn't like and what could be changed . . . like maybe grammar mistakes or non-organized writing." Others explain that they now understand how to organize their writing better. One player talked, for example, about how learning to be a journalist helped her with her science lab notebook:

> In science we write lab notes and everything, so I kind of like take notes too before I write out my lab . . . [and] organize what I want. . . . [In the game] I just wrote down a whole bunch of stuff from my notes in the exact order of my notes, but then afterwards I realized that I have to organize it.

For some, the effects were even broader. One player said, "I ask people a lot of questions now. . . . Even people I don't know I just go up to them like: 'How are you doing? What's your name?' " Another player felt more confident in science class and in school generally: "It makes me feel as if I am a better student, that I know more in class now. So it makes me feel like I can answer questions and I will get good grades."

In other words, playing *science.net* didn't transform these players into professional journalists. They were, in the end, still middle school students. But the game did teach them to think and to feel like journalists, and to use the skills, knowledge, and values that go with that way of thinking to help them in school.

Epistemic Frames

Impacts that transfer from one context to another are, in some sense, the holy grail of education, and certainly the ultimate goal in the development of educational games. As Dewey pointed out more than half a century ago: "Every experience influences in some degree the objective conditions under which further experiences are had."[23] A key question—and perhaps *the* key question—for any educator who wants to design games for learning has to be: How does one experience change another? The premise of education writ large is that it is possible for one experience to influence another in this general sense. Otherwise there is no education, in school or otherwise. There is no learning. There is no continuity, no culture, nothing beyond the immediate here and now.

One way to think about what happens in *science.net* is to say that by taking on the role of a reporter in a journalism practicum, players become people who care about science because it matters in the lives of others; they become people who ask questions, who critique writing, and who think about how to organize ideas. And certainly in one sense this must be the case: Many players do these things after playing the game. But rather than thinking about the game in terms of the kind of person that players became—that is, in terms of their identity— it is more accurate to think what the game did for players' identit*ies*.

IDENTIT*IES*

Gee has argued that every game gives players an opportunity to try on new iden- tities. A game, he points out, is always about a relationship between two differ- ent identities: what he calls the *real identity* of the player and the *virtual identity* of the character or role the player has in the game. This relationship is enacted through a third *projective identity*, which is the kind of character the player wants to be in the world of the game.[24] The game gives players a chance to see them- selves as a different person—in the case of *science.net*, to see themselves as a per- son who asks questions in class, who cares about science, and so on.

In the study of development, identity is often conceptualized in terms of three kinds of different (though related) identities. From a developmental per- spective, my sense of identity comes from how I see myself, how others see me, and how both of those relate to broader social categories. Adolescents go through a process of defining themselves in terms of social roles—of under- standing who they are by understanding where and how they fit into the social world around them.[25]

A key part of this development is acquiring what psychologists Hazel Markus and Paula Nurius call *possible selves:* "individual's ideas about what they might become, would like to become, and what they are afraid of becoming."[26] Possible selves give form to a person's hopes for mastery, power, status, or belonging and to a person's fears of incompetence, failure, and rejection. They are images of what we might become, but not generic images. They are images that a particular person has based on his or her own past experiences, hopes, dreams, and worries.

Epistemic games can give adolescents new possible selves that are based on authentic experiences with innovative thinking that matter in the world. Adolescents are in the process of working out exactly the kinds of identity issues that professional practica are all about: becoming a particular kind of person in the larger social world; learning to care about people and issues that matter to society at large; developing expertise and being respected for that expertise. An epistemic game gives players a chance to see themselves as innovative professionals—and, as in any practicum, to be seen by others as professionals. And all of that seeing is, by definition, relative to a broader social (and socially valued) group.

What Hatfield and Magnifico found in their tests of *science.net*—and what has been true in studies of epistemic games in general—is that getting players to take on the identity of a professional is relatively easy. In fact, there is a kind of recipe—a heuristic or rule of thumb—for how to get someone to see themselves as a professional, and for others to see them in that way. To make players feel like a *professional X* in an epistemic game, it seems that they need someone to tell them they are a professional X. They need a badge of office or prop of profession X. They need to do something that they expect a professional X to do. They need to learn about something that a professional X does that they didn't know was part of the profession and then do that thing. They need someone they know (a peer, perhaps, or a parent) to see them as a professional X. And the virtual world of the game in which they are a professional X needs to be consistent in treating them like professionals rather than school students.

In *science.net*, a professional journalist tells the players that they are going to be working as journalists, and gives them a press pass, a reporters' notebook, and a pencil. They learn right at the start how a journalist conducts an interview, and then interview someone right away. They learn what a story lead is and how it is constructed, and then write a story using one. The virtual world of the game mimics the conditions of a real journalism practicum, and concludes when friends and family see the newsmagazine the players create.

So in the end, making players feel like journalists is easy. What makes *science.net* powerful as an epistemic game is not that two-thirds of the players who finished the game over one summer said they "felt like a journalist sometimes" when they were interviewed back in school. About the same number had started the game feeling that way. What was impressive is that they still felt like journalists even though they had come to understand how complex and difficult journalism is—and how much more is involved in being a journalist than they first believed. The possible selves these players took away from the game were not just about feeling like a journalist; they were based on an authentic experience of becoming a journalist.

The persistence of a new sense of identity, in other words, is only part of the story of *science.net*. The game is modeled on a professional practicum that links a new identity with the skills, knowledge, values, and epistemology of a profession. What transferred was not just a new identity but the *collection* of professional skills, knowledge, identity, values, and epistemology that the game created. What transferred was the *epistemic frame* of the profession.

FRAMES

In the 1970s, sociologist Erving Goffman described the concept of *frame analysis*.[27] He argued that any activity is interpreted in terms of a frame: the organizational rules and premises, partly existing in the minds of participants and partly in the structure of the activity itself, that shape the perception of those involved in the activity. We always have some set of assumptions, understandings, beliefs, expectations, actions, justifications, and sense of self that we use to make sense of what we are doing and what is happening around us. This set of organizing premises is the frame we are using to structure what we are doing at any given moment.

From this perspective, saying that someone is a particular kind of professional means that he or she interprets ongoing activities (or is able to do so) through a particular kind of frame: the epistemic frame of the profession.

The term *frame* in this sense is an apt description, since the epistemic frame of a profession acts like a pair of glasses that color the world in particular ways: making some things seem more important and others less so; marking some concepts, events, and objects with relevant terms of art and leaving others unnamed; making obvious some courses of action and dismissing others as not relevant or productive; setting the terms by which actions, decisions, and claims are judged and justified; and ultimately identifying the wearer as someone who has and uses that way of caring, knowing, acting, and thinking in the world.

The epistemic frame of a profession is the combination—linked and interrelated—of values, knowledge, skills, epistemology, and identity that people have when they become that kind of professional. For example, lawyers act like lawyers, identify themselves as lawyers, are interested in legal issues, and know about the law. These abilities, affiliations, habits, and understandings are made possible by looking at the world in a particular way: by thinking like a lawyer. This is a two-way street, of course. Thinking like a lawyer is made possible by these abilities, affiliations, habits, and understandings.

This is not to say that epistemic frames are hegemonic any more than identities are. As social psychologists Sheldon Stryker and Peter Burke point out, individuals have multiple identities, which can reinforce one another or compete and conflict.[28] Lawyers don't *only* think like lawyers. They may also be parents, and video gamers, and sports fans, and amateur carpenters. They are able to take on these other epistemic frames and to think and act in these ways as well.

The same is true for doctors and engineers—and army Rangers, plumbers, bricklayers, commodities traders, politicians, and drug dealers—but for different ways of thinking. A community of practice is always a group with a local culture, and the epistemic frame is the grammar of that culture—the ways of thinking and acting, the things someone knows and cares about—that individuals internalize when they become acculturated. And once an individual develops the epistemic frame of a community of practice, he or she can use that frame to see, think, and act in the world in other settings, including those outside the original community. The epistemic frame is what we get when we internalize the community and carry it with us.[29]

Epistemic frames are thus a level of description between and across the schema-based and community of practice-based views of thinking and learning. They describe how seeing oneself as a member of a community and learning to do what people in the community do requires learning what people in a community know and care about—and learning to decide, explain, and justify decisions and actions according to the norms of that community. The concept explains how neither learning to solve isolated problems nor merely participating in the activities of a community is sufficient to explain the kind of effects that we see in a professional practicum—or in an epistemic game.

The idea that cultures and communities have a common way of seeing the world is not new, of course. Anthropologist Karin Knorr-Cetina uses the term *epistemic cultures* to describe places where new formal knowledge is created, such as particle physics or molecular biology laboratories. In his influential book *The Structure of Scientific Revolutions*, Thomas Kuhn argued that scientific disciplines have a shared paradigm that defines what questions to ask, what to observe, and how to interpret the results of such observation. David Perkins has written about *epistemic understanding* as knowledge about how to justify and explain ideas within a particular discipline. Alan Collins and his colleagues at Northwestern University describe a discipline in terms of *epistemic forms* (the forms of knowledge appropriate to a discipline) and *epistemic games* (the rules for manipulation of knowledge in these forms). Philosopher Michel Foucault argued that every era has an *episteme:* a particular relationship between discursive practices (how people interact) and structures of knowledge that exists at the level of the culture as a whole, across domains of knowledge and forms of practice in a particular era: the classical episteme, the modern episteme, and so on. Sociologist Pierre Bourdieu described the nondiscursive structure of a culture as *habitus:* the habits, tastes, preferences, styles, and other things that "go without saying" for members of a community.[30]

Describing the skills, knowledge, identities, values, and epistemology of a community as its epistemic frame is useful, however, because it emphasizes that this structure is:

→ INTERPRETIVE. It makes some things seem more important and others less so, some courses of action possible and desirable and not others.

→ STABLE. It persists over time and across contexts. Once we develop an epistemic frame, it is something that stays with us—although if we rarely use it, its power diminishes.

→ TRANSIENT. Although it persists, it is not always in place. People can change epistemic frames and move between them, using different ones in different settings, or even seeing the same situation from two different points of view.

→ GENERATIVE. Epistemic frames are easier to use in situations that are similar to the ones in which they were created, but once developed, an epistemic frame does not depend entirely on its original context.

→ UBIQUITOUS. Epistemic frames are at the core of any community—not just cultures as a whole, and not just traditional academic disciplines or research communities.

And perhaps most important, epistemic frames are:

→ EPISTEMOLOGICAL. Epistemic frames are about setting the terms by which actions, decisions, and claims are judged and justified. They are a particular way of doing and of thinking, of deciding what is worth knowing and doing and of making those decisions.

In other words, epistemic frames are stable structures that explain how experience in the cultural context of one community can influence how people think and act in another. They explain how some things we learn in one setting can help us work in another.

From the schema point of view, we might say that an epistemic frame is just a set of facts and rules that can actually transfer across settings. Perhaps. But if so, then it is a very particular kind of schema, with elements that are not traditionally included in the description of how people solve the kind of word problems and puzzles usually associated with schema-based theories of learning. From the communities-of-practice point of view, we might say that identity always implies certain skills, and vice versa, and that both always require some kind of values, knowledge, and epistemology. Quite so; that is almost certainly true. But taking that as a starting premise assumes away the most important question from an educational point of view: How do these things get put together in one way and not another? Epistemic frames let us talk explicitly about what it means to think and work as a member of a community—and about how doing that means developing and integrating the skills, knowledge, identity, values, and epistemology of the community.

FRAMES OF INNOVATION

By this definition, of course, *any* game has an epistemic frame, because the community of players of any game has some particular culture. To play a game well, you have to be able to do certain things, to know certain things, to see yourself as someone who plays the game, to care about the things that matter in it, and to be able to explain or justify things in terms that make sense in it. That is, to play a game well, you have to have its skills, knowledge, identities, values, and epistemology—its epistemic frame.

To be clear, though: The epistemic frame is a property of the *game*. Simulations do not have epistemic frames; games do. A deck of cards does not have an epistemic frame, but the game of *Poker* does—and the easiest way to see that is to think about how the skills, knowledge, identities, values, and epistemology involved in a *Poker* game are different when I play in a casino than they are when I play in the basement with some friends on *Poker* night.

Any game creates a virtual world using some simulation: It is all of the things we do with, in, and around a simulation, the roles we play when interacting with a simulation, the norms we follow, the rules we obey. The epistemic frame is a property of the communities we inhabit in and around that virtual world, not a property of the simulation that makes it possible. So players can acquire an epistemic frame from the *Digital Zoo*, not *SodaConstructor* by itself; from *Escher's World*, not the *Geometer's Sketchpad*; from *science.net*, not *Byline*; and so on.

But if any game has an epistemic frame, what do I mean by an epistemic game? Simply put:

> An *epistemic game* is a game that deliberately creates the *epistemic frame* of a socially valued community by re-creating the process by which individuals develop the skills, knowledge, identities, values, and epistemology of that community.

And that definition explains the potential power of epistemic games. They are based on frames of innovation. Frames of efficacy in a high-tech, digital world. Frames of mastery. They give players realistic images of a possible self that are constructive, motivating, and tied to the skills, knowledge, values, and ways of thinking that will prepare them for success in school and later in life.

The point of such games is not to train young people in specific Professions in the traditional sense of vocational education. Epistemic games let players learn to work (and thus to think) in the ways of innovation. Developing the epistemic frames of innovation through epistemic games lets players see the world in ways that are fundamentally grounded in meaningful activity and well aligned with the core skills, habits, and understandings of a postindustrial society. Put another way, the point is not to train young people to *be* professionals, but to train them to be the kind of people who can *think* like professionals when they want and need to.

The epistemic frame of a professional is built during a professional practicum, and epistemic games based on these practicum experiences can develop these innovative ways of thinking and working for students who otherwise would be memorizing facts for standardized tests. Once built, these frames seem to last: They become valuable tools in a player's kit of skills, knowledge, identities, values, and epistemologies. They are ways of seeing and solving problems that matter in society and that have the power to help shape how young people see themselves and the world around them.

For Parents, Teachers, and Mentors

Science.net is not currently available for wide distribution, although David Hatfield is working on developing a version of *Byline* that could be used in schools, community centers, libraries, and after school and summer programs. There are, however, a growing number of commercial games that develop professional expertise and professional ways of thinking. One excellent example is *Full Spectrum Warrior*.[31] The game is based on a U.S. Army training simulation, but it is not a typical first-person shooter game. To survive in the game, you have to act—and think—like a modern professional soldier. The player controls two squads of soldiers, who can move in formations; the player selects the best position for them and decides what objectives they should achieve and how to go about pursuing them, within the rules of engagement that the U.S. Army uses for soldiers in the field. The excitement comes less from blowing things up than from avoiding death or injury for the soldiers in your squad. To do that means learning some modern military doctrine about things like suppression fire and how the concept applies in different contexts, what it has to do with solving particular kinds of problems, and how it relates to other practices of modern warfare, such as the injunction against shooting while moving. As the game manual explains dramatically: "Everything about your squad is the result of careful planning and years of experience on the battlefield. Respect that experience, soldier, since it's what will keep your soldiers alive."[32] The game lets players understand what it feels like to be a squad commander, lets them see how things look from that perspective, and lets them ask whether that way of looking at the world is one they like. Whether players decide that this possible identity is a good one for them or not, the game is about understanding the frame of an important professional practice.

Of course, some people may not want to expose their children to the identity of a professional soldier. The game is rated M (mature), and intended for players over seventeen years old. But certainly it could help adolescents considering a military career make more informed decisions about their career paths.

Whether *Full Spectrum Warrior* is the best example of a game that can develop a professional identity is less important, though, than recognizing that the identities that players develop in a game matter:

→ Young people grow and develop, in part, by exploring possible selves: by trying on different images of who they are and how they might act in the world. Talk with them about the kind of person a game encourages them to be and about the pros and cons of the different identities they find in the games they play.

→ Open-ended games that can be played in many different ways give players more of an opportunity to explore who they want to be and how they want to act than very scripted games. Part of understanding possible selves through games is trying to be different kinds of people in the same setting. Innovation can't be scripted, nor can learning to think like an innovator.

→ Think about the epistemic frame that a game creates. What kinds of skills, knowledge, identities, values, and epistemology does the game encourage? How does the game bring those together? Remember: The game is what players do with the simulation. Since the way of thinking is part of the game, not the simulation, you can influence what players learn by talking with them about the game, by playing it with them and thinking together about the kind of person you become while playing.

CHAPTER SIX

The future:
Urban Science

So far we've looked at five epistemic games, each of which shows the importance of one of the elements of an epistemic frame. With these illustrations I've argued that epistemic frames are a new way of thinking about thinking, and epistemic games like *Digital Zoo, Escher's World, The Pandora Project*, and *science.net* offer a new way of thinking about learning—one that is critical to education in the high-tech, digital world of global competition. Computers are making the capacity for innovative thinking more essential than ever before. And the ability of computers to make epistemic games widely available provides an opportunity to think about our system of education in new ways to meet that challenge.

The question is: How do we get there from here?

At the end of each chapter I suggest that commercial games exist that can help young people develop important skills, knowledge, identities, values, and ways of innovative thinking. There are many games out there that are fun to play and that can help children learn. This final chapter looks at what makes epistemic games special by comparing two excellent games about cities: *SimCity*, one of the top fifty computer and video games of all time, and *Urban Science*, an epistemic game originally designed by Kelly Beckett and expanded by Elizabeth Sowatzke, researchers at the University of Wisconsin.[1]

Thus far we have focused on the skills, knowledge, identities, values, and epistemology that players can take away from epistemic games—and at how many of these elements can be found or brought to current commercial games. A comparison of *SimCity* and *Urban Science* shows the particular power of linking ways of doing, knowing, being, caring, and thinking into a complete and coherent epistemic frame based on a real professional practicum. More important, though, the comparison shows how the next steps toward education for the digital age may not come in schools or even at home, but from a different and perhaps unexpected direction.

Building Cities

Building things is fun. With sand, Lego bricks, Lincoln Logs, paper, scissors, and, tape, clay, papier mache, wooden blocks, cardboard, paper bags, paint paper and glue, or bailing wire and twine. Building things is so much fun, in virtual worlds as in the real one, that some of the most popular computer and video games let players build things. In these games—which go by the unfortunate moniker *God Games* for reasons I will explain in a moment—players can design and run complex projects over time, developing and managing a business (which is why so many of them have the word "Tycoon" in their title), or, in the case of *SimCity*—the most famous construction game of all—building and leading a municipality as it grows from tiny hamlet to urban sprawl.

My daughters have a particular fondness for building cities in the sand when they are at the beach. At home, they focus on zoos, made from Playmobile, stuffed animals, and a Fisher Price barn. So perhaps it is not surprising that one of their favorite computer games is one of these construction games, *Zoo Tycoon*.

ZOO TYCOONS

In *Zoo Tycoon*, players get to landscape and build paths through their zoo property. They put up fences and buy animals for the exhibits, choose food for their animals and place water in the exhibits, place benches, bathrooms, concession stands, and donation boxes for zoo patrons to use, hire and manage staff, and monitor the zoo's cash flow through a fairly sophisticated budgeting process. While building, players can switch to guest mode and walk through the zoo, watch the animals (and the patrons), and take pictures for a scrapbook. The key to success in the game is making the zoo an intriguing, healthy, clean, and appealing place—a process that sometimes involves going into guest mode and cleaning up after people and animals alike.

Which is why I found it so interesting one day when I overheard a conversation between one of my daughters and a friend who was playing the game with her.

"Put an ice cream stand there," said the friend.

"I will," said my daughter. "Really. Sometimes I do. And then you have to clean up garbage. I don't like doing that."

"Then we won't do it," said her friend.

"No, but it's okay," was my daughter's answer. "I can clean up garbage."

To which her friend said: "Then we'll get more money!"

What was so interesting about the conversation, first off, was that it showed clearly how the game was bigger than the virtual world itself. The game they were playing was shaped by the virtual world, to be sure. But it was about the interests they were bringing to the world, the goals they were setting for their activities in it, and the conversations they were having about those activities as much as it was about the activities themselves. The game was more than what came in the box or could be found on the screen.

What was also fascinating was that in that brief but clear exchange, these kindergarteners were starting to grapple with the trade-offs among money, time, waste, and satisfaction that are built into the simulation that underlies the game. And, of course, this is precisely why games like *Zoo Tycoon* and *SimCity* seem so appealing as educational games.

To be fair, these are *great* games. They are fun. They are interesting. They are about things that matter in the world. And they involve complex and important concepts in mathematics, science, history, sociology, economics, and even zoology (in *Zoo Tycoon*) and urban and regional planning (in *SimCity*). But they are not epistemic games. And understanding why they are not helps explain why the next steps to a system of education based on epistemic games may not be through either school or the arcade.

WHY NOT *SIMCITY?*

The game *SimCity* is based on a simulation that models complex urban systems. Players take control of an urban grid. They design and run a city by maintaining a balance among a growing population, environmental changes, urban and economic development, and social issues such as crime and transportation. They play a role that incorporates elements of mayor, urban planner, and city government official, planning and managing the growth of the city over decades and even centuries.

Just as my daughter and her friend began to see interdependencies and trade-offs as they made choices in running a zoo, players in *SimCity* begin to understand the complexities of urban ecology. They see what happens when they make changes in an urban ecosystem. For example, if you put more parks in a city, the cost of public utilities goes up because you have to keep the parks clean. If you put an industrial site next to residential housing, the residential land values fall and the crime rate rises. As a result, players must decide whether to raise taxes, decrease the green space, move the industry, or risk urban flight— or, more realistically, decide which combination of these choices and in what measure will lead to the best long-term outcomes for the city. In this way *SimCity* makes visible how human choices affect environmental outcomes and lets players see how those outcomes then shape future choices.

Studies have shown that *SimCity* can help students learn about urban geography and community planning in social studies classes.[2] But while such a game can help players think about complex systems, there are also real limitations in using this particular game—and more generally this *kind* of game—for educational purposes.

In *SimCity*, the city that you create and maintain does not always represent an actual place—and certainly not the places in which most children live. The simulation model may represent realistic patterns of great complexity, but the issues are not necessarily issues that resonate to the world players inhabit outside the game. Space is compressed and time is dramatically expanded in the game. Changes occur on a wide-ranging geographical scale, presenting a macrolevel view of how cities function. Players manage an entire city that undergoes dramatic transformation in a matter of minutes or hours, whereas real cities grow and change slowly. Because we know that complex ecological and social processes look very different at different time scales, the fast-paced changes may give a distorted picture of how problems are resolved in the real world.[3]

Most troubling, though, for *SimCity* as a context for learning about the world—if we ignore the monster attacks and alien invasions that are part of the game—is that players act as virtual dictators. Much of the work of planning and running a real city depends on responding to the needs of constituents and interest groups that often do not even understand clearly what their own goals and agendas are for urban development, or how they may be mutually contradictory. Thus, much of the work of running a city is in trying to figure out what people want and then incorporating those desires into a workable plan for action through the political process: a process that is almost completely absent from the game. There is no context (a planning or city council meeting, for example) in which players explain and justify their actions—why they place industrial sites adjacent to residential ones, or fund road construction instead of greenspace— or submit their plans and intentions for approval.[4]

This is why *SimCity* is called a God Game. Players are not responsible for any social process of decision making within the virtual world. They face consequence for their actions, but they are free to do whatever they want, however irrational, destructive, or unrealistic.

URBAN PLANNING

SimCity is fun to play and helps players develop intuitions about urban issues. But it is not an epistemic game because players are not learning to think about how cities work from the perspective of any real professional community. Let's consider, then, *Urban Science*, a game about urban ecology that actually *does* get players thinking the way professionals think about the complex and ill-defined problems that urban areas face.

Beckett and Sowatzke, the developers of the game, began by asking: What group of people knows how to think about and solve problems of urban ecology? Their answer was urban planners.

Urban planners are great examples of innovative professionals. They develop land use plans that meet the social, economic, and physical needs of their communities. To do their job, urban planners have to have a deep understanding of both social and scientific issues. They use sophisticated tools to solve complex problems, including geographic information systems (GIS) that make it possible to ask creative what-if questions. Learning to think and work like an urban planner means learning to use GIS models and other tools to solve complex real-world problems in which science, society, economics, and technology intersect.

According to the American Planning Association, urban planning involves "developing plans for how land is used . . . working with the public . . . analyzing problems, visualizing futures, comparing alternatives and describing implications, so that public officials and citizens can make knowledgeable choices . . . managing the planning process itself, in order to involve interest groups, citizens, and public officials . . ., [and] being technically competent and creative."[5]

Several of these important characteristics are missing from the game *SimCity*, notably working with the public, describing implications so that public officials and citizens can make knowledgeable choices, and managing the planning process itself. Part of the mandate of the association is that its members be creative, because, like all professionals, planners cannot simply follow a rulebook to solve problems.

Planners develop the epistemic frame of their particular form of innovative thinking through a practicum, working to solve problems with the help of peers and mentors, and the epistemic game Beckett and Sowatzke developed was based on such a practicum.

URBAN SCIENCE

The game begins when players get a project directive from the mayor to the city planning department: create a detailed redesign for the local pedestrian mall in their city. They get a city budget plan and letters from concerned citizens about issues such as crime, revenue, jobs, waste, traffic, and affordable housing. Players go to the pedestrian mall, where they conduct a site assessment, as real planners do, and have a chance to hear from concerned citizens and community groups, such as the Urban League, Chamber of Commerce, a historical preservation association, and so on. In the original version of the game that Beckett developed and studied, players saw videotaped interviews with representatives of the various groups interested in the redesign of the street. In Sowatzke's updated version, players use handheld computers with a global positioning system link to get information from virtual representatives of these groups during the site visit.

Next, players use *iPlan*, a planning microworld that contains an interactive GIS model of the downtown area, to create a redevelopment plan. With *iPlan* they develop a *preference survey*: an instrument planners use to assess the response of community stakeholders to possible planning alternatives. Based on the responses they receive from surveys of the different stakeholder groups, players develop a plan to address the interests of the different groups.

For example, if a player wants to raise the number of jobs to satisfy the Chamber of Commerce, she might rezone part of the pedestrian mall for a large retail store. *iPlan* would show her that the number of jobs projected for the neighborhood goes up under that plan, but the model also would show how other issues, such as waste and traffic, are affected by the new store—issues that might be problematic for other stakeholders. Just like real planners, players have to balance the overall impact of their proposals against the costs and benefits—economic, social, and environmental—of alternative choices. And they have to do so within the social, economic, and ecological system of the city. After completing a land use plan, including a revised downtown zoning map, players present their proposals to a representative from the city planning office, justifying their plans.

In other words, this is a game played by the rules of an urban planning practicum: a city planning simulation that, to use Beckett's evocative phrase, is "augmented by reality."[6] The virtual world of the game is modeled on the real world of the city players live in and the real work of planners who shape that city. Players are redesigning a city, but it is *their* city. They can see and touch the places they are redesigning and can see how those changes might make their lives and the lives of those around them richer and more satisfying. However, their choices are constrained by the economic, social, and physical realities of life in a city and by the norms and practices of the profession of urban planning.

BECOMING PLANNERS

Beckett tested *Urban Science* as part of the PEOPLE Program—the same summer enrichment program for at risk students where *Digital Zoo* and *science.net* were tested, although Beckett's study worked with older adolescents. In the study, eleven high school students played for a total of ten hours over the two days of a single weekend in the summer, including time for lunch and other breaks. Four of the players were female, seven were male. Eight were African American, two were Latino/a, and one was of Asian descent. All had volunteered to play the game in exchange for community service credit in the PEOPLE program.[7]

Beckett interviewed players before and after the game, asking about ecology and urban planning, and players were given urban planning transfer scenarios (like those used in *The Pandora Project* and *science.net*) to assess whether they could use concepts, skills, and values from the game to solve problems like an urban planner. Players also completed concept maps representing diagrammatically their understanding of the issues and interest groups relevant to their city.

Beckett's interviews showed that these players knew very little about urban planning before they started the game. In the course of the game, though, they learned to read and interpret documents the way urban planners do. They learned to conduct a site assessment, to create a land use plan, and to make a project presentation. And they learned to put these skills together, as urban planners do, to create a convincing proposal for the development and renewal of their city. They developed these skills and abilities in the same way urban planners do, supported by adults who held them accountable to professional standards of excellence.

Beckett found that after the game, players had a better understanding of ecology. Before, less than 10 percent of the players could explain what the word *ecology* meant. After the game, more than 80 percent could, and, like this player, they understood what it meant to think about the ecology of a city the way an urban planner does:

> [Ecology is] the study of the ecosystem. Basically how one thing will affect the other thing. If something is removed or placed here or something like that. Like increasing population might lead to a lack of jobs for people, and then it leads to more waste and traffic. . . . [T]hat's like ecology in the city.

After the game, players' thinking about urban issues as measured in concept maps became more complex, including on average 72 percent more connections between issues and stakeholders and taking into account on average 20 percent more factors that impact city planning.[8] Players' explanations of their concept maps also showed the change in the complexity of their thinking. For example, describing the role of "jobs" in the concept map he drew before the game, one player said: "Jobs are connected to the greenspace, if you're a gardener or someone who takes care of the parks."

After the game, the same player said:

> Jobs would mean more people. More people would mean more pollution, [and] . . . more crime. . . . When the city grows and the city has more people its going to need like buildings to house them. . . . [I]f there are more buildings, there will be more traffic. . . . You can't really change one thing without changing another.

More important, in the process of learning about urban ecology, players came to see themselves as planners and see the world through the epistemic frame of planning. After the game, every single player Beckett interviewed said, in one way or another, that playing had changed the way they think about their city. After playing the game, one player said that now, walking down the street, she tended to "notice things, like, that's why they build a house there, or that's why they build a park there." Another said:

> I'm looking at connections a lot closer now. Usually you'll see connections but you don't think about them. . . . I really noticed how . . . when they think about building things, urban planners also have to think about how the crime rate might go up, or the pollution, or waste depending on choices.

It is in the transfer scenarios, though, that Beckett found the most dramatic evidence that players had begun to develop the epistemic frame of planning. One scenario was about a small town that had too much waste for its landfill. Before the game, one player's solution was just to "look for a new landfill." This high school student had, in effect, been thinking less about interconnectedness and trade-offs than my daughter and her kindergarten friend were while playing *Zoo Tycoon.*

After the game, though, the same player gave a much more detailed response to a similar problem dealing with the closing of the town recycling station:

> Okay, well, first of all, they should have not closed down the recycling plant. They could have cut other stuff, or they could've raised taxes to increase revenue. . . . I think they should keep a recycling plant because they should be helping to reduce the amount of waste. . . . They could export the trash, but then that would cost a lot more money too, and they're making budget cuts. . . . I'd say fundraising. . . . You could rent the fairgrounds, charge for parking, and they can get a certain percentage from the fair people.

Notice how the proposed solution after the game is specific, technical, and innovative about how to solve this planning dilemma. The player analyzes the problem using knowledge and values from the planning profession. She uses planning skills to frame the problem in terms of different alternatives (raise taxes, export the trash, or cut the budget). She considers each alternative and how it might impact the many dimensions of a complex urban ecology. That is, after playing the game, this player is able to see the problem and develop an innovative solution within the epistemic frame of the profession of urban planning.

DIFFERENT GAMES

SimCity is a commercial game, designed primarily for entertainment. *Urban Science* is designed to re-create an urban planning practicum. Both create epistemic frames, but one creates an indeterminate frame based on the culture of the game and the practices of . . . well, of some form of (hopefully, enlightened) urban despot. The other develops the epistemic frame of the profession of urban planning.

SimCity can be a useful educational tool for starting discussions about the interconnectedness of urban systems. It can help players understand basic urban issues such as crime and traffic, learn to think about budgets, revenue, and taxation, and more generally appreciate the difficulties in controlling events in a complex system. But it was designed primarily to be fun to play and thus to sell well in the marketplace of commercial games. *Urban Science* was designed to develop innovative thinking.

We know the training practices of urban planners do the work of building the professional epistemic frame of planning. And as Beckett's study showed, players can use that frame, as the planning association suggests, to be "technically competent and creative . . . to envision alternatives to the physical and social environments in which we live." The game is fun, but it was designed primarily as a tool for learning.

Fun and learning can be quite compatible, of course. Racing enthusiasts can use the high-fidelity simulation in the racing game *Gran Turismo 4* to learn about a car's driving dynamics and a track's layout.[9] But the focus of a game matters in the end, and in the most extreme cases, commercial games can give dangerously inaccurate portrayals of the way things work in the real world. A recent reviewer of the game *Phoenix Wright: Ace Attorney*, for example, said it was his "favorite game of the year" but noted: "The most outrageous episodes of [the television series] 'Ally McBeal' exhibited a more faithful portrayal of the legal system. . . . Perjury is treated as mildly inappropriate, and witnesses receive great leeway if they hand the judge a box lunch."[10]

What makes epistemic games special is that they are based on what we already know about how people learn to be innovative thinkers and on how that kind of thinking is used to solve real problems in the world outside of the game.

Building Epistemic Games

Building from existing models is different from building from first principles or building from scratch. We know that professionals develop the skills, knowledge, identities, values, and epistemology of innovation in professional practica: places where novices work on professional problems and reflect on that work with peers and mentors. In this general sense, the architectural design studio, mock negotiations, and capstone courses in engineering, journalism, and urban planning are all similar in their overall structure. But the specific kinds and forms of reflection-on-action in each practicum matter, because they provide a map of the different professional vision of each practice. The reflection-in-action, or thinking on the fly, of a professional is formed as cycles of action and explicit reflection-on-action are internalized—that is, made part of the epistemic frame of the profession that guides future action.

Thus, we can analyze a practicum through *epistemography*: by looking at the kinds of action and the kinds of reflection-on-action that develops the epistemic frame of the profession. Such an analysis is important because most professional practica are evolved rather than designed. By that I mean that no one person or group of people sat down to decide how best to train architects, engineers, urban planners, and other professionals. Over time, different people tried different approaches. Those that were effective persisted, and those that were not eventually got left behind. Practica are not necessarily ideal, because learning is a complex process. So it is likely that some less-than-ideal elements of practica persist because they are either too hard to eliminate or facilitate doing something else important. Biological evolution often works that way, proceeding not according to a master plan but by incremental changes. Such changes generally become better adapted to local conditions but may also preserve things that are problematic: for example, the position of the human larynx, which makes possible both speaking and choking.[11]

What this means, though, is that we can't explain a practicum entirely by reference to principles of learning. We can see principles at work and recognize some features of the practicum as being more essential than others in developing the epistemic frame of the profession, but we can't extract general principles of learning that can be used anywhere.

Remember the Oxford Studio, the basis for *Escher's World?* An analysis of the Oxford Studio showed that students worked on projects in depth, in a series of iterative design episodes, over an extended period of time, in consultation with peers and mentors in desk crits. These projects gave students a great deal of creative control, and they were presented publicly for discussion and assessment. The analysis thus provided a long list of guidelines about how projects worked in the studio, but they were not principles of learning in the usual sense. Rather, they were attempts to describe explicitly some key aspects of the Oxford Studio that helped develop the epistemic frame of design—and that therefore were critical structures to preserve in adapting the practices of the design studio for younger students. Similarly, *science.net* was based on J-828 as a whole and not only on the war stories, news meetings, and copy editing that were central to the development of an epistemic frame of journalism.

Epistemic games create virtual worlds based on existing professional train-ing using key features as explicit markers rather than designing from scratch based on a set of principles extracted and abstracted from existing practica.

NOT ONE FROM GROUP A

Several decades ago psychologist Ann Brown and her colleagues developed an innovative curriculum called Facilitating Communities of Learners, or FCL for short.[12] FCL incorporated a number of new teaching techniques, including *reciprocal teaching* (in which students in a small group take turns asking each other guiding questions while reading) and *jigsaws* (in which students break into groups to learn about different aspects of a topic and then come together in new groups containing one student with expertise in each aspect of the original topic).

Much to the dismay of Brown and her colleagues, teachers and other researchers took reciprocal teaching and jigsaws and started using them as part of other curricula. Brown's dismay was not that people were stealing her ideas but that they were stealing only some of them. They were using reciprocal teaching and jig-saws without also using the rest of the FCL curriculum plan, and as a result the activities were not working. Brown and her colleague Joe Campione argued, for example, that a jigsaw works in FCL only because it is part of a consequential task. If they do not need the information to complete some other meaningful activity, students merely go through the motions of exchanging information in a jigsaw. And completing a meaningful activity happens only when the teacher and curriculum designers understand that one of the fundamental principles of learning in FCL is that students learn by working together on problems that matter to them.

Brown and Campione responded by suggesting that learning takes place only as part of a coherent system, and many failed attempts to implement good educational ideas have been the result of seeing what should be a coherent whole as a set of isolated parts—what they described as a "Chinese menu . . . one from Group A, one from Group B" approach to education.

A similar danger exists in studying professional practica. One of the impor-tant features of epistemic games is that they explicitly do not try to extract good educational practices from professional training and then incorporate them into existing school settings. The point of *Escher's World* is not that desk crits are a great way to talk about work with students. Rather, in the game, desk crits are part of a larger system of acting and reflecting on action that produces a particular epistemic frame. Similarly, the point of *science.net* is not that journalistic copy editing can be lifted out of context and used in a traditional English class.

Epistemic games are based on the idea that practica have evolved, over time, sophisticated techniques for helping novices take on the epistemic frame of a profession—and that these techniques depend on one another in an often-delicate balance. These are not practices to adopt in isolation but coherent systems that can, with new technologies, be adapted so that younger students can start developing the epistemic frames of innovation at an early age.

QUESTIONS

Epistemic games are always built by asking a series of questions. The questions may seem obvious once stated, but they are, in fact, made possible only by the power of computers to create virtual worlds and by thinking about thinking in terms of epistemic frames.

Any epistemic game starts with the question: What is worth being able to do in the world? There are many things that we want young people to be able to accomplish in life. Some things matter for economic reasons, such as being able to balance a checkbook. Some are more practical, such as being able to change a flat tire. Others are about self-actualization: being able to appreciate a work of art or a piece of music. Or about interpersonal relationships, as in being able to talk constructively about conflict. Some are about citizenship and some about health and some, like learning to read, are about more than one of these things in different ways at different times.

Whatever is worth doing, though, some group of people in society knows how to do it. If there is not such a group, one has to assume the thing is not worth doing. Or if it still is worth doing, it seems strange that we would expect children to do what adults can not. So the second question is: Who knows how to do this kind of thing, and how do *they* learn how to do it? This question leads to the kind of epistemographic study described earlier, a careful investigation of how the skills, knowledge, identities, values, and epistemology are created and linked into the epistemic frame of a group of people who solve some important kind of problem in the world.

Finally, we ask: How can we make these learning practices available for others? Computers make it possible to create virtual worlds, so what kind of virtual world will make it possible to act—and to reflect on that action—to develop the epistemic frame that lets people see and address this kind of problem? The solution almost always involves some piece of technology that makes a simulation possible, but it also always involves more than just technology, because a game is always about more than just the underlying simulation. The virtual world of an epistemic game re-creates learning practices that almost always involve people as well as things, reflection with peers and mentors as well as action.

The examples we've looked at show that this kind of analysis and game design are possible across a range of "things worth doing"—and thus suggest that epistemic games may be a way to rethink, and perhaps rebuild, our system of education.

Rebuilding Education

With epistemic games, young people don't have to wait to begin their education for innovation until college, or graduate school, or their entry into the workforce. *Digital Zoo, Escher's World, The Pandora Project, science.net,* and *Urban Science* show what effective learning might look like in a high-tech, global, digital, postindustrial world. To make that image a reality, games like these will need to change our understanding of classrooms and commercial games, formal and informal learning. And one path to those changes is to think about epistemic games in third places.

The term *third place* was coined by sociologist Ray Oldenburg to describe cafés, community centers, coffee shops, and general stores. These are neither homes nor work, and thus are the "third places" in people's lives, where people regularly go to talk with friends and "hang out"—to build community, share triumphs and losses, and in the process deal with issues, problems, and concerns that can't be fully expressed within the confines of the family or the structures of a job.[13] Television watchers will quickly recognize the bar in the comedy

Cheers—where, as the theme song says, "everybody knows your name"—as a prototypical third place. Similarly for Central Perk, the coffee shop in *Friends*, Monks, the diner in *Seinfeld*, or Ten Forward or Quarks in *Star Trek*. The attraction of showing third places on television is precisely that they are where people talk about things that matter and are free to be (and to become) who they really are, separate from the expectations of home and work.

Currently, epistemic games are a kind of third place—or perhaps more appropriately a third *space*—between formal schooling and more traditional commercial games.[14] In describing *Urban Science* and other epistemic games that have been developed and tested, you may notice that I have said very little about playing these games in schools. Although some have been used and tested in school settings—notably *The Debating Game* and *The Pandora Project*—most have been developed and played elsewhere: after school hours at a community center, on weekends as part of an outreach program, in conjunction with the 4H or Girl Scouts, or as part of a summer program for kids.

More than 2.5 million elementary and middle school students in the United States spend time in organized after-school programs every week. The main purpose of such programs has been to provide a safe place for children between the time school ends and the time their parents come home from work. But many of these programs are also trying to provide opportunities for students to continue their education in a different—and perhaps more meaningful—fashion. One way to do this is through video or computer games like the ones I have described. Perhaps in the not-too-distant future, epistemic games may also be a part of what games researcher Constance Steinkuehler has called *virtual third places:* multiplayer online worlds like *Second Life* or *Quest Atlantis* where young people and adults can gather from across the world, rather than across a city or neighborhood, to work on meaningful projects.[15]

The reason I focus on how these games are played out of school is that schools, as currently organized, make it difficult to prepare kids for innovation through epistemic games. Game scholar Kurt Squire has written in some detail about how the culture of games does not fit well with the culture of schools, and some of the same arguments apply to epistemic games as well.[16] It is hard for teachers to spare the time from getting students ready for the next standardized test, and, not surprisingly, innovation is difficult to accomplish in forty-minute chunks of time, spread from room to room and subject to subject throughout the day. So to develop and test epistemic games we look outside of schools, to places where children have time to work on complex problems in depth—and where adult mentors in these games can focus on students' innovative thinking rather than on their performance on tests of basic skills.

THIRD SPACES IN THIRD PLACES

Right now, epistemic games are something different from school and different from most commercial games. They work best in the childhood equivalent of third places: clubs, after-school programs, summer camps, and community centers. There, these games can develop according to their own intrinsic logic, to explore the highest potential of what learning might be—and what education could become—in the digital age. As a third space between formal instruction and free play, epistemic games can explore what can happen to games when the primary focus is on *learning* rather than on market forces in commercial game production or on the institutional imperatives of schools as they currently exist.

Some will argue, no doubt, that this is a copout: What is the point of developing ideal educational games without taking into consideration who would pay for them or how they would work as part of a comprehensive system of education? Shouldn't epistemic games be tested in rigorous, randomized trials to see if they are better at improving test scores than traditional instruction?

In the current video game market, new titles are costly to produce—and are becoming more so each year. Thus the scope of experimentation is relatively low. Even within the industry, game developers like Eric Zimmerman have been calling for the development of indie games, much like independent films that explore new ideas in filmmaking through lower-budget movies with smaller audiences.[17]

Our modern school system is similarly difficult to change, because innovation is politically as well as financially expensive. If schools are going to adapt to new social and economic conditions, we need to develop viable alternative models of learning that excite parents, teachers, administrators, business leaders, politicians, and others who care about what happens in schools. And of course it would be important that these alternatives actually help prepare kids to be innovative thinkers in a complex, postindustrial world. We can develop epistemic games outside of the network of traditional schooling, not to compete with the schools but to show what can happen when we think—quite literally— outside the boxes of the traditional school building, classrooms, schedules, subjects, and curricula. If this puts pressure on schools, or helps us see a way to help schools do a better job of preparing students for life in a high-tech, digital, world of global competition, so much the better.

Epistemic games in the third places of childhood are one way to address the need to create incentives for students to take advanced courses in technical subjects in school, which is one of the recommendations of a recent national report on responses to globalization.[18] More generally, as we've seen, such experiences are productive for adolescents and for middle school students in particular. As psychologist Albert Bandura points out, middle school marks a difficult transition for many students. Leaving the relatively protected world of elementary education, many face their first experiences of academic, athletic, or social difficulties. Mastery experiences like those that come through playing epistemic games reinforce adolescents' sense of self and self-efficacy in a critical period of academic and career development. Middle school is when many students begin to opt out of mathematics and science, and studies suggest that the career trajectory for many students gets crystallized quite early.[19] Moreover, as science education researchers Jayne Stake and Kenneth Mares have shown—and as we have seen in study after study of epistemic games—students returning to school after enrichment programs have a *splashdown effect*, seeing the school in a new and more productive way.[20] Epistemic games can thus help young people take important steps toward success in school and in life in the digital age of global competition.

But the point of epistemic games is not that they can do the same things that schools do only better—or, for that matter, that they can do the same thing that commercial games do only with more math, science, and social studies in them. The point is that they are a fundamentally different way of thinking about learning based on a fundamentally different way of thinking about thinking.

They are about the kind of thinking and learning that kids need in a changing world.

EPISTEMIC GAMES AND SCHOOL

Of course, both schools and commercial games might benefit from becoming more like epistemic games. It is certainly possible to imagine that schools might someday be more about epistemic games and less about the game of *School* and its standardized answers to standardized assessments. That would begin to address the problem of preparing young people for innovative thinking in a competitive world. But education based on epistemic games could also go a long way toward solving other problems that plague our schools today.

We know that what kids learn in school doesn't stick with them very well. It doesn't transfer very well beyond the tests students take. Sometimes it doesn't even transfer that far. Most people study mathematics every year beginning in first grade, but many can't do much more than perform (often poorly) the functions that are already built into a 99-cent calculator. In the most recent Trends in International Mathematics and Science study, only 7 percent of students in the United States scored at the most advanced level in mathematics.[21]

But this disconnect between facts and rules that students memorize and knowledge they can use to solve real problems simply does not happen in epistemic games, which are based on making and applying knowledge. Instead of learning facts, information, and theories first and then trying to apply them, the facts, information, and theories are learned and remembered because they were needed to play the game—that is, to solve some real-world problem—in the first place.

Of course, epistemic games like *Urban Science* are about facts, and lots of them. Students playing the game had to learn a complex set of zoning codes and to understand what they meant and how to use them. They had to figure out the relationships among complex variables such as the crime rate, housing stock, land values, tax revenue, waste, transportation, and pollution. But this information was not merely a set of facts to be memorized; it was knowledge put to use as part of a professional way of thinking—the kind of learning that students need to prepare for innovative work.

EPISTEMOLOGY MATTERS

The biggest change, though, in organizing schools around epistemic games would be to stop thinking about the goal of school as learning math, science, and social studies in the first place.

This seems like a radical thing to say because the traditional intellectual disciplines have been the focus of schooling since we have had modern schools. Whatever the hidden curriculum of social discipline may be, the explicit curriculum of school is about learning *the basics:* the fundamental ways of thinking that students will use no matter what they choose to do after school.

But wait a minute. If mathematics, science, and history matter because they are *ways of thinking*, then accounting, medicine, and journalism matter too. They are also ways of thinking. That's what it means to say that frames are *epistemic*. Mathematicians, scientists, and historians have epistemic frames through which they see the world: frames that incorporate skills, knowledge, and values within particular ways of deciding what is important and explaining and justifying the things they do.

The epistemic frame of a professional research mathematician is not any more fundamental than that of a statistician, though. Or an accountant. Or a surveyor. Professionals in those fields use mathematics too, but they learn and use knowledge and skills about numbers and objects in space in the context of solving different kinds of problems from professional mathematicians. Accountants and surveyors don't have much use for formal proofs, for example, geometric or otherwise. It may be important to them that someone be able to do such proofs, but they think about quantitative and spatial information in a different way. Similarly, it is not important to a professional mathematician to use logistic regressions to find patterns in complex data or to accurately map complex parcels of land based on aging and out-of-date records. But it is important to him or her that someone be able to do it—assuming he or she ever wants to buy a house. All of these professions are important.

But which ones are more fundamental—in the sense that everyone should learn to think using that epistemic frame—is an open question.

Computers now make it possible for young people to learn through epistemic games based on the way professionals train for innovative thinking. So the question is no longer: How can we make sure every student learns math—or science, or history? Rather, we need to ask: Which epistemic frames should students develop to become fully actualized and empowered citizens in a postindustrial society?

It may be that learning to develop the epistemic frame of academic mathematicians, historians, and research scientists is an important end of the educational process. Or it may be that the epistemic frames of (for example) accountants, journalists, and foundation program officers are more useful general ways of thinking about issues numeric, civic, and scientific in the body politic. Or we might decide fundamental skills for life in a global society and economy include a wide range of epistemic frames and that different combinations matter for different students. The fact is that we won't know until we have enough epistemic games (and enough players) to see which ones are the most interesting, most transformative, and most useful, how different games fit with one another, or how to organize a whole curriculum of such games.

Which frames we focus on is a practical and a moral—and thus ultimately a political—question. But it is a question that points toward a very different kind of education, and away—far, far away—from the direction in which our schools are moving now.

INNOVATION FOR ALL

In 1955 Rudolf Flesch wrote *Why Johnny Can't Read*, arguing that phonics was the one true way to teach reading. Fifty years later, this is the new gospel of our schools. Conservatives applaud. Progressives lament. But the truth is that Johnny—and Johnny's parents, and teachers, and every one of us—has bigger things to worry about.

It is absolutely critical that schools make sure all children learn to read and write. But in today's world, it is, quite simply, not enough. It is not enough for our children or for our economic survival if education is only about giving kids basic skills for jobs that no longer exist. We have to start preparing children—all children, rich and poor, at risk and gifted, urban, suburban, and rural—for the challenge of innovative work.

And epistemic games are a way to do that.

They use the power of new technologies to change the way we think about education. In these games, the same technologies that place a premium on innovative practices make those practices accessible to young people as never before. The same technologies that make industrial schools largely irrelevant in preparing students for productive and satisfying lives make it possible to invent a new way of teaching and learning. Epistemic games may not be the only way to do that, but they are one way.

I have said little, thus far, about who the players of epistemic games have been, what kinds of schools they attend, and what neighborhoods they live in. That is because these games have been played by a wide range of young people: from wealthy families and poor ones, from good schools and bad, from urban and suburban neighborhoods. Kids from different ethnic backgrounds. Kids who do well in school, and kids who don't. When these games become more widely available and more young people are playing them, we will surely learn more about how different kinds of players experience them in different ways. Thus far, however, we have seen few systematic differences in what these young people get out of the epistemic games they've played.

It matters that these games work for young people from many different backgrounds and with many different interests because in the end, developing epistemic games and making them widely available is as much a question of equity as it is of pedagogy. If we surrender to the challenge of preparing children for innovative work, the burden will fall disproportionately on the poor. If we do not invest in rebuilding our educational system to prepare students to be innovators, then well-off parents will surely make up the difference for their kids, and the withering of public education, which is the foundation of a democratic society, will be all but complete.

If Johnny can't learn to innovate, it will be because *we* weren't willing to innovate. It will be because we were not willing to reinvest in Johnny's education by thinking about learning in new ways.

SOME AND SOMETHING

None of this is meant to suggest that epistemic games are an all-or-nothing proposition; far from it. The concept of epistemic frames that guides these games is a powerful way of thinking about learning. It has great potential to make commercial games more compelling and educationally relevant, and it has the potential to make school curricula more interesting and more effective.

As one might imagine, I am contacted with some frequency by game developers interested in producing games for learning—or the "educational market" as they sometimes describe it. Some of these games are good. Some are not so good. But one of the things that I always do when someone starts describing an idea they have for a game is to try to understand what epistemic frame they are trying to create and how they are going about that task. Often it becomes clear in the process that the developers have thought a lot about some aspects of the frame and less about others. As you might expect, the games I see are mostly about knowledge and skills and, more rarely, in good games, about identity and values.

One developer recently asked me for advice on a very interesting game he was designing about marine biology called *Uncharted Depths*. Players were going to be scientists, and the design document described a storyboard in which players travel in a submersible in a virtual ocean to come up with interesting research questions. They submit grant proposals to fund research and then return to the virtual sea to collect specimens, from which they gather data in their virtual laboratory. They present their findings, successful projects lead to more funding, and so on.

In talking about *Uncharted Depths*, it became clear that the developer was concerned about the attitudes toward ocean life players might develop from the game. Would they think that it was acceptable to perform any kind of experiments on animals? Would they mistreat the virtual animals in their virtual lab, and how might that negative learning carry over from the game?

I suggested that the developer look at the actual training practices of marine biologists to see how this link between skills of experimentation and value of respect for animal subjects gets formed. Not surprisingly, of course, biologists who apply for grants (and biology students working on funded projects) have to submit their research for review. They prepare a formal document describing what they are going to do in their experiments, and a committee has to agree that their research methods will treat the animals in the experiment fairly. In other words, one way to make the game more effective as a tool for learning was to take a closer look at the actual practice of marine biology research.

The process of thinking in terms of epistemic frames and epistemic games can be similarly useful in developing school curricula. For example, a student in one of the courses I teach recently did a final project about an elementary school science classroom. She observed the class for several weeks while they did a science unit in which they were "being scientists." The teacher had these first graders make observations of plants growing, drawing the plants at various stages, talking about the different parts of the plant and how they worked. The teacher referred to the students as scientists during the unit: "Okay, scientists, now it is time to make our observation for the day." She explained their activities in terms of things a scientist does: "A good scientist always puts an experiment away carefully."

As the student analyzed these activities from the perspective of epistemic frames, she concluded that the teacher was, in effect, creating a kind of epistemic game, but one that could have been more deliberate and consistent in letting these first graders play an authentic role of scientists.

I have suggested throughout the book that one of the best things adults can do to help children learn from computer and video games is to play the games with them. Doing that will surely mean letting them teach you about the game, and how to play, and what you need to know and do to be good at it. But it also means having an opportunity to talk about the games together and to be explicit about the epistemic frame—good or bad—that the game creates. *SimCity* is not *Urban Science*, but it becomes a much better opportunity for learning when you talk about what happens in the simulation the way a planner does.

Epistemic frames and epistemic games are not only powerful tools for rethinking education, they are also a useful way of improving existing games and existing curricula along the way.

CLEANING UP THE GARBAGE

There are, of course, some who feel that video games are a passing fad—or perhaps worse, a pernicious drug, stupefying players young and old into wasting hours of time and millions of dollars on mindless, senseless, and often violent activities.[22]

The case has already been made by others—notably though by no means exclusively by Gee in his book *What Video Games Have to Teach us about Learning and Literacy* and Johnson in *Everything Bad Is Good for You*—that video games are complex, challenging, and, in the end, important.[23] Here I have argued that more than just being complex and challenging, computer and video games are significant because they let us think in new ways.

Computers make it possible to create virtual worlds and to think and learn by inhabiting those worlds. They represent a change in thinking on the order of the development of the printing press, or writing, or even language itself. The new kinds of games that computers make possible are a form of communication, of interaction, of play uniquely suited to the high-tech, digital, on-demand and just-in-time postindustrial world of global competition that information technologies are creating.

The virtual worlds of video and computer games are also occasions for learning. They make it possible for players to learn by doing things that matter in the world on a massive scale. People who do things that matter in the world— professionals in the broad sense of anyone who uses judgment to solve complex problems that can't be addressed by rote formulas—learn to think through practica. In these practica, professionals-to-be take action and reflect on that action with peers and mentors. In the process, they develop the skills, knowledge, identities, values, and epistemology—the epistemic frame—of their profession. They develop a professional way of seeing, thinking about, and acting on important problems.

The virtual worlds of computer and video games can re-create these practica and make them available to young people through epistemic games: games designed to create the epistemic frames of innovative thinking. These games make it possible to move beyond disciplines derived from medieval scholarship and taught in schools designed for the Industrial Revolution—a new model of learning for a digital culture and a global economy.

Seymour Papert wrote that when it comes to learning, what *can* be done is a technological question, what *should* be done is a pedagogical question, and what *will* be done is a political question.[24] The future of education depends not only on whether epistemic games work, but on whether we have the will to change how we think about thinking and learning in a changing society.

The other day I walked past the computer as my daughter was playing *Zoo Tycoon*—which is still her favorite game almost a year after we first bought it. She was walking through her newest, most elaborate zoo happily scooping up trash from the concession stands and cleaning up after the animals.

She saw me watching and said: "I really like cleaning up now!"

"Really!" I replied. "That's great!"

But what I was thinking was: Maybe there is hope after all.

For Everyone

In the end, the best hope for a better way of educating children for life in the digital age is for adults to think about learning in a new way: to think about helping young people develop the epistemic frames of professional innovation. I've described a number of games here: epistemic games and commercial games; games in school, games at home, and games in after-school and summer programs; games about science and history and writing and business and engineering and a host of other valued practices in the world. But whether any of these is the "best" example of an educational game or not, the take-home message is that games matter:

→ There are plenty of bad games out there, just as there are plenty of bad books. But there are plenty of good ones too, and the only way you can help young people become discerning players is to become literate yourself. Find some games—at least one, and preferably more—that you think are good, that you enjoy playing, and that make you think in interesting ways. When you can't read, it is hard to tell whether a book is bad or whether you just don't know enough to read it. The same is true for games.

→ Remember that what comes in a box is always a simulation. The game is what the players make of it. Play games with your children, starting when they are very young—just as you read with them well before they are able to understand the words of the book or perhaps even make sense of the pictures. Those experiences help children see reading as enjoyable, social, and important. It gives you a chance to shape their habits and attitudes toward reading early on. The same can be true for games. Use simulations in the classroom as an opportunity for students to do things that really matter in the world. These are the kinds of experiences that can help children learn to think in productive, creative, innovative ways with new technologies.

→ Think about the skills, knowledge, identities, values, and especially the epistemology of the games you play and the games your children play. What is worth doing in the world? What kinds of thinking will matter to young people's success, happiness, and ability to make the world a better place? These are the things worth learning—and thus the games worth playing.

Notes

Introduction

1. The report was prepared by the National Academies' Committee on Science Engineering and Public Policy (2006).

2. National Science Board (2005) shows that science and engineering degrees earned by U.S. citizens declined from 17,300 in 1998 to 16,100 in 2001.

3. Reports on the coming economic and educational crisis include Antráas et al. (2005), Blunden (2004), Burgess & Connell (2006), Hagel & Brown (2005), Hunter (2006), Kanter (2001), Kehal & Singh (2006), Markusen (2005), and the National Science Board (2005). These works discuss offshoring and outsourcing across a wide array of fields. Friedman (2005) is perhaps the best known and most popular treatment of the issue.

4. The quotation is in Overby (2003), which is available online.

5. The examples are from Friedman (2005); see pp. 239–241. Castells (2000), and Kelly (1998) write more generally about the impact of computer and information technologies on outsourcing.

6. Drucker (1993), Gee et al. (1996), Kelly (1998), and Rifkin (2000) discuss the importance of innovation and knowledge about innovation in a post-industrial economy.

7. For problems of retaining foreign students, see AAC&U News (2004).

8. China's growing industrial and innovative capacity is described in Judson (2005), as well as Friedman (2005).

9. "Good chemistry" (2006).

10. Friedman (2005).

11. The study, Bridgeland et al. (2006), also shows that nearly half of the dropouts found it hard to get a "good job" without a diploma, and three-quarters said they would finish school if they could relive the experience.

12. The argument that computers are a transformative technology is now well established. McLuhan (1962, 1964) is perhaps the most widely known techno-profit of the cultural and social changes that new media bring. Shaffer & Clinton (in press) and Shaffer & Kaput (1999) write about the specific ways in which computers change thinking. J. Murray (1999) looks at the future of storytelling; Kaput (1992) at mathematics; diSessa (2000) at science; Olson (1994) at literacy; Mitchell (2000) at social, economic and cultural organization; Clark (2001, 2003) at cognition; and Turkle (1995) at identity in an age of computers, hypermedia, and simulations. For a more skeptical view, see Postman (1993).

13. Dreyfus & Dreyfus (1986) provide a succinct overview of computer-aided instruction and other early approaches to computers in education.

14. Papert (1980).

15. Thoreau (1995) and McPhee (1971) are classic works on environmentalism and ecological thinking.

16. In *School and Society* (1915) Dewey wrote: "In critical moments we all realize that the only discipline that stands by us, the only training that becomes intuition, is that got through life itself."

17. For more on the sophistication of children's culture, see Johnson (2005). The importance of these early cultural and technological experiences for future learning are discussed in Gee (2003) and Shaffer et al. (2005).

18. The comparative complexity of television and movie plots and of video games is discussed in more detail in Johnson (2005). He points out that *Mary Poppins* has far fewer characters and storylines than *Finding Nemo*. Similarly, the amount of information required to explain *Pacman* is far less than the 53,000 words of one *Grand Theft Auto* guidebook.

19. Piaget (1937, 1948, 1966) wrote about the importance of play in several contexts. Vygotsky (1976, 1978) and his views on play and development are discussed in more detail in chapter 1. Bruner (1976) discusses the importance of play as an arena for cognitive and developmental exploration without consequences. For more on play and its developmental role see also Garvey (1990), Lillard (1993), Sutton-Smith (1979), and Sylva et al. (1976).

20. The data come from Crowley & Jacobs (2002), the seminal paper on building islands of expertise in everyday family activity. In the study, parents and children visiting the museum were videotaped talking about a set of replica fossils. The

excerpt of dialog is from page 345, and I have added a pseudonym for the boy to make the conversation easier to refer to later.

21. Witt & Baker (1997) argue that after-school programs are increasingly important in children's social and intellectual development because of the lack of adult role models for adolescents, particularly inner-city youth.

22. Cuban (1986, 2001) argues that the basic structure of schooling remains the same despite the influx of new technologies over time. This issue is discussed in more detail in chapter 1.

23. McLuhan (1964) made famous the phrase "the medium is the message," by which he meant that the content of a medium (the story in a novel or the plot in a movie) is less important than the structure of the medium itself.

24. Turkle (1995) describes the centrality of simulations in our interaction with computers in talking about digital culture as a *culture of simulation*.

25. The importance of this "offloading" of work—particularly cognitive work—onto the computer is discussed in detail in Shaffer & Kaput (1999) and Shaffer & Clinton (in press).

26. Although surely not the gold standard for academic achievement, *Time Magazine's* list of the one hundred most important people of the twentieth century includes only one psychologist, Piaget.

27. The key readings in Piaget's voluminous corpus of work are available in the ably edited Gruber & Voneche (1995). For a short and apt summary of Piaget's work—including a discussion of the concept of genetic epistemology—see Gardner (1982).

28. Dewey (1915, 1916, 1938) are some of the better-known of his many works on his philosophy of education. His work is discussed in more detail in chapter 4.

29. Rodgers (2002) and Schutz (2001) are examples of the many scholars who update, use, and otherwise apply Dewey in contemporary contexts.

30. The quotation is the title of Papert (2005).

31. Interested readers are welcome to visit the Web site http://epistemicgames.org, which has the latest information about the games described here and others being developed.

32. The studies are described in Autor et al. (2003) and Autor et al. (2006).

33. The study by Rao et al. (2001) shows a strong positive relationship between measures of innovation (notably, patents), productivity, and gross domestic product per capita. More innovative countries are wealthier and grow wealthier faster.

Chapter One

1. For more on the first televised debate, see Schlesinger et al. (2003).
2. Throughout the text I make reference to specific people playing games or to professionals in their training. Out of respect for their privacy, all of the names of players, students, and others described in the book have been changed. No demographic information (age, gender, ethnicity, socioeconomic status, and so forth) should be read into or from any of the pseudonyms.
3. Papert (1980) characterized "hard fun" in his original discussion of the LOGO programming language to explain why people are willing to take on difficult tasks in pursuit of ends they care about.
4. Suits (1967) offers a definition of games that does not focus primarily on pleasure, as does Gee (2003) more recently, although both emphasize the goal-directedness of games that for reasons I discuss in the text may not be central to the notion of a game. Vygotsky (1978) characterizes play in terms of rules and explicitly rejects the notion that play is centrally about enjoyment.
5. Johnson (2005) describes in detail the frustrations and difficulties of playing many modern games.
6. The taxonomy that Bartle (1990, 1996) developed is well-known within the multiplayer online game community, although it has been questioned and expanded upon by other researchers. See, for example, Steinkuehler (2005a).
7. Players in *World of Warcraft* do hold competitions, including ladder tournaments in which players are ranked over time against each other. For example, see www.battle.net/war3/tournaments/season3.shtml.
8. *Dungeons and Dragons* can be played as a competition, as can life itself. But for most players the game is about what one does rather than whether one wins.
9. See Vygotsky (1978), p. 94.
10. By this definition, of course, any system of social activity can be viewed as a game—a position consistent with Goffman (1963, 1967, 1974, 1981), who analyzed social interaction in terms of games, Wittgenstein (1963), who viewed all language as a game, and of course, M. Donald (2001), who describes careers as extended role-playing games. As described in the text, neither fun nor victory appears to be defining characteristics of games. Nor does safety. Games can have consequences: injuries in *Football*, losses in gambling games. Game scholars such as Juul (2003) argue for

a more specific definition of a "game," but for every additional criteria, there are exceptions. Some theorists—for example, Lindley (2005)—have attempted to construct typologies of games, but all include some form of roles and the rules that constrain action within those roles.

11. Although this example may seem morbid to adult ears, children often play games about things that worry—and thus fascinate—them. The Grimms' fairy tales are well-known examples of children's fictions about dark themes: Hansel and Gretel are repeatedly abandoned by their father to die, for example. *Orphans* was one of my daughters' favorite games for several weeks after seeing the movie *Annie* for the first time. For more on children's fantasy themes, see Bettelheim (1977).

12. The full example and discussion can be found in Vygotsky (1978).

13. According to the game's producers, Electronic Arts (www.ea.com), in early 2002 *The Sims* had sold 6.3 million copies worldwide. It was the best-selling PC game of both 2000 and 2001, and has been translated into at least thirteen different languages.

14. Vygotsky (1978), p. 94.

15. Bruner (1976) argued that play provides an occasion to examine alternatives, although his work focused on physical rather than social situations. For more on play and its developmental role, see also Garvey (1990), Lillard (1993), Sutton-Smith (1979), Sylva et al. (1976).

16. Dreyfus & Dreyfus (1986), p. 30.

17. Wallbank et al. (1977), p. 535–536.

18. Wineburg (1991), p. 75.

19. Quotations in the preceding paragraphs are from pp. 83–84 in Wineburg (1991). Emphasis is in the original.

20. Wineburg (1991), p. 84.

21. Wineburg (1991), p. 84.

22. Wineburg (2001) has written at length about the nature of historical thinking, and there is, of course, a much broader historiographical literature on the subject, from the classic Collingwood & Knox (1946) to more contemporary writing such as Morris-Suzuki (2005) or Doel & Sèoderqvist (2006).

23. Perkins (1992), p. 85. In analyzing his results, Wineburg (1991) similarly refers to Schwab's (1978) concept of *syntactic knowledge*, which Wineburg describes as "knowledge of how to establish warrant and determine validity of competing truth claims in a discipline" (p. 84).

24. Buehl & Alexander (2005) studied the domain specificity of epistemological beliefs from a psychological perspective: whether and how students have different understandings of the nature of justification and explanation in different disciplines. Donald (2002) has looked at the differences in the epistemological organization of fields of study at the collegiate level. In both cases, different disciplines and practices are characterized by different structures of argument and different criteria for verification of claims.

25. For a summary of Piaget's concept of cognitive stages, see Gardner (1982).

26. Wineburg (1991), p. 73.

27. The data in this section are from Tyack (1974), an authoritative overview of the development of the modern school system.

28. Tyack (1974), pp. 74, 40, and 29.

29. The concept of the grammar of schooling is discussed in Tyack & Cuban (1996) and Tyack & Tobin (1994).

30. For more on the way in which technology is used as a metaphor for social, natural, and psychological phenomena, see Tichi (1987).

31. Tyack (1974), p. 43.

32. Tyack (1974), pp. 55–56.

33. Tyack (1974), p. 54.

34. Fried (2005) describes school as a game and outlines the rules by which it is played. Not surprisingly, he concludes that much of what students learn is about "playing the game." While that may be an essential ability in itself, it comes at the expense of other skills, understanding, and habits of mind that will prepare them for success later in life. See also Tripp (1993).

35. The idea of a hidden curriculum originated in Jackson (1968).

36. Educational theorists Paul Zoch (2004) and Robert Fried (2005) both describe the passivity, epistemological uniformity, and rigidity of contemporary schooling.

37. J. S. Brown & Duguid (2002), p. 95.

38. Davenport (2005).

39. The statistics come from Davenport (2005). Although specific numbers in both categories depend on exactly what is counted as knowledge work and complex thinking skills, even conservative estimates show there is already a gap between the jobs available in the economy and skilled workers to fill them. Evidence that computer technologies are responsible for the high skill demands of the modern workforce can be found in Autor et al. (2003).

40. Readers interested in debate activities in history classes might consult Wineburg & Wilson (1991), which analyzes a master teacher's approach to debate, or MacArthur et al. (2002), which looks at debate in the context of students with learning differences.

41. Squire (2004a, forthcoming), has written extensively about the game *Civilization* and its use as a tool for learning historical thinking. Diamond (2005) describes a form of historical analysis based on resource allocation and structural differences between civilizations in different geographic areas rather than the more traditional focus on ideologies or prominent political actors that dominate accounts in many textbooks. In this sense, the game *Civilization* is a particularly rich context for thinking about one particular epistemology of historical inquiry.

Chapter Two

1. The game is described in more detail below and in Svarovsky & Shaffer (in press). Available online at www3.interscience.wiley.com/cgi-bin/abstract/112655434/ ABSTRACT.

2. See Svarovsky & Shaffer (2006).

3. The weekend version was tested twice, each time with six players recruited from middle schools in Madison, Wisconsin. The players volunteered for "an after school program on engineering and physics." They came from a variety of socioeconomic backgrounds. There were ten males and two females; five participants were students of color. The first group of players were seventh graders, the second group were sixth graders. For the summer game, thirteen students in the PEOPLE Program were assigned to the game for their summer enrichment experience. Svarovsky collected data on the students willing to participate in a study of the game. More information on the PEOPLE Program is available online at www.diversity.wisc.edu/people/mainpage/.

4. Crowley & Jacobs (2002) use the term *explanatoids* to describe the short fragments of explanatory talk between a parent and child. Svarovsky uses the term *exploratoids* to describe the short recurring interactions with *SodaConstructor* that collectively built expertise in a topic, and argues that they can play a similar role in developing an island of expertise.

5. There were some improvements, enhancements, and other changes made to the first level as it moved from being a stand alone ten-hour game to part of a longer game. Most of the essential structure remained the same, however.

6. Although it may seem odd to talk about the "cost" of creatures designed in a simulation, additional computer cycles are required to compute the motion and interaction of each additional element in a creature. More complex creatures take more time (and thus more money) to render in a finished move. Thus while there is no cost associated with building creatures in *SodaConstructor* (and additional design elements do not make the creatures move more slowly in these simple models), an important requirement from the client's point of view is that the creatures have as few structural elements as possible.

7. For more on cross-functional teams in the business context, see Parker (1994). For a discussion of how schooling can (and cannot) prepare students to participate in business practices such as these, see Gee (2004).

8. Prensky (2003), p. 9.

9. This body of work is discussed in Gardner (1991). McDermott (1998) provides a comprehensive overview of research on students' conceptions and misconceptions about physics.

10. Goodwin (1994).

11. Data here are from Dickinson & Neuman (2006) and Schleppegrell (2004). For more on the importance of academic language skills for school and career success, see Gee (2004).

12. See Hirsch et al. (1988).

13. The discussion that follows about cognitive evolution is made in more detail in Shaffer & Kaput (1999) and in Shaffer & Clinton (in press), both building on M. Donald (1991).

14. This is, of course, a lesson we sometimes need to learn again as adults, as when the Zen master reminds us to concentrate on the moon, not on the finger that points to it.

15. This is partly due to the fact that most people grow up relying on words rather than gestures as a primary means of communication, so there is a practice effect at work in such comparisons. Communication can be accomplished quite efficiently using sign languages, although the demands of life on the savannah in evolutionary times may have emphasized the advantages of words over gestures more than is the case today.

16. Bruner (1986, 1996) and Nelson (1996) discuss the significance of oral cultures in more detail, as does M. Donald (1991).

17. Kaput & Roschelle (1998), and Schmandt-Besserat (1978, 1992, 1994) as well as Olson (1994) discuss the origins and impact of writing in more depth.

18. Newton's laws of gravitation were based on empirical work by Kepler on planetary motion and by Galileo on the motion of objects on earth. His grand synthesis was to see both these local and celestial phenomena as the result of the same basic physical force.

19. For more on the link between medicine and writing, see Shaffer et al. (2002).

20. There is a large literature more generally about the tight link between technology and cognition—that is, how we think and the tools we think with—see Clark (2003), Engestrom (1999), Latour (1996, 2000), Norman (1993), Pea (1993), Wertsch (1998).

21. FAQs are lists of *frequently asked questions* and their answers collected by game players and users of other kinds of software. *Cheat codes* are information about how to unlock advanced features or levels in a game. While the name sounds derogatory, such codes are often an expected part of game play at advanced levels. See Johnson (2005) for a more detailed discussion of these issues.

22. The term is introduced in Shaffer & Kaput (1999) and described in more detail in Shaffer & Clinton (in press).

23. See Salomon (1993).

24. If we should learn to do everything by hand before we use technology to do it for us, then presumably we should learn the algorithm for extracting square roots too, so we really understand square roots. Of course, someone does need to understand the underlying algorithms in order to program the computers in the first place, but that doesn't mean everyone has to learn everything. After all, most of us learn to *use* a refrigerator, not *build* one. Computers similarly change the importance of many of the topics we now take for granted in the school curriculum.

25. Papert (1980).

26. The example is from Noss & Hoyles (1996).

27. This body of work includes studies of mathematics and science in symbolic microworlds such as *LOGO* by Harel & Papert (1991), *StarLogo* by Resnick (1994), and *Boxer* by diSessa (2000), or direct manipulation environments such as the *Geometer's Sketchpad* by Goldenberg & Cuoco (1998), Serra (1997), and Shaffer (2002); civics, economics and urban planning in simulations such as *SimCity* by Adams (1998); history in games such as the *Oregon Trail* by Smith-Gratto & Fisher (1999) and *Civilization* by Frye & Frager (1996), and Squire (2004a, forthcoming). The interactive properties of microworlds are described particularly in Hoyles et al. (2002), and Noss & Hoyles (1996).

28. Gee (2003).

29. Zoch (2004) describes the difficulties with learning "formal and abstract knowledge via an informal discovery approach in a structureless environment" (p. 593). See also Shaffer et al. (2005). The psychological term for this kind of generalization is the *Einstellung effect*, a condition in which the repetition of one pattern of problem solving biases a learners approach to future problems that share similar features but require different solution strategies; see J. R. Anderson (1980).

Chapter Three

1. More information on *Escher's World* can be found in Shaffer (1997a, 1997b, 2003a). The study of the studio on which Escher's World was based is available as Shaffer (2002, 2003b, forthcoming).

2. Nathan & Petrosino (2003) have provided ample documentation of the problems of abstraction in mathematics teaching and learning, and particularly the tendency of experts to teach using abstraction.

3. Gardner (1982).

4. Boaler (1993) gives an overview of word problems and the difficulties children have with them.

5. Albers (1971).

6. Desk crits are described in more detail in the context of the Oxford Studio in Shaffer (2002, 2003b, forthcoming), and more generally in Schon (1983, 1985).

7. There is a rich literature on design practices, including work on design education such as Anthony (1987), Briggs (1996), Chafee (1977), Frederickson & Anderton (1990), Haider (1990), Ledewitz (1985), Sheppard (1999), Uluoglu (2000), Wingler (1978).

8. For more on the mathematics of M. C. Escher's work, see Schattschneider (1990). The underlying mathematics of transformational geometry has been amply discussed by Loeb (1993), and the role of geometry in the mathematics curriculum is covered in Lindquist & Clements (2001) and Wu (1996).

9. The program is commercially available, and the publisher has a number of activity books that describe how to use the program as part of the mathematics curriculum.

10. The properties of *Geometer's Sketchpad* are described in more detail from a theoretical perspective by Goldenberg & Cuoco (1998). For its uses in more traditional classroom settings, see King & Schattschneider (1997).

11. One way to construct a square in *Sketchpad* is to make segment AB, then to construct lines perpendicular to AB through points A and B. A circle with center at A and radius of length AB gives point C at the intersection of the circle and the line. Constructing a line perpendicular to AC through point C gives point D, the final vertex of the square.

12. Students' scores on paper-and-pencil tests of transformational geometry knowledge rose significantly between pre- and post-interviews (mean pre — 58%, mean post = 72%; p < .01). These gains were stable in final interviews three months later (mean final = 72%). Scores on three control problems about algebra were not different among pre, post, or follow-up interviews (p > .50 for all three comparisons). See Shaffer (2005c).

13. Bandura (1997).

14. Silver et al. (1995).

15. The bicycle example and a more detailed discussion of procedural and declarative knowledge can be found in Dreyfus & Dreyfus (1986).

16. For more on the distinction between (and importance of) knowing how and knowing that—that is, declarative and procedural knowledge—see Broudy (1977).

17. To be fair, mathematics tests often require that a student compute or deduce an answer, and in this sense are testing procedural rather than declarative knowledge. However, in most cases the work is only assessed based on the answer produced; the process by which the answer was reached is never seen by the examiner, nor is it judged in scoring the test. This is why test-prep schools and guides emphasize raising test scores by learning tricks and techniques for solving test items rather than developing the general understanding that the tests are trying measure. The mathematics advanced placement tests (Calculus AB and BC) are notable exceptions in this regard, giving credit for process as well as product.

18. Dewey (1915), p. 33. Dewey says earlier in the same work (p. 26), that "it is our present education system which is highly specialized, one-sided, and narrow. It is an education dominated almost entirely by the mediaeval conception of learning. It is something which appeals for the most part simply to the intellectual aspect of our natures, our desire to learn, to accumulate information . . . not to our impulses and tendencies to make, to do, to create, to produce."

19. See Marshak (2003)

20. For a discussion of the developmental importance of personal mastery experiences, see B. J. Zimmerman & Cleary (2006). These results are supported in studies by

Silver et al. (1995), which show that prior experiences of mastery increase a person's sense of self-efficacy.

21. Friedman (2005).

22. See Dewey (1934/1958) and Gardner (1982). Sawyer (2006) provides a comprehensive overview of research on creativity.

23. Simpson (1988). The speech was covered in the New York Herald Tribune, June 2, 1964.

24. Lévi-Strauss (1982) came to this conclusion after studying the ceremonial masks of Northwest American Indians. See Gardner (1982) for a more detailed discussion of how all expressions—artistic, technological, or linguistic—are meaningful and creative only within a larger system of signifiers. That is, innovation is always new and different relative to some existing body of work.

25. Rabinow is quoted in Csikszentmihalyi (1996), pp. 49–50. Csikszentmihalyi's quote is from p. 51.

26. Gardner (1982) was talking specifically about artistic creativity, but he argued, following Goodman (1968, 1978) that the arts are symbolic systems, and follow the same general rules of use and development as more scientific representational forms. That is, art and science are different in their particulars but not in the ontological status or functional relationships of their symbol systems and developmental pathways. Csikszentmihalyi (1996) makes the same argument regarding the similarity of the process of innovation across symbolic domains.

27. Although master carpenters and surgeons both solve problems that are always different and thus require the exercise of professional discretion, the consequences of poor judgment are often higher for surgeons, which is part of the justification traditionally given for their higher salaries and status. Sociologists of the Professions such as Freidson (2001) argue that the status of Professionals is due to a combination of restricted access to the occupation (through the mechanisms of Professional training and certification) and their traditional service to elite interests. However, Stacey (1992) argues for the separation of *professionalism* (how professionals do their work) from *professionalization* (the financial and social position and mechanisms of the Professions). Here and throughout, I use the term *Professional* (capitalized) to refer to the formal Professions, and the term *professional* (lowercase) to refer to professional ways of thinking and acting, regardless of job title or social status. For more on this distinction, see Abbott & Wallace (1990).

28. For more on total quality management as the professionalization of work across the production process, see Berry (1991), Teare (1997).

29. Rose (2004), p. 1.

30. Schon (1985), p. 27.

31. My own research into this concept is described below in chapter 5, and in more detail in Shaffer (2004a, 2005a, 2005d), Shaffer et al. (2005). Ryan et al. (1996) provide an overview of research on professional practica, and Sullivan (2005) a discussion of the current state of the Professions and professional training.

32. The term was coined by Philips (1972). Shaffer (2005d) provides a description of participant structure in the more specific sense it is used here as a domain-specific form of interaction.

33. The zone of proximal development is described in detail in Vygotsky (1978). For a more contemporary treatment of the topic, see Bransford et al. (2000).

34. Bereiter & Scardamalia (1993) write about the importance of continual learning and extension of skills in professional thinking. See also Davenport (2005) on the risk taking of high-performing knowledge workers.

Chapter Four

1. The Pandora Project has been described at more length in Shaffer (2004a, 2004b, 2006).

2. A number of books are available on the science and particularly the ethical issues raised by xenotransplantation, including on the science side Cooper (1997), Molnar (2006), and Platt (2002) and from the ethical point of view McLean & Williamson (2005), Rollin (2006), Rothblatt (2004), and Suconik (2000).

3. Information on these epidemics is available on the World Health Organization Web site, www.who.int.

4. Details are available in Bosch (2001), Sykes et al. (2004), and World Health Organization (2005).

5. In the case of late stage organ failure, recent advances in biomedical technology suggest that xenotransplantation may not be the only way to "grow" organs for transplantation. According to recent news reports (e.g., www.cnn.com/2006/HEALTH/conditions/04/03/engineered.organs/index.html), researchers can now harvest

human bladder cells from a patient and grow new tissue for use in surgical repairs to the organ. Once again, the rate at which new ideas, tools, and techniques are developed is such that specific knowledge is less useful than understanding how to think about innovation and its consequences for real world problems.

6. The mutual gain approach is described in Fisher et al. (1997). For more on teaching mutual gains negotiation, see Susskind & Corburn (2000). There is also a literature of negotiation theory and practice as applied in the teaching and practice in various fields, including international relations in Torney-Purta (1998) and environmental policy in Susskind (1994), Susskind et al. (2000), Susskind et al. (1997).

7. A second study was conducted with students at an inner-city charter school. The results from both studies were similar. We did not collect demographic information on the players in either study. More information about the study can be found in Shaffer (2004a, 2004b, 2006).

8. The mean number of nodes on players' maps increased from 9.6 to 10.6; $p < .05$. The mean number of links increased from 12.8 to 18.5; $p < .01$. For more on these results, see Shaffer (2004b).

9. Each of these transfer problems came as part of a matched pair of problems with different stories that had the same basic format. We used matched pairs so that answers after the game wouldn't be influenced by the fact that players had seen the problem before. We also varied the order of problems and which version of each problem players saw before and after the game.

10. Dewey (1915), pp. 36, 37, and 58.

11. Dewey (1915), p. 38.

12. Dewey (1934/1958), p. 60.

13. Csikszentmihalyi (1996).

14. Dewey (1934/1958), p. 60.

15. For more on the lab school, see Menand (2001).

16. Cuisenaire rods are rectangular rods in ten lengths, with each length corresponding to a different color. Students traditionally use the rods to explore elementary school mathematical concepts: whole numbers, fractions, measurement, area, perimeter, symmetry, and patterns. See Davidson (2002).

17. For more on these activities, see Lichtfield et al. (1997), Evans et al. (2001), *The Political Machine* (2004), and *Grand Theft Auto: Vice City* (2004).

18. Dewey (1933), p. 150.

19. Dewey (1915), pp. 38ff.

20. Dewey (1915), p. 111.

21. Dewey (1916), p. 215.

22. Wineburg (1991), p. 84.

23. Dewey (1938), p 88. My claim that the scientific model of reasoning was the end-point for all educative experience in Dewey's work is a controversial one. It is consistent with how Jewett (2003), and Rorty (1982) read Dewey and opposed by others, such as Hickman (1990). For more on the perspective described here see Shaffer (2005b).

24. Kegan (1982), p. 191.

25. See Csikszentmihalyi & Larson (1984) and Csikszentmihalyi & Schneider (2000). The quotation is from Csikszentmihalyi et al. (1997), p. 219.

26. See, for example, Davenport (2005).

27. Kroger (2000), p. 31. Kroger provides an overview of these developmental issues. A recent edited volume by Pajares & Urdan (2006) discusses the importance of self-efficacy in adolescent development.

Chapter Five

1. Franklin (1986), Gardner et al. (2001), D. M. Murray (2000), and Stewart (1998) discuss the personal transformation that reporters undergo in becoming practicing journalists. Halberstam (1994) provides a particularly engaging account of his own personal growth and development as a journalist.

2. Rhodes & Davies (2003) discuss the importance of and role of capstone courses in journalism training. The term *osmosis* in this context comes from Halberstam (1994).

3. For more on the origins of journalism see Gardner et al. (2001) and Kovach & Rosenstiel (2001).

4. Murray (2000).

5. Edgerton (1997).

6. Giles (1969).

7. Murray (2000), pp. 25–26.

8. Gardner et al. (2001).

9. Gardner et al. (2001), p. 50.

10. Kovach & Rosenstiel (2001), p. 111.

11. Bunton et al. (1999), p. iv.

12. Franklin (1986), p. 71.

13. Franklin (1986), pp. 75, 181, and 181, respectively.

14. Some key works on information processing or schema theories of learning include J. R. Anderson (1980, 1993), Bruner (1973), Chi et al. (1981), Cobb (1987), and Pinker (1997).

15. The canonical work on communities of practice is Lave & Wenger (1991), from which the examples in the next paragraph are drawn. There are many other equally excellent studies and accounts, including Bourdieu (1977), Hutchins (1995), Lave (1988), Rogoff (1990), and Wenger (1998).

16. We chose Journalism 828 by interviewing former journalists who were teaching at the school, who said that the intermediate courses play a critical role in their program by developing the skills necessary for entry into successful journalism careers. We selected two intermediate-level courses for observation and also observed the introductory journalism course and work at one of the school's student newspapers. We conducted in-depth interviews with students in the courses being observed and also with reporters and editors at the student newspaper and at a local newspaper.

17. Sullivan (2005), pp. 207–210.

18. On the problem of transfer, see J. R. Anderson (1980) and Dreyfus & Dreyfus (1986). For a good overview of current theories of learning, including this issue, see Bransford et al. (2000).

19. Hutchins (1995).

20. *Byline* was developed by David Hatfield, and in described in more detail in Hatfield & Shaffer (2006).

21. Ten students in the PEOPLE Program were assigned to the game for their summer enrichment experience. Hatfield and Magnifico collected data on those students willing to participate in a study of the game. We did not collect more specific demographic information about the players in either of these studies.

22. From preinterview to postinterview, the mean number of players' references to science as a school subject went down from 2.21 to 1.14 and the mean number of references to science as a social force went up from 0.29 to 1.50 ($p < .05$ for both results). See Shaffer & Squire (2006).

23. Dewey (1938), p. 37.

24. Gee (2003).

25. Halverson (2005) provides a useful overview of the interactions among these dimensions of identity. For a more general overview of adolescent identity development, see Kroger (2000). There is, of course, a great deal of research, both developmental and sociocultural, on theories of identity, including Feldman & Elliott (1990), Sadowski (2003).

26. For more on possible selves see Markus & Nurius (1986). The quote is from p. 954.

27. See Goffman (1974, 1963). Game scholar Gary Fine (1983) used frame analysis to examine the relationships among real, virtual, and projective identities; see also Gee (2003). Fine's work focused on noncomputational role-playing games. My analysis extends this work by looking at games that re-create the frames of valued social practices see Shaffer (2004, 2005a, 2005d).

28. See Stryker & Burke (2000) for more on multiple identities.

29. The concept of a community of practice as a group with a local culture is described in Rohde & Shaffer (2004).

30. The concepts of culture and community are discussed far more broadly than there is space to explore here, of course. Some seminal ideas come from Collins & Ferguson (1993), Foucault (1972), Geertz (1973), Knorr-Cetina (1999), Kuhn (1963), Perkins (1992), Schon (1987).

31. The game is described in more detail from the perspective of professional identity development in Gee (2005) and Shaffer et al. (2005).

32. The quotation is from p. 2 of the game manual and can also be found in Shaffer et al. (2005), p. 107.

Chapter Six

1. The top 100 games were ranked by IGN in 2005. The rankings are available at http://top100.ign.com/2005/index.html.

2. Adams (1998) describes the benefits of using the game in geography class. Frye & Frager (1996) looked at elementary- and secondary-level social studies classes and found improvements in cognitive skills and in reading comprehension.

3. Latour (2000) and Lemke (2000) discuss the importance of timescales in ecological and social systems. They argue that different patterns of interaction and processes of

change occur over the span of minutes than do in evolutionary time, for example. Short time spans focus on local interactions. Long time spans focus on larger patterns of change. Each highlights different features of the system as being important. For example, in the long run a deteriorating school system leads to dramatic changes in the demographics of a city. But that tells you little about what specific decisions the school board should make in any given budget cycle.

4. For more on the advantages and disadvantages of *SimCity*, see Starr (1994) and also Beckett & Shaffer (in press).

5. The full description can be found in Beckett & Shaffer (in press).

6. For more on the concept of "augmented by reality," see Beckett & Shaffer (in press).

7. The study is reported in more detail in Beckett & Shaffer (in press).

8. Overall, there was a statistically significant difference ($p < .05$) in the links and nodes players added to their concept maps from pre- to post-interview. Links, which measure the complexity of the map, went from an average of 6.55 to 11.27. Nodes, which represent different factors that impact city planning, went from an average of 6.90 to 8.27.

9. See Ford GT vs. GT4 (2006).

10. Herold (2005), p. 7.

11. Gould & Lewontin (1979) describe how features of an organism can be preserved despite their lack of direct evolutionary advantage.

12. Brown & Campione (1996) discuss the Facilitating Communities of Learners curriculum, its adoption, and curricular coherence more generally. See also Shaffer (2005c).

13. Oldenburg (1989).

14. The idea of games as third places comes from the work of Steinkuehler (2005), although her focus is primarily on massively multiplayer online games and the way in which the simulated world of the game functions as a third place in the more traditional sense of a place that is neither home nor school. Boyd (2004) describes the web in general as a third space. Here I argue that games are powerful activities within the third places of childhood (which might include online spaces of the kind Steinkuehler and Boyd describe), and on how epistemic games in particular create a niche distinct from formal school and informal play.

15. See Steinkuehler (2005).

16. Squire (2004b, 2005a, 2005b), and Squire & Jenkins (2004) have discussed the differences between school culture and game cultures, and the topic is discussed in relationship to epistemic games in Shaffer et al. (2005).

17. For more on indie games, see Zimmerman (2002).

18. See the report of the Committee on Science Engineering and Public Policy (2006).

19. Bandura (2006) provides a useful overview of these developmental challenges.

20. The effect is described in Stake & Mares (2005).

21. Friedman (2005).

22. For an overview of these criticisms see Anderson (2004).

23. See Gee (2003) and Johnson (2005).

24. Papert (1980).

Bibliography

AAC&U News. (2004). Facts and figures: surveys show declining foreign enrollment at U.S. colleges and universities. Retrieved July 10, 2005, from www.aacuedu.org/aacu_news/AACUNews04/November04/facts_figures.cfm

Abbott, P., & Wallace, C. (1990). The sociology of the caring professions. New York: Falmer Press.

Adams, P. C. (1998). Teaching and learning with SimCity 2000. Journal of Geography, 97(2), 47–55.

Albers, J. (1971). Interaction of color. New Haven: Yale University Press.

Anderson, C. A. (2004). An update on the effects of playing violent video games. Journal of Adolescence, 27, 113–112.

Anderson, J. R. (1980). Cognitive psychology and its implications. San Francisco: Freeman.

Anderson, J. R. (1993). Rules of the mind. Hillsdale, NJ: Erlbaum.

Anthony, K. H. (1987). Private reactions to public criticism: Students, faculty, and practicing architects state their views on design juries in architectural education. Journal of Architectural Education, 40(3), 2–11.

Antráas, P., Garicano, L., Rossi-Hansberg, E., & National Bureau of Economic Research. (2005). Offshoring in a knowledge economy, from http://papers.nber.org/papers/W11094.

Autor, D. H., Katz, L. F., & Kearney, M. S. (2006). The polarization of the U.S. labor market. Retrieved April 1, 2006, from http://post.economics.harvard.edu/faculty/katz/papers/akk-polarization-nber-txt.pdf

Autor, D. H., Levy, F., & Murname, R. J. (2003). The skill content of recent technological change: An empirical exploration. Quarterly Journal of Economics, 118(4).

Bandura, A. (1997). Self-efficacy: The exercise of control. New York: W. H. Freeman.

Bandura, A. (2006). Adolescent development form an agentic perspective. In F. Pajares & T. Urdan (Eds.), Self-efficacy beliefs of adolescents. Greenwich, CT: Information Age Publishing.

Bartle, R. A. (1990). Who Plays MUAs? Comms Plus! 18–19.

Bartle, R. A. (1996). Hearts, clubs, diamonds, spades: Players who suit MUDs. Journal of MUD Research, 1(1).

Beckett, K. L., & Shaffer, D. W. (in press). Augmented by reality: The pedagogical praxis of urban planning as a pathway to ecological thinking. Journal of Educational Computing Research.

Bereiter, C., & Scardamalia, M. (1993). Surpassing ourselves: An inquiry into the nature and implications of expertise. Chicago: Open Court.

Berry, T. H. (1991). Managing the total quality transformation. New York: McGraw-Hill.

Bettelheim, B. (1977). The uses of enchantment: The meaning and importance of fairy tales. New York: Vintage Books.

Blunden, B. (2004). Offshoring IT: The good, the bad, and the ugly. Berkeley, CA: Apress.

Boaler, J. (1993). The role of contexts in the mathematics classroom: Do they make mathematics more "real"? For the Learning of Mathematics, 13(2), 12–17.

Bosch, X. (2001, October 4). Vatican approves use of animal transplants to benefit humans. Nature, 413, 445.

Bourdieu, P. (1977). Outline of a theory of practice. New York: Cambridge University Press.

Boyd, S. (2004). Being wired encourages human contact: The Third Space, from www.corante.com/getreal/archives/004843.html.

Bransford, J., Brown, A., & Cocking, R. R. (Eds.). (2000). How people learn: Brain, mind, experience, and school. Washington, DC: National Academy Press.

Bridgeland, J. M., DiIulio, J. J., Jr., & Morison, K. B. (2006). The silent epidemic: Perspectives of high school dropouts. Washington, DC: Civic Enterprises.

Briggs, D. C. (1996). Reform the design studio. Architecture, 85(8), 75–76.

Broudy, H. (1977). Types of knowledge and purposes of education. In R. C. Anderson, R. J. Spiro & W. E. Montague (Eds.), Schooling and the acquisition of knowledge (pp. 1–17). Hillsdale, NJ: Lawrence Erlbaum.

Brown, A. L., & Campione, J. C. (1996). Psychological theory and the design of innovative learning environments: On procedures, principles and systems. In L. Schauble & R. Glaser (Eds.), Innovations in learning: New environments for education (pp. 289–325). Mahwah, NJ: Erlbaum Associates.

Brown, J. S., & Duguid, P. (2002). The social life of information. Boston: Harvard Business School Press.

Bruner, J. S. (1973). Beyond the information given: Studies in the psychology of knowing. New York: Norton.

Bruner, J. S. (1976). Nature and Uses of Immaturity. In J. S. Bruner, A. Jolly, & K. Sylva (Eds.), Play, its role in development and evolution. New York: Basic Books.

Bruner, J. S. (1986). Actual minds, possible worlds. Cambridge, MA: Harvard University Press.

Bruner, J. S. (1996). The culture of education. Cambridge, MA: Harvard University Press.

Buehl, M. M., & Alexander, P. A. (2005). Motivation and performance differences in students' domain-specific epistemological belief profiles. American Educational Research Journal, 42(4), 697–726.

Bunton, K., Connery, T. B., Kanihan, S. F., Neuzil, M., & Nimmer, D. (1999). Writing across the media. Boston: Bedford/St. Martin's.

Burgess, J., & Connell, J. (2006). Developments in the call centre industry: Analysis, changes, and challenges. New York: Routledge.

Castells, M. (2000). The rise of the network society (2nd ed.). Malden, MA: Blackwell Publishers.

Chafee, R. (1977). The teaching of architecture at the École des Beaux-Arts. In A. Drexler (Ed.), The architecture of the École Des Beaux-Arts. New York: Museum of Modern Art.

Chi, M. T. H., Feltovich, P., & Glaser, R. (1981). Categorization and representation of physics problems by experts and novices. Cognitive Science, 5(2), 121–152.

Clark, A. (2001). Mindware: An introduction to the philosophy of cognitive science. New York: Oxford University Press.

Clark, A. (2003). Natural-born cyborgs: Minds, technologies, and the future of human intelligence. Oxford: Oxford University Press.

Cobb, P. (1987). Information-processing psychology and mathematics education—A constructivist perspective. Journal of Mathematical Behavior, 6(1), 3–40.

Collingwood, R. G., & Knox, T. M. (1946). The idea of history. Oxford: Clarendon Press.

Collins, A., & Ferguson, W. (1993). Epistemic forms and games. Educational Psychologist, 28(1), 25–42.

Committee on Science Engineering and Public Policy. (2006). Rising above the gathering storm: Energizing and employing America for a brighter economic future. Washington, DC: National Academies Press.

Conrad, D., & Hedin, D. (1982). Youth participation & experiential education. New York: Haworth Press.

Cooper, D. K. C. (1997). Xenotransplantation: The transplantation of organs and tissues between species (2nd ed.). New York: Springer.

Crowley, K., & Jacobs, M. (2002). Building islands of expertise in everyday family activity. In G. Leinhardt, K. Crowley, & K. Knutson (Eds.), Learning conversations in museums. Mahwah, NJ: Lawrence Erlbaum.

Csikszentmihalyi, M. (1996). Creativity: Flow and the psychology of discovery and invention. New York: HarperCollins.

Csikszentmihalyi, M., & Larson, R. (1984). Being adolescent: Conflict and growth in the teenage years. New York: Basic Books.

Csikszentmihalyi, M., Rathunde, K. R., & Whalen, S. (1997). Talented teenagers: The roots of success and failure. New York: Cambridge University Press.

Csikszentmihalyi, M., & Schneider, B. L. (2000). Becoming adult: How teenagers prepare for the world of work. New York: Basic Books.

Cuban, L. (1986). Teachers and machines: The classroom use of technology since 1920. New York: Teachers College Press.

Cuban, L. (2001). Oversold and underused: Computers in the classroom. Cambridge, MA: Harvard University Press.

Davenport, T. H. (2005). Thinking for a living: How to get better performance and results from knowledge workers. Boston: Harvard Business School Press.

Davidson, P. S. (2002). Idea book: Mathematics activities for Cuisenaire rods at the primary level ([Rev.]. ed.). Vernon Hills, Ill.: ETA/Cuisenaire.

Dewey, J. (1915). School and society. Chicago: University of Chicago Press.

Dewey, J. (1916). Democracy and education: An introduction to the philosophy of education. New York: Macmillan.

Dewey, J. (1933). How we think, a restatement of the relation of reflective thinking to the educative process. Boston: D. C. Heath.

Dewey, J. (1934/1958). Art as experience. New York: Capricorn Books.

Dewey, J. (1938). Experience and education. New York: Collier Books.

Diamond, J. M. (2005). Guns, germs, and steel: The fates of human societies. New York: Norton.

Dickinson, D. K., & Neuman, S. B. (2006). Handbook of early literacy research. New York: Guilford.

diSessa, A. A. (2000). Changing minds: Computers, learning, and literacy. Cambridge, MA: MIT Press.

Doel, R. E., & Sèoderqvist, T. (2006). The historiography of science, technology and medicine: Writing recent history. New York: Routledge.

Donald, J. G. (2002). Learning to think: Disciplinary perspectives. San Francisco: Jossey-Bass.

Donald, M. (1991). Origins of the modern mind: Three stages in the evolution of culture and cognition. Cambridge, MA: Harvard University Press.

Donald, M. (2001). A mind so rare: The evolution of human consciousness. New York: W.W. Norton.

Dreyfus, H. L., & Dreyfus, S. E. (1986). Mind over machine: The power of human intuition and expertise in the era of the computer. New York: Free Press.

Drucker, P. F. (1993). Post-capitalist society. New York: HarperBusiness.

Edgerton, L. (1997). The editing book. Dubuque, IA: Kendall/Hunt.

Engestrom, Y. (1999). Activity theory and individual and social transformation. In Y. Engestrom, R. Miettinen, & R.-L. Punamaki (Eds.), Perspectives on activity theory (pp. 19–38). Cambridge: Cambridge University Press.

Evans, C. A., Abrams, E. D., & Rock, B. N. (2001). Student/scientist partnerships: A teachers' guide to evaluating the critical components. American Biology Teacher, 63(5), 318–323.

Feldman, S. S., & Elliott, G. R. (1990). At the threshold: The developing adolescent. Cambridge, MA: Harvard University Press.

Fine, G. A. (1983). Shared fantasy: Role-playing games as social worlds. Chicago: University of Chicago Press.

Fisher, R., Ury, W., & Patton, B. (1997). Getting to yes: Negotiating an agreement without giving in (2nd ed.). London: Arrow Business Books.

Ford GT vs. GT4. (2006). Retrieved April 1, 2006, from www.edmunds.com/inside-line/do/Features/articleId5107485?mktcat5insideline&kw5HTML&mktid5NL990 467&DARTmail.

Foucault, M. (1972). The archeology of knowledge (A. M. Sheridan Smith, trans.). New York: Harper Colophon.

Franklin, J. (1986). Writing for story: Craft secrets of dramatic nonfiction by a two-time Pulitzer Prize winner. New York: Atheneum.

Frederickson, M. P., & Anderton, F. (1990). Design juries: A study on lines of communication. Journal of Architectural Education, 43(2), 22–8.

Freidson, E. (2001). Professionalism: The third logic. Chicago: University of Chicago Press.

Fried, R. L. (2005). The game of school: Why we all play it, how it hurts kids, and what it will take to change it. San Francisco: Jossey-Bass.

Friedman, T. (2005). The world is flat: A brief history of the twenty-first century. New York: Farrar, Straus and Giroux.

Frye, B., & Frager, A. M. (1996). Civilization, colonization, SimCity: Simulations for the social studies classroom. Learning and Leading with Technology, 24(2), 21–23, 32.

Gardner, H. (1982). Art, mind, and brain: A cognitive approach to creativity. New York: Basic Books.

Gardner, H. (1991). The unschooled mind. New York: Basic Books.

Gardner, H., Csikszentmihalyi, M., & Damon, W. (2001). Good work: When excellence and ethics meet. New York: Basic Books.

Garvey, C. (1990). Play. Cambridge, MA: Harvard University Press.

Gee, J. P. (2003). What video games have to teach us about learning and literacy. New York: Palgrave Macmillan.

Gee, J. P. (2004). Situated language and learning: A critique of traditional schooling. London: Routledge.

Gee, J. P. (2005). What will a state of the art video game look like? Innovate, 1(6), www.innovateonline.info.

Gee, J. P., Hull, G. A., & Lankshear, C. (1996). The new work order: Behind the language of the new capitalism. St. Leonards, NSW: Allen & Unwin.

Geertz, C. (1973). The growth of culture and the evolution of mind. In The interpretation of cultures: Selected essays (pp. 3–30). New York: Basic Books.

Giles, C. H. (1969). The student journalist and feature writing. New York: Richard Rosen Press.

Goffman, E. (1963). Behavior in public places: Notes on the social organization of gatherings. New York: Free Press of Glencoe.

Goffman, E. (1967). Interaction ritual: Essays on face-to-face behaviour. Garden City, NY: Anchor Books.

Goffman, E. (1974). Frame analysis: An essay on the organization of experience. New York: Harper & Row.

Goffman, E. (1981). Forms of talk. Philadelphia: University of Philadelphia Press.

Goldenberg, E. P., & Cuoco, A. A. (1998). What is dynamic geometry? In R. Lehrer & D. Chazan (Eds.), Designing learning environments for developing understanding of geometry and space (pp. 351–368). Mahwah, NJ: Lawrence Erlbaum.

Good chemistry. (2006, February 4). The Economist, 58.

Goodman, N. (1968). Languages of art: An approach to a theory of symbols. Indianapolis: Bobbs-Merrill.

Goodman, N. (1978). Ways of worldmaking. Indianapolis: Hackett.

Goodwin, C. (1994). Professional vision. American Anthropologist, 96(3), 606–633.

Gould, S. J., & Lewontin, R. (1979). The spandrels of San Marco and the Panglossion paradigm: A critique of the adaptationist programme. Proceedings of the Royal Society of London, 205(1161), 581–598.

Grand Theft Auto: Vice City. (2004). Rockstar Games.

Gruber, H. E., & Voneche, J. (Eds.). (1995). The essential Piaget. New York: Basic Books.

Hagel, J., & Brown, J. S. (2005). The only sustainable edge: Why business strategy depends on productive friction and dynamic specialization. Boston: Harvard Business School Press.

Haider, J. (1990). Design education: An interdisciplinary perspective. Design for Arts in Education, 92(2), 41–49.

Halberstam, D. (1994). The education of a journalist. Columbia Journalism Review, 33(4), 29–34.

Halverson, E. R. (2005). InsideOut: Facilitating gay youth identity development through a performance-based youth organization. Identity: An International Journal of Theory and Research, 5(1), 67–90.

Harel, I., & Papert, S. (Eds.). (1991). Constructionism. Norwood, NJ: Ablex.

Hatfield, D. L., & Shaffer, D. W. (2006). Press play: Designing an epistemic game engine for journalism. In S. Barab, K. Hay, & D. Hickey (Eds.), Proceedings of the Seventh International Conference of the LearningSciences. Mahwah, NJ: Lawrence Erlbaum.

Herold, C. (2005, December 7). Puppies to pet, monsters to battle, movies to make. New York Times.

Hickman, L. (1990). John Dewey's pragmatic technology. Bloomington: Indiana University Press.

Hirsch, E. D., Kett, J. F., & Trefil, J. S. (1988). Cultural literacy: What every American needs to know. New York: Vintage Books.

Horwood, B. (1995). Experience and the curriculum. Boulder, CO: Association for Experiential Education; Kendall Hunt.

Hoyles, C., Noss, R., & Adamson, R. (2002). Rethinking the microworld idea. Journal of Educational Computing Research, 27(1&2), 29–53.

Hunter, I. (2006). The Indian offshore advantage: How offshoring is changing the face of HR. Burlington, VT: Ashgate Publishing.

Hutchins, E. (1995). Cognition in the wild. Cambridge, MA: MIT Press.

Jackson, P. W. (1968). Life in classrooms. New York: Holt.

Jewett, A. (2003). Science and the promise of democracy in America. Daedalus, 132(4), 64–70.

Johnson, S. (2005). Everything bad is good for you: How today's popular culture is actually making us smarter. New York: Riverhead Books.

Judson, H. F. (2005/2006 December–January). The great Chinese experiment. Technology Review.

Juul, J. (2003). The game, the player, the world: Looking for a heart of gameness. In M. Copier & J. Raessens (Eds.), Level up: Digital games research conference proceedings (pp. 30–45). Utrecht: Utrecht University.

Kanter, R. M. (2001). Evolve! Succeeding in the digital culture of tomorrow. Cambridge, MA: Harvard Business School Press.

Kaput, J. J. (1992). Technology and mathematics education. In D. A. Grouws (Ed.), Handbook of research on mathematics teaching and learning (pp. 515–556). New York: Maxwell Macmillan International.

Kaput, J. J., & Roschelle, J. (1998). The mathematics of change and variation from a millennial perspective: New content, new context. In C. Hoyles & R. Noss (Eds.), Mathematics for a new millenium. London: Springer Verlag.

Kegan, R. (1982). The evolving self: Problem and process in human development. Cambridge, MA: Harvard University Press.

Kehal, H. S., & Singh, V. P. (2006). Outsourcing and offshoring in the 21st century: A socio-economic perspective. Hershey, PA: Idea Group Publishing.

Kelly, K. (1998). New rules for the new economy: 10 radical strategies for a connected world. New York: Viking.

King, J. R., & Schattschneider, D. (Eds.). (1997). Geometry turned on! Dynamic software in learning, teaching, and research. Washington, DC: Mathematical Association of America.

Knorr-Cetina, K. (1999). Epistemic cultures: How the sciences make knowledge. Cambridge, MA: Harvard University Press.

Kovach, B., & Rosenstiel, T. (2001). The elements of journalism: What newspeople should know and the public should expect. New York: Crown.

Kroger, J. (2000). Identity development: Adolescence through adulthood. Thousand Oaks, CA: Sage Publications.

Kuhn, T. S. (1963). The structure of scientific revolutions. Chicago: University of Chicago Press.

Latour, B. (1996). Pursuing the discussion of interobjectivity with a few friends. Mind, Culture, and Activity, 3(4), 266–269.

Latour, B. (2000). When things strike back: A possible contribution of "science studies" to the social sciences. British Journal of Sociology, 51(1), 107–123.

Lave, J. (1988). Cognition in practice: Mind, mathematics, and culture in everyday life. Cambridge: Cambridge University Press.

Lave, J., & Wenger, E. (1991). Situated learning: Legitimate peripheral participation. Cambridge: Cambridge University Press.

Ledewitz, S. (1985). Models of design in studio teaching. Journal of Architectural Education, 38(2), 2–8.

Lemke, J. L. (2000). Across the scales of time: Artifacts, activities, and meanings in ecosocial systems. Mind, Culture, and Activity, 7(4), 273–290.

Lévi-Strauss, C. (1982). The way of the masks. Seattle: University of Washington Press.

Lichtfield, D., Goldenheim, D., & Dietrich, C. H. (1997). Euclid, Fibonacci, and Sketchpad. Mathematics Teacher, 90(1), 8–12.

Lillard, A. S. (1993). Pretend play skills and the child's theory of mind. Child Development, 64, 348–371.

Lindley, C. A. (2005). The semiotics of time structure in ludic space as a foundation for analysis and design. Game Studies, 5(1).

Lindquist, M. M., & Clements, D. H. (2001). Geometry must be vital. Teaching Children Mathematics, 7(7), 409–415.

Loeb, A. (1993). Concepts and images: Visual mathematics. Boston: Birkhauser.

MacArthur, C., Ferretti, R., & Okolo, C. (2002). On defending controversial viewpoints: Debates of sixth graders about the desirability of early 20th-century American immigration. Learning Disabilities Research & Practice, 17(3), 160–172.

Markus, H., & Nurius, P. (1986). Possible selves. American Psychologist, 41(9), 954–969.

Markusen, J. R. (2005). Modeling the offshoring of white-collar services from comparative advantage to the new theories of trade and FDI, from http://papers.nber.org/papers/w11827.

Marshak, D. (2003). No Child Left Behind: A foolish race to the past. Phi Delta Kappan, 85(3), 229–231.

McDermott, L. C. (1998). Students' conceptions and problem solving in mechanics. In A. Tiberghien, E. L. Jossem & J. Barojas (Eds.), Connecting research in physics education with teacher education. Available from the International Commission on Physics Education at www.physics.ohio-state.edu/~jossem/ICPE/TOC.html.

McLean, S., & Williamson, L. (2005). Xenotransplantation: Law and ethics. Burlington, VT: Ashgate.

McLuhan, M. (1962). The Gutenberg galaxy: The making of typographic man. Toronto: University of Toronto Press.

McLuhan, M. (1964). Understanding media: The extensions of man. New York: Mentor Books.

McPhee, J. A. (1971). Encounters with the archdruid. New York: Farrar.

Menand, L. (2001). The metaphysical club. New York: Farrar Straus & Giroux.

Mitchell, W. J. (2000). e-topia: "Urban life, Jim—but not as we know it." Cambridge, MA: MIT Press.

Molnar, E. M. (2006). Stem cell transplantation: A textbook of stem cell xenotransplantation. Sunshine, MD: Medical and Engineering Publishers.

Morris-Suzuki, T. (2005). The past within us: Media, memory, history. New York: Verso.

Murray, D. M. (2000). Writing to deadline: The journalist at work. Portsmouth, NH: Heinemann.

Murray, J. (1999). Hamlet on the holodeck: The future of narrative in cyberspace. Cambridge, MA: MIT Press.

Nathan, M. J., & Petrosino, A. J. (2003). Expert blind spot among preservice teachers. American Educational Research Journal, 40(4), 905–928.

National Science Board. (2005). Science and engineering indicators 2004. Washington, DC: NSF Publications.

Nelson, K. (1996). Language in cognitive development: Emergence of the mediated mind. Cambridge: Cambridge University Press.

Norman, D. A. (1993). Things that make us smart: Defending human attributes in the age of the machine. Reading, MA: Addison-Wesley.

Noss, R., & Hoyles, C. (1996). Windows on mathematical meanings: Learning cultures and computers. Dordrecht, The Netherlands: Kluwer Academic Publishers.

Oldenburg, R. (1989). The great good place: Cafés, coffee shops, community centers, beauty parlors, general stores, bars, hangouts, and how they get you through the day. New York: Paragon House.

Olson, D. R. (1994). The world on paper. Cambridge: Cambridge University Press.

Overby, S. (2003, December 15). The future of jobs and innovation. CIO Magazine, from www.cio.com/archive/121503/jobfuture.html.

Pajares, F., & Urdan, T. (Eds.). (2006). Self-efficacy beliefs of adolescents. Greenwich, CT: Information Age Publishing.

Papert, S. (1980). Mindstorms: Children, computers, and powerful ideas. New York: Basic Books.

Papert, S. (2005). You can't think about thinking without thinking about thinking about something. Contemporary Issues in Technology and Teacher Education, 5(3/4), 366–367.

Parker, G. M. (1994). Cross-functional teams: Working with allies, enemies, and other strangers. San Francisco: Jossey-Bass.

Pea, R. (1993). Practices of distributed intelligence and designs for education. In G. Salomon (Ed.), Distributed cognitions: Psychological and educational considerations. Cambridge: Cambridge University Press.

Perkins, D. (1992). Smart schools. New York: Free Press.

Philips, S. U. (1972). Participant structures and communicative competence: Warm Springs children in community and classroom. In C. B. Cazden, V. John-Steiner, & D. H. Hymes (Eds.), Functions of language in the classroom (pp. 370–394). New York: Teachers College Press.

Piaget, J. (1937). The construction of reality in the child. In H. E. Gruber & J. Voneche (Eds.), The essential Piaget. New York: Basic Books.

Piaget, J. (1948). The child's conception of space. In H. E. Gruber & J. Voneche (Eds.), The essential Piaget. New York: Basic Books.

Piaget, J. (1966). The semiotic or symbolic function. In H. E. Gruber & J. Voneche (Eds.), The essential Piaget. New York: Basic Books.

Pinker, S. (1997). How the mind works. New York: W. W. Norton.

Platt, J. L. (2002). Xenotransplantation: Basic research and clinical applications. Totowa, NJ: Humana Press.

Political Machine, The. (2004). Ubi Soft.

Postman, N. (1993). Technopoly: The surrender of culture to technology. New York: Vintage Books.

Prensky, M. (2003). Escape from planet Jar-gon: Or, what video games have to teach academics about teaching and writing. On the Horizon, 11(3).

Rao, S., Ahmad, A., Horsman, W., & Kaptein-Russell, P. (2001). The importance of innovation for productivity. International Productivity Monitor, 2, 11–18.

Resnick, M. (1994). Turtles, termites, and traffic jams: Explorations in massively parallel microworlds. Cambridge, MA: MIT Press.

Rhodes, S., & Davies, D. (2003). Advanced reporting. In M. D. Murray & R. L. Moore (Eds.), Mass communication education. Ames: Iowa State Press.

Rifkin, J. (2000). The age of access: The new culture of hypercapitalism, where all of life is a paid-for experience. New York: J.P. Tarcher/Putnam.

Rodgers, C. (2002). Defining reflection: Another look at John Dewey and reflective thinking. Teachers College Record, 104(4), 842–866.

Rogoff, B. (1990). Apprenticeship in thinking: Cognitive development in social context. New York: Oxford University Press.

Rohde, M., & Shaffer, D. W. (2004). Us, ourselves, and we: Thoughts about social (self-) categorization. Association for Computing Machinery SigGROUP Bulletin, 24(3), 19–24.

Rollin, B. E. (2006). Science and ethics. New York: Cambridge University Press.

Rorty, R. (1982). Consequences of pragmatism. Minneapolis: University of Minnesota Press.

Rose, M. (2004). The mind at work: Valuing the intelligence of the American worker. New York: Viking.

Rothblatt, M. A. (2004). Your life or mine: How geoethics can resolve the conflict between public and private interests in xenotransplantation. Burlington, VT: Ashgate.

Ryan, G., Toohey, S., & Hughes, C. (1996). The purpose, value and structure of the practicum in higher education: A literature review. Higher Education, 31(3), 355–377.

Sadowski, M. (2003). Adolescents at school: Perspectives on youth, identity, and education. Cambridge, MA: Harvard Education Press.

Salomon, G. (1993). No distribution without individuals' cognition: A dynamic interactional view. In G. Salomon (Ed.), Distributed cognitions: Psychological and educational considerations. Cambridge: Cambridge University Press.

Sawyer, R. K. (2006). Explaining creativity: The science of human innovation. New York: Oxford University Press.

Schattschneider, D. (1990). Visions of symmetry: Notebooks, periodic drawings, and related work of M. C. Escher. New York: W. H. Freeman.

Schleppegrell, M. J. (2004). The language of schooling: A functional linguistics perspective. Mahwah, N.J.: Lawrence Erlbaum.

Schlesinger, A. M., Israel, F. L., & Frent, D. J. (2003). The election of 1960 and the administration of John F. Kennedy. Philadelphia: Mason Crest Publishers.

Schmandt-Besserat, D. (1978). The earliest precursor of writing. Scientific American, 238(6), 50–58.

Schmandt-Besserat, D. (1992). Before writing. Austin: University of Texas Press.

Schmandt-Besserat, D. (1994). Before numerals. Visible Language, 18(2), 48–60.

Schön, D. A. (1983). The reflective practitioner: How professionals think in action. New York: Basic Books.

Schön, D. A. (1985). The design studio: An exploration of its traditions and potentials. London: RIBA Publications.

Schön, D. A. (1987). Educating the reflective practitioner: Toward a new design for teaching and learning in the professions. San Francisco: Jossey-Bass.

Schutz, A. (2001). John Dewey's conundrum: Can democratic schools empower? Teachers College Record, 103(2), 267–302.

Schwab, J. J. (1978). Education and the structure of the disciplines. In I. Westbury & N. J. Wilkof (Eds.), Science, curriculum, and liberal education (pp. 229–272). Chicago: University of Chicago Press.

Serra, M. (1997). Discovering geometry: An inductive approach (2nd ed.). Berkeley, CA: Key Curriculum Press.

Shaffer, D. W. (1997a). Escher's world: Learning symmetry through mathematics and art. Symmetry: Culture and Science, 8(3–4), 369–393.

Shaffer, D. W. (1997b). Learning mathematics through design: The anatomy of Escher's World. Journal of Mathematical Behavior, 16(2), 95–112.

Shaffer, D. W. (2002). Design, collaboration, and computation: The design studio as a model for computer-supported collaboration in mathematics. In T. Koschmann, R. Hall & N. Miyake (Eds.), Computer support for collaborative learning 2 (pp. 197–222). Mahwah, NJ: Lawrence Erlbaum.

Shaffer, D. W. (2003a). Pedagogical praxis: The professions as models for learning in the age of the smart machine (WCER Working Paper No. 2003-6). Madison: University of Wisconsin-Madison, Wisconsin Center for Education Research.

Shaffer, D. W. (2003b). Portrait of the Oxford Design Studio: An ethnography of design pedagogy (WCER Working Paper No. 2003-11). Madison: University of Wisconsin-Madison, Wisconsin Center for Education Research.

Shaffer, D. W. (2004a). Pedagogical praxis: The professions as models for post-industrial education. Teachers College Record, 106(7), 1401–1421.

Shaffer, D. W. (2004b). When computer-supported collaboration means computer-supported competition: Professional mediation as a model for collaborative learning. Journal of Interactive Learning Research, 15(2), 101–115.

Shaffer, D. W. (2005a). Epistemic Games. Innovate, 1(6), www.innovateonline.info.

Shaffer, D. W. (2005b). Multisubculturalism: Computers and the end of progressive education (WCER Working Paper). Madison: University of Wisconsin-Madison, Wisconsin Center for Education Research.

Shaffer, D. W. (2005c). Studio mathematics: The epistemology and practice of design pedagogy as a model for mathematics learning (WCER Working Paper Series No. 2005–3). Madison: University of Wisconsin-Madison, Wisconsin Center for Educational Research.

Shaffer, D. W. (2005d). Epistemography and the participant structures of a professional practicum: A story behind the story of Journalism 828 (WCER Working Paper Series

No. 2005–8). University of Wisconsin-Madison, Wisconsin Center for Educational Research.

Shaffer, D. W. (2006). Epistemic frames for epistemic games. Computers and Education, 46(3), 223–234.

Shaffer, D. W. (forthcoming). Learning in design. In R. Lesh, J. Kaput & E. Hamilton (Eds.), Foundations for the future: The need for new mathematical understandings & abilities in the 21st century. Hillsdale, NJ: Lawrence Erlbaum.

Shaffer, D. W., & Clinton, K. A. (in press). Toolforthoughts: Reexamining thinking in the digital age. Mind, Culture, and Activity.

Shaffer, D. W., & Kaput, J. J. (1999). Mathematics and virtual culture: An evolutionary perspective on technology and mathematics. Educational Studies in Mathematics, 37, 97–119.

Shaffer, D. W., Kigin, C., Kaput, J., & Gazelle, G. (2002). What is Digital Medicine? In R. Bushko (Ed.), Future of Health Technology. Amsterdam: IOS Press.

Shaffer, D. W., Squire, K., Halverson, R., & Gee, J. P. (2005). Video games and the future of learning. Phi Delta Kappan, 87(2), 104–111.

Shaffer, D. W., & Squire, K. D. (2006). The Pasteurization of Education. In S. Tettegah and R. Hunter (Eds.), Education and technology: Issues in policy, administration and application. London: Elsevier.

Sheppard, S. D. (1999, November). Design as cornerstone and capstone. Mechanical Engineering Design, 44–47.

Silver, W. S., Mitchell, T. R., & Gist, M. E. (1995). Responses to successful and unsuccessful performance: The moderating effect of self-efficacy on the relationship between performance and attributions. Organizational Behavior and Human Decision Processes, 62(3), 286–299.

Simpson, J. B. (1988). Simpson's contemporary quotations. Boston: Houghton Mifflin.

Smith-Gratto, K., & Fisher, M. M. (1999). An aid to curriculum and computer integration: Prototypes for teachers. Computers in the Schools, 15(2), 61–71.

Squire, K. D. (2004a). Sid Meier's Civilization III. Simulations and Gaming, 35(1).

Squire, K. D. (2004b). Video games and next-generation learners. Paper presented at the Education and Information Systems Conference, Orlando, FL.

Squire, K. D. (2005a). Game-based learning: Present and future of state of the field. Retrieved May 31, 2005, from http://www.masie.com/xlearn/Game-Based_Learning.pdf.

Squire, K. D. (2005b). Game cultures, school cultures. Innovate 1(6), www. innovateonline.info.

Squire, K. D. (forthcoming). Civilization III as a world history sandbox. In M. Bittanti (Ed.), Civilization and its discontents: Virtual history, real fantasies. Milan, Italy: Ludilogica Press.

Squire, K. D., & Jenkins, H. (2004). Harnessing the power of games in education. Insight, 3(1), 5–33.

Stacey, M. (1992). Regulating British medicine: The General Medical Council. New York: Wiley.

Stake, J. E., & Mares, K. R. (2005). Evaluating the impact of science-enrichment programs on adolescents' science motivation and confidence: The splashdown effect. Journal of Research in Science Teaching, 42(4), 359–375.

Starr, P. (1994). Seductions of sim: Policy as a simulation game. The American Prospect, 5(17), 19–29.

Steinkuehler, C. A. (2005a). Cognition & learning in massively multiplayer online games: A critical approach. Unpublished doctoral dissertation, University of Wisconsin.

Steinkuehler, C. A. (2005b). The new third place: Massively multiplayer online gaming in American youth culture. Tidskrift Journal of Research in Teacher Education, 3, 17–32.

Stewart, J. B. (1998). Follow the story. New York: Simon & Schuster.

Stryker, S., & Burke, P. (2000). The past, present and future of identity theory. Social Psychology Quarterly, 63, 284–297.

Suconik, J. B. (2000). Animals: Why they must not be brutalized. Elmhurst, IL: Nuark Publishing.

Suits, B. (1967). What is a game? Philosophy of Science, 34.

Sullivan, W. M. (2005). Work and integrity: The crisis and promise of professionalism in America (2nd ed.). San Francisco: Jossey-Bass.

Susskind, L. E. (1994). Environmental diplomacy: Negotiating more effective global agreements. New York: Oxford University Press.

Susskind, L. E., & Corburn, J. (2000). Using simulations to teach negotiation: Pedagogical theory and practice. In M. Wheeler (Ed.), Teaching negotiation: Ideas and innovations (pp. 285–310). Cambridge, MA: PON Books.

Susskind, L. E., Levy, P. F., & Thomas-Larmer, J. (2000). Negotiating environmental agreements: How to avoid escalating confrontation, needless costs, and unnecessary litigation. Washington, DC: Island Press.

Susskind, L. E., Moomaw, W., & Hill, T. L. (1997). Global environment: Negotiating the future. Cambridge, MA: Program on Negotiation at Harvard Law School.

Sutton-Smith, B. (Ed.). (1979). Play and learning. New York: Gardner Press.

Svarovsky, G., & Shaffer, D. W. (2006). Engineering girls gone wild: Developing an engineering identity in Digital Zoo. In S. Barab, K. Hay, & D. Hickey (Eds.), Proceedings of the Seventh International Conference of the LearningSciences. Mahwah, N.J.: Lawrence Erlbaum.

Svarovsky, G., & Shaffer, D. W. (in press). SodaConstructing knowledge through exploratoids. Journal of Research in Science Teaching.

Sykes, M., d'Apice, A., & Sandrin, M. (2004). Position paper of the Ethics Committee of the International Xenotransplantation Association. Transplantation, 78(8), 1101–1107.

Sylva, K., Bruner, J. S., & Genova, P. (1976). The role of play in the problem-solving of children 3–5 years old. In J. S. Bruner, A. Jolly, & K. Sylva (Eds.), Play: Its role in development and evolution. New York: Basic Books.

Teare, R. (1997). Teamworking and quality improvement: Lessons from British and North American organizations. Herndon, VA: Cassell.

Thoreau, H. D. (1995, reprint). Walden, or, life in the woods. New York: Dover Publications.

Tichi, C. (1987). Shifting gears: Technology, literature, culture in modernist America. Chapel Hill: University of North Carolina Press.

Torney-Purta, J. (1998). Evaluating programs designed to teach international content and negotiation skills. International Negotiations, 3, 77–97.

Tripp, R. L. (1993). The game of school: Observations of a long-haul teacher. Reston, VA: Extended Vision Press.

Turkle, S. (1995). Life on the screen. New York: Simon & Schuster.

Tyack, D. (1974). The one best system: A history of American urban education. Cambridge, MA: Harvard University Press.

Tyack, D., & Cuban, L. (1996). Tinkering towards utopia. Cambridge, MA: Harvard University Press.

Tyack, D., & Tobin, W. (1994). The grammar of schooling: Why has it been so hard to change? American Educational Research Journal, 31(3), 453–479.

Uluoglu, B. (2000). Design knowledge communicated in studio critiques. Design Studies, 21, 33–58.

Vygotsky, L. S. (1976). Play and its role in the mental development of the child. In J. S. Bruner, A. Jolly, & K. Sylva (Eds.), Play: Its role in development and evolution. New York: Basic Books.

Vygotsky, L. S. (1978). Mind in society. Cambridge, MA: Harvard University Press.

Wallbank, T. W., Schrier, A., Maier-Weaver, D., & Gutierrez, P. (1977). History and life: The world and its people. Glenview, IL: Scott, Foresman.

Warren, K., Sakofs, M. S., & Hunt, J. S. (1995). The theory of experiential education (3rd ed.). Dubuque, IA: Kendall/Hunt.

Wenger, E. (1998). Communities of practice: Learning, meaning, and identity. Cambridge: Cambridge University Press.

Wertsch, J. V. (1998). Mind as action. New York: Oxford University Press.

Wineburg, S. S. (1991). Historical problem solving: A study of the cognitive processes used in the evaluation of documentary and pictorial evidence. Journal of Educational Psychology, 83(1), 73–87.

Wineburg, S. S. (2001). Historical thinking and other unnatural acts: Charting the future of teaching the past. Philadelphia: Temple University Press.

Wineburg, S. S., & Wilson, S. M. (1991). Models of wisdom in the teaching of history. History Teacher, 24(4), 395–412.

Wingler, H. M. (1978). The Bauhaus: Weimar, Dessau, Berlin, Chicago. Cambridge, MA: MIT Press.

Witt, P., & Baker, D. (1997). Developing after-school programs for youth in high risk environments. Journal of Physical Education, Recreation & Dance, 68(9), 18–20.

Wittgenstein, L. (1963). Philosophical investigations (English text reprint ed.). Oxford: Blackwell.

World Health Organization. (2005). Animal to human transplantation—future potential, present risk. Retrieved April 1, 2006, from www.who.int/mediacentre/news/notes/2005/np08/en/index.html.

Wu, H.-H. (1996). The Role of Euclidean Geometry in High School. Journal of Mathematical Behavior, 15(3).

Zimmerman, B. J., & Cleary, T. J. (2006). Adolescent's development of personal agency: The role of self-efficacy beliefs and self-regulatory skill. In T. Urdan (Ed.), Self-efficacy beliefs of adolescents. Greenwich, CT: Information Age Publishing.

Zimmerman, E. (2002). Do independent games exist?, from www.ericzimmerman.com/texts/indiegames.htm

Zoch, P. A. (2004). Doomed to fail: The built-in defects of American education. Chicago: I. R. Dee.

Index

Acknowledgments

Designing and studying games is almost never done in isolation, and this work is no exception. The studies I have described here depended first and foremost on the many young people who played these games and on the willingness of their parents to let us talk with them about their experiences. Epistemic games are also based on the work of professionals, and the games described here could not have been made without the many students and professionals who let us watch how they learn to think and patiently explained to us what they were doing and why.

None of this would have been possible either without the students and colleagues—mentors, fellow teachers, co-investigators, and friends—who contributed to this work. I am sincerely grateful for all the help I have received and can only hope that, in return, I have been similarly generous with my time, fellowship, and whatever insights I might be so fortunate to have had into their work. I would particularly like to thank Jim Gee and the faculty and students of the Games and Professional Practice Simulations research group at the University of Wisconsin Academic Advanced Distributed Learning Co-Laboratory, who have done so much for my own personal, professional, and intellectual development as a game scientist and who helped make epistemic games a reality.

Similarly, this work owes a great debt to the generous support provided by funders, including the Foundation for Ethics and Technology, the LEGO Corporation, the Spencer Foundation and National Academy of Education, the MacArthur Foundation, the Wisconsin Alumni Research Foundation, the Academic Advanced Distributed Learning Co-Laboratory, and the National Science Foundation through a Faculty Early Career Development Award (REC-0347000).

Despite all of this help, the opinions, findings, and conclusions—and, more important, any mistakes—are my own. They do not necessarily reflect the views of the funding agencies, cooperating institutions, or other individuals.

And finally, of course, most of all, I would like to thank my family, for everything.